M000288360

Faith
WITHOUT
RELIGION

The Kingdom Quest

Secret Spiritual Keys to The Kingdom
The Judgement and Rewards

Frank Atkins

Copyright © 2018 by Frank Atkins

ISBN: 978-1-7326798-0-1

To ALLIE,

I pray that God will
speak to you through these
words.

Blessings!

PREFACE

There is an entire book of miraculous stories to be told about life before my wife and I came to the USA, but for now I will give you a very brief thumbnail and cover just one story in detail, the one that is most relevant to the contents of this book. This story we call 'May 10th'

I grew up in London in the swinging sixties. At the age of three and a half, I discovered that my birth mother had left when I was a baby never to return. It was only many years later that I began to realize the part that news had played in the way my life unfolded and let's just say there were a lot of ups and downs.

Fast forward to the early nineties, a near death experience in a Johannesburg hospital leads to a series of miraculous events through which I had my own personal encounter with God and started an entirely new phase of my life as a born-again believer.

As I mentioned, the amazing litany of miraculous stories that I have experienced are for another book. Meeting my wonderful wife is one of the most remarkable, especially the way God orchestrated everything. From the first time I met her, I knew that she was the one He had promised me and that was before I even knew her name. After a literal 'whirlwind romance' I knew we were to be together forever and I could not wait to meet her parents and get their approval to my proposal.

Ronald Sydney Valentine was an interesting man; Larger than life, successful in his career, passionate about his country and sport and loved to sing and play his guitar. He absolutely adored his son and daughter and was very proud of their accomplishments.

Little did I know, when I went to ask his permission and blessing to marry his daughter that he had already been battling the evil cancer for a couple of years. What I also didn't know was that before we had even met, my wife had prayed to God that He would find her the right husband as well as keep her dad Ronnie alive till he could walk her down the aisle on her wedding day.

We got married on May 10, 1996 at 4:30 in the afternoon. Ronnie Valentine passed away on May 10, 1997 early afternoon, exactly one year to the day and almost the same hour that we were married. God had miraculously extended his life and he was able to see his daughter get married.

Death from cancer is often an ugly ritual and my wife was right there at the bed as death crept upwards from his ice-cold feet and legs, moving through his entire body. She was praying relentlessly pleading with God that her dad would not die without her knowing confidently *where he was going*. He liked to go to church on some Sundays but never spoke much about it and she wasn't certain that he was born again as talking about church or politics was taboo in the day.

Both she and her brother moved away from their home in Namibia to South Arica after high school to study further. When the family did get together over those years, conversations were more about life at home and education and careers.

After her dad contracted cancer he travelled from Namibia to Johannesburg for treatment and she spoke to him about faith and God but never asked in depth questions as everyone was overwhelmed by the situation. He was doing well for about a year when she suddenly received a call from her mom "I don't think your dad will live until tomorrow". After speaking to him just the day before, this came as shock, as he literally went from his office to the hospital and in 24 hours became 'confused and incoherent'. She and her brother left immediately for the airport and it was a troubling 2-hour flight.

By the time they got home he was falling in and out of a coma and was alive for 3 more days. On the third and final day she returned from a break to find a stranger that has appeared earlier in the day. The hospital said he was a 'standby Pastor' as Ronnie's pastor was out of town and they sat together on a bench in front of his bed. They talked about Ronnie's life and also the great things God had done for her throughout her life.

What she described next sounded like something out of a science-fiction movie. The hospital room in which he was lying suddenly became filled with a *Presence* and there was a substance to it, the atmosphere was like a thick 'jelly cloud' that was filled with millions of little sparkly crystals, like a gold speckled cloud. This *cloud* began to engulf her dad and as he became immersed in it, he passed away in its midst.

Obviously, no one wants to witness death, especially of a loved one, but the spectacular spiritual awesomeness of what went on in that hospital room and being present to witness such a *supernatural* event brought a temporary peace to her heart.

The next few days before the funeral were once again tormented by feelings of doubt and uncertainty and she cried out to God 'Is he saved, where did he go, how will I know?" as she never heard him confess his faith in Christ.

Then late afternoon after the funeral, she walked to a convenience store close by the family home. On the way back, she crossed a large open space and cried out aloud to God with the agony of uncertainty. Suddenly, in a loud voice, which she describes as being so loud, (like a megaphone announcement) that it could be heard all around, the Lord started speaking to her loud and clear. He has spoken to her in a similar way on 5 previous occasions, but this was different as He was quoting a direct passage from the Scriptures. Not remembering exactly which book and verse the Word was quoted from she rushed home and verified it was from the book of Corinthians 3:10-15

"By the grace God has given me, I laid a foundation as a wise builder, and someone else is building on it. But each one should build with care, for no one can lay any foundation other than the one already laid, which is Jesus Christ. If anyone builds on this foundation using gold, silver, costly stones, wood, hay or straw, their work will be shown for what it is, because the Day will bring it to light. It will be revealed with fire, and the fire will test the quality of each person's work. If what has been built survives, the builder will receive a reward. If it is burned up, the builder will suffer loss but yet will be saved—even though only as one escaping through the flames."

We returned to Johannesburg holding on to the comfort that although she really didn't know what her dad had *built on his foundation*, she was confident that he had died in Christ.

Ronnie believed and knew that Jesus died for his sins (in many conversations after his death her mom confirmed it) and he had an *awareness* of God and his power, but he wasn't focused on it and really didn't give much time to seeking after the things of God. Within a day after we got back home, my wife received a call from her friend Joan who said she had a book that God had urged her to give to us. This book not only served to confirm the words God had spoken about her father's final destination, but also it became the catalyst for us to embark on a quest to learn the truth about The Kingdom and what it means to each and every believer.

For several years we hunted for every scrap of knowledge that we could get on these subjects: the judgement seat of Christ, the coming Kingdom and the positioning of believers in that 1000-year reign of Christ on earth and the destiny of worldly believers.

4

We wanted to know why it wasn't being taught or even talked about in most churches. Many of the writings we could find were written in old English from so long ago that it was difficult to share with others.

In late 2002, God started speaking directly to me about these subjects. I had developed the habit of spending quiet time with him first thing in the morning. I would soak in the Presence of His Spirit and pray, just talking to Him and listening.
I had also begun journaling during these times and one day I found myself writing as usual when everything suddenly switched and I was writing as though someone else was guiding me about what to write.

I didn't give it too much thought at first, but it continued so I started to show these writings to my wife. She was astonished, mainly because she knew that as someone without "formal religious education" or training, who had not grown up in a church going family, there was no way that I could have come up with the profound truth and wisdom contained in these writings on my own.

Initially, I saw it as Gods way of teaching us things. He was explaining in understandable language, what we needed to know in order to understand the reality of His system of *judgments and rewards* and what they will mean in the coming Kingdom.

After a number of years and an ever-growing pile of journals, we both realized that this material was too important to keep to ourselves and that it is our divine calling and purpose to share it with those 'who have eyes to see and ears to hear'.

We (mostly me) resisted for years the idea of getting the material into the hands of others for whatever reason I could come up with. In the end, and really a testament to my precious wife's seemingly unending patience and continuous encouragement, I finally realized that this was exactly what I was supposed to be doing and that it was just too important to ignore any longer.

God told me exactly what I was to do with these messages and teachings and I knew that we had to help as many people as possible to make sure that they know these profound truths in the Word concerning the coming 1000-year Kingdom and start their own *Kingdom Quest*.

INTRODUCTION

There is no particular sequence to these messages and you can literally read any page on any day and find something of value. Every message also contains one or more scripture references as we always want to point you back to the source of all truth which is His life-giving Word that is all power and all might at all times and will never fail you.

Every word in this book is written for two reasons. Firstly, to bring you the comfort of knowing that God, the creator of the universe and everything in it is still speaking to us today. That He is looking at the lives of seemingly ordinary people and speaking to them and through them, giving wisdom and guidance to those that will listen.

That's right, God is speaking to you today because He wants your attention and He wants to be more involved in your life and help you with everything you do. He wants to pour out His blessings upon you and to see you thrive and prosper.

He wants to help you prepare, to get you ready for what will be coming when His Son returns to the earth to set up His Millennial Kingdom where He will rule and reign among us for 1000 years.

We have to be prepared for that and be made ready for the role that we are going to fulfill in that Kingdom. That is why God wants to get our attention now, because only those that are ready and that have been properly prepared will be able to take up positions of significance in that Kingdom.

Only believers in Christ have any possibility of sharing that inheritance with Him, but outside of the salvation that faith assures, there is an important 'race' for every believer to run in pursuit of the rewards available to those who complete it. Salvation is not a prize or reward, it is a *free* gift given to all who believe. The race, to be run by every believer, begins after the receipt of the gift of salvation.

'Many are called but few are chosen' and we need to know what that really means.

That brings us to the second reason for the words in this book. As referenced earlier, everything that the Father has given us to write in these pages, points you back to the one source of all truth; to the Scriptures, the living, breathing, life giving Word of God.

He wants you to awaken to the Truth of His Word, to consume it as the essence of life itself. Not to regard it as an accessory to religion, or a textbook, but to revere and honor it for its true substance.

'In the beginning was the Word, and the Word was with God and the Word was God'

The Word is the revelation of the essence of Christ. Sustenance to feed us while we wait for His literal return. He left us with His Spirit, through whom the true depth of the Word is revealed. He walked among us as the Word made manifest. Now, through His Spirit, we can complete the cycle and honor God in the way that He has asked that we serve Him.

Our prayer is that through this book, you will hear what the Father is saying *to you* today and that you will realize that the time is short. We must return to the root of the truth and prepare ourselves for what is soon to come.

NOTES FROM THE WRITER

This book is for everyone that believes in God and that He sent His Son to save us from the penalty of sin so that we can have eternal life.

Whether you have been a believer for your whole life or since yesterday does not matter, there is something in this book that will affect your life because everything in here points you back to the life-giving truth of His written Word.

What you will read here are things that I was inspired to write down during times of prayer over a period of many years. For most of those years I have been involved in business as an entrepreneur and the way God has explained certain concepts to me will sometimes reflect that.

God speaks to each of us in the manner that we can individually understand so if the language sometimes doesn't mirror your own vernacular, I encourage you to look past that and get to the truth of *what* He is saying and how that can benefit you and your own life journey.

There is no index or table of contents, so you can explore it in any way that feels good for you. If you read something that sounds like it was written especially for you, it probably was! In some places, words have been put into italics or quotes for emphasis. I have used "inverted commas" to make clear the beginning and end of where God was speaking.

At the beginning and throughout the book, there are references to a 'Formula'. This refers to a structured blueprint that He showed me.

Following this formula and including all of its steps will lead us into a closer, deeper relationship with God and put us firmly on the right track to run our own 'race' for the Kingdom and the rewards that await.

When God told me to write down this *formula*, it didn't make much sense at first but then He explained how each step leads to the next. Like a recipe for a cake, each of the ingredients form a necessary and important part so you cannot miss any of them out.

My hope for this work is that it will help you to recognize the importance of the times we are in. We are indeed involved in a *race* the outcome of which will affect our lives significantly in the coming age. The messages in this book will help you to see that you can be victorious in *your* race.

You do not have to join anything, you do not have to change careers or churches or become 'religious'. All you need to do is get a full understanding of God's coming Kingdom and what is available to those that make the decision that they want themselves and everyone that they know and love to be part of it and to pursue the rewards that are available in that Kingdom.

Colossians 2:2-3

[2] My goal is that they may be encouraged in heart and united in love, so that they may have the full riches of complete understanding, in order that they may know the mystery of God, namely, Christ, [3] in whom are hidden all the treasures of wisdom and knowledge.

THE FORMULA

WORD - SPIRIT - CROSS - WORD - SPIRIT IN GREATER MEASURE – ACTION – SEEDS – HARVEST – BLESSINGS - SEED IN GREATER MEASURE – REWARDS – KINGDOM

WORD

"Feed and nourish yourself from the truth in My Word"

SPIRIT

"Unite My Spirit to yours every minute of every day through Prayer"

CROSS

"Take up your cross and carry it at all times. Set aside your own plans and follow your eternal purpose through the Truth in My Word"

WORD

"Embrace it and act on what it prompts you to do, let the Truth fill you constantly and you will be able to bring love and value to others"

SPIRIT IN GREATER MEASURE

"The more Truth you consume the greater measure of My Spirit you will see operating in your life"

ACTION

"You will feel compelled and emboldened to act on what My Spirit directs you to do"

SEED

"The result of these actions will produce seed for you to sow for yourselves and also to sow into the lives of others"

HARVEST

"The seed that you sow and nurture will produce a harvest"

BLESSINGS

"Through the harvest you will be blessed and be able to bless others"

SEED IN GREATER MEASURE

"Now you will be able to save some seed from the fruit of your harvest and use that to produce even more seed that you can plant and distribute to those in need"

REWARDS

"Now you can use some of the fruit from that seed to store up treasures in Heaven by using it for good purpose and blessing others"

KINGDOM

"This is the righteous formula that will lead to you receiving a good report in the Kingdom to come"

IF YOU TRULY FOLLOW ME

"Sow seed and expect that I will create a harvest from it and that the harvest will be an abundant crop says God. I am not concerned about your past failure, I am concerned about your future faithfulness. Only faithfulness in your daily walk can produce the lasting permanent changes that you seek. True desire means putting aside all else in pursuit of what you really want. If you truly want My favor, I must be the biggest thing in your life. I must be at the forefront of your mind all of the day. You must begin the day with Me, confront the challenges of the day with Me and end the day with Me. I am all things to all men, but you must make the choice to let Me be all things to you. Through that choice comes the abundance and the contentment that you desire. Get your own mind out of the way and let My Spirit lead you. Let My Spirit show you the path to true righteousness.

Until you start with the sowing I cannot nurture the seeds and produce the crop. Know Me, that I am God. Be still and hearken to My Words. Seek earnestly after Me and I will seek more earnestly after you. Glorify My name and I will elevate your name, expand your territories and increase your abundance.

Goodness comes from knowing your leader. Greatness comes from glorifying your leader. Spirit led accomplishments come from diligently seeking My counsel before any step or action that you take.

My wisdom will become your wisdom when your steps become My steps. Rid yourself of all guilt and of all doubt and of any shame. Remorse is important, but confession and repentance are more important. Staying close to Me and being led by My Spirit is even more important. All things will come from wisdom.

This wisdom can only be imparted to you in direct proportion to your proximity to the source. You cannot sunbathe in the shade.

Love is the essence of wisdom.

Love is wisdom in action. I am the author of your contentment and your prosperity and your opportunity to seek Kingdom rewards. You must become the page-turners. Your hands cannot even touch the Life Book if they are soiled with the ills of this world. Cleanse yourselves and I will write new pages for you. Unite My Spirit to yours every minute of every day. This is what I mean when I say, 'take up your cross'. When I ask you to do that, you may notice that I do not tell you to put it down. You must carry it with you at all times. It brings you light, it separates you from the world, it makes My Spirit even more able to abide with you and instruct you. By taking up My Cross, being proud of it and keeping it with you at all times, I can relate to you as true family. You will truly be numbered among My Children.

Where do you find the cross? The burden of My Cross is contained in My Word. Embrace the Word to your heart, let it dwell in you and you will become My instrument. I always give My best and most rewarding assignments to the Cross bearers for they have proven themselves to be most worthy. Success leaves clues, there is a clear path to the righteousness you seek.

Word – Spirit – Cross - Word - Spirit in greater measure - Action – Seeds – Harvest – Blessings - Seeds in greater measure – Rewards - Kingdom

It all starts with the Word. Then the Spirit and the burden of the Cross takes care of everything else. If you feel yourselves straying out of the anointing, simply come back to this formula, it is truly the 'Key to the Kingdom'. If you truly follow it, you will run a good race.

Your potential to attain a prize is without question. Whether or not you succeed and the degree to which you succeed will be in direct proportion to your ability to choose to follow the formula. Every distraction will divert you from the path if you choose to let it distract you.

Stay focused, and the only way to stay as focused as you know you need to be is to be led by My Spirit. The more you carry your Cross and the more you are filled by the light of My Word, the more My Spirit will abide in you and bring you the wisdom needed to make the right choices.

Now the enemy will come and try to divert you from this new zeal. He will try to bring doubt and uncertainty upon you. Be prepared; don't be fooled by thinking that if you are filled with My Spirit you will not be attacked. It is *because* you are filled with My Spirit that you will be attacked. The enemy will try to create enmity with the people in your life, be prepared and stand strong. The enemy will try to attack your life, your business and your family. Stand strong. Resist him and he will flee from you says God.

Beware of flatterers and strange temptations. I never send people into your path that will bring alarm to your spirit. Test every new relationship, idea or action by applying My wisdom to any decision. Ask yourself what you would do if you could see Me standing beside you. The same when you go about your daily tasks. Work in the manner you would if you could see Me watching your every move. Be constantly aware of My presence and be very aware of the sensitivity of My Spirit. Pray clearly so that I may know how to help you for that is My true desire."

1 Corinthians 9:24
Hebrews 12:1
Genesis 15:1
Ephesians 3:17-19, 6:10-18
James 4:7

KINGDOM & MILLENNIUM

"It does not matter how zealously My children attach themselves to the plans and programs of ambitious men and women. If they do not have a fundamental understanding of the truth in connection with the Kingdom to come and the importance of being ready, they are missing so much says God.

Mammon centered ministry is in abundance today, it all amounts to the same thing which is deception. Yes, there is a place for organized structured ministry, even a need for it, but they have to eliminate mammon from their lives before they can have impact and true purpose.

You have to act on your own calling, I cannot call any louder, I cannot call at a more convenient time, I cannot come back later after you have had time to be successful in your worldly pursuits. You made the commitment to leave behind the things of the world. You must now leave them behind and seek only after the supernatural. You have spent years doing your best to leverage whatever worldly capital you perceived to possess. Now you must leverage your Spiritual capital.

You can no longer write down your intended actions and then not act upon them. Do you think that not acting on a written word declaring your intentions is any less disappointing to Me than a spoken promise that is broken"?

Revelation 3:11-13

ACTION MUST BE TAKEN

"Once words are freed from the mind either verbally or in writing, they are compelled to produce, there is no silence in the spiritual realm; a thought and a shout have the same volume.

There is only one that creates with only a word says God. For all others, the words spoken or written must be followed up by action. If the action is of My Spirit, the fruit will be as well. If the action is from the enemy, the fruit will be bad. If there is no action, there will be no fruit. No fruit and bad fruit are the same in My eyes, says God.

Action must be taken and this is of great importance says God. Everything will appear differently from the spiritual perspective.

It is much easier to see the wider picture when you remove the narrow constraints of the worlds system. You cannot measure spiritual progress from a worldly perspective.

Give time and attention to fellow warriors. You will know them by their fruit. Align yourself with those that you can see will be part of your eternal picture, those who will not, will be very obvious.

Take certain action today and every day. Be accountable to each other. Do not engage in procrastination. A day lost, an hour lost, a minute lost, none of them can be regained. There are no do-overs with time.

It is either used effectively or not. You are less likely to waste time if it is planned.

Everything I do is planned says God. There are no accidents, and nothing is left to chance. As you know, I know the *end* from the *beginning*, so I am not taken by surprise. You need to eliminate surprises from your life. They only serve to remind you that there was lack of preparedness".

James 2:17

WHAT IS THE KINGDOM ABOUT?

"It is now time for you to set your life apart from the lies of this world and the deceptions of 'feel-good theology' that are being spread all over the world says God. There is more joy to be found in living out My living Word in your daily life than in any worldly pursuit. Your time on the earth is nothing more than a preparation for your position in the coming Kingdom.

Yes, there will be positions but they are not the same for all people. Kingdoms have structure and hierarchy. Earthly kingdoms were meant to be pointers to the structure of the coming Kingdom. Look closely at the structures and it is obvious that I am a God of structure and order.

Without structure and order, chaos rules. Chaos is of the evil one and his confederates. There will be no chaos within the safety of My Kingdom. Those not in the Kingdom will suffer from much chaos until the end. If there is a choice, who would choose chaos over peace, joy and love of the eternal Kingdom?

There is a choice. You demonstrate your choice daily by your actions.

'But we made our choice when we gave our lives over and became saved!'

That decision earned you the right to be a producer of fruit in My garden says God. What are you producing? Is your fruit of the highest quality? Does it transcend the earthly realm? If not, of what use is it? Is your fruit ripe and bursting with seed that will reproduce more of the same?

Ask yourself this; if I remove you from the earth tomorrow, what impact will your fruit have in your absence? Or, if I return to the earth tomorrow, how will your fruit make an impact on the Kingdom that I come to establish?

Hard questions. If you do not like them now, how much less will you like them if you have to hear them from Me face to face?

If you do not like the answers you are getting from yourself, then change what you are doing right now says God. Remember the rich young prince? He was astounded at what he realized would be necessary to follow My path. You may also be shocked, but rather be shocked now and make changes than to be shocked on the Day and carry regret with you into judgment.

'But, I hear you say, we will not have any judgment, because we are saved and our sins are paid for'

Yes, you are saved and protected from the penalty of your sins, which for the unsaved is eternal damnation, but there is going to be a judgment. Why else would I say so in My Word? There are going to be rewards for some and not for others. Why else would I say so in My Word? There will be some that suffer loss, why else would I say it in My Word?

Everything in My Word has proven to be true. Why then would these things not be true? Truth does not change just because it is not convenient to the human mind.

My eternal plan is not to be altered and manipulated to satisfy the fleshly desires of mankind. If you do not know these things from My Word to be true, you do not know My Word. If you spend more time pursuing the things of this world that you live in physically, than the world you live in spiritually, which one do you think you will know the most about?

I provided all truth and all answers in the Words that I caused to be written. Let those that are ready feed on their fruit. To those that are not ready, they will taste bitter and unpalatable. They cannot absorb the nutrients. They need to flush out their bodies with My Spirit cleansing and they need to eat 'raw food'; My unadulterated living Word.

It is the only source of true nutrition. Earthly food fuels the earthly body, but this spiritual food feeds the spiritual body. Do not leave the earthly realm with an undeveloped Spiritual body and no fruit".

Acts 14:22
2 Corinthians 5:10
1 Corinthians 3:10-15
Romans 14:10-12
1 Peter 1:17
Mark 10:17-30
Revelation 20:6, 21:1-8

SWIMMING AGAINST THE TIDE

"Are you 'going with flow?' asks God. Examine your life very carefully and look for any areas of friction. These are activities or ideals that you maintain that appear to be completely opposite to the positions or actions taken by almost everyone else. It is this friction that shapes you and polishes you into one of My prized possessions.

It illuminates you with a *glow* that is distinct and different to most others. It is brightness, a shimmering sheen that will stimulate curiosity in the hearts of many that do not possess it. On the other hand, if you are simply following the pack, moving in the same direction as everyone else, there will be no friction says God.

Therefore, there will be no shaping and polishing. Everything about you will 'blend in' and there will be no distinction, no separateness or differences through which you can be used as a light or a beacon to others.

You will be 'in' the world and 'of' the world and will ultimately see the spirit of Esau manifest in your life. He that refuses to be shaped and directed by My Word, will ultimately relinquish his birthright, his inheritance in the Kingdom to come for the equivalent of a 'bowl of food'. The food for which Esau traded his privileged position, is represented today through the temporal, material objectives that are the focus of the actions of most people today. They pursue assets and 'things' using far more effort and focus than they use in pursuing a relationship with Me.

What foolishness is this? There is a nation of Esau's springing up around you. They will indeed 'perish through lack of knowledge' because My Word is true and infallible. Do not confuse friction with stress says God. Stress is meant for destruction. It breaks down the physical body and is an instrument of the enemy.

The pursuit of the world's purposes will always produce stress for the called and the lost alike. Many are rendered ineffective through this stress because their eyes are on the world and not on Me.

They try to take the easy path, the one that most people are on. They see a light in the distance and proceed towards it in the deception that it shines from the throne room. It does not! One of the most difficult parts of running the race is the fact that there are so many that are running the wrong way on the track. These can be more of a challenge to you than even the lost. They will obstruct you, bump you, try to turn you around and they make your own race more arduous.

This again brings to the fore the importance of the friction in your life. The more perfectly shaped and highly polished you are, the better equipped you will be to deal with the buffeting and jostling that you will experience while running. Any sense of 'certainty' regarding the outcome of your race should serve as a warning to you says God.

Certainty breeds complacency and will always lead to costly mistakes.

It is the friction which keeps the wedding garment presented in pristine condition, it is the friction that can take the dull, meaningless things of the world and turn them into the gold silver and precious stones to be laid upon your eternal foundation.

It is the friction that rubs the 'olive' of your soul and keeps your lamps brimming with oil avoiding the loss of the 5 foolish virgins.

The friction keeps you focused on polishing and growing your talents so that you hear the good report of the faithful servant and not the suffering of loss reserved for those counted among the wicked servants because they took the easy path. They went with the flow and did not follow My instructions".

1 Corinthians 3:12, 9:24-27
Philippians 3:12
Matthew 25

THE POWER OF THE SOWN SEED

"If you understand the power of the sown seed, you will look to *plant* something every day says God. The more seeds that are planted, the more harvests you can reap. The more harvests you reap, the more you will have to set aside as seed. The seeds are the core of your faith. Faith with no seeds is unproductive and stagnant, what are you having faith in? What are you waiting for?

The farmer that looks at the ground in which he has planted nothing, can stare at that ground until the passing of time. Nothing will spring forth because 'nothing' produces nothing. Just one seed, correctly used, planted in faith, harvested in love, with some of the crop set aside for more seed, can produce abundance as to the *type* of the seed. However, wheat will not produce apples, nor can figs produce olives. Like for like is the principle. Be wise in your choices. Plant your seeds earnestly and sincerely and with clarity and I will grant you the favor that you ask for. There are people I am pouring out favor upon because they truly understand the principles of sowing and reaping.

Chase after charity and kindness with an earnest heart, as without charity and kindness, everything is pointless. Embrace these things, understand them and acquire the heart to practice them enthusiastically. Plan the steps of your day the night before and I will confirm to you in the early part of the next day that your steps are well planned".

Galatians 6:7-8
Genesis 26:12
2 Corinthians 9:6

25

THE ONLY TRUE WISDOM IS THE WORD

"Wash yourself in My Word at every opportunity for the dirt and grime of this world clings to you and has a foul odor.

My Word will keep your body and your mind clean and it contains all the wisdom that you are seeking, says God.

Do not rely only on the authors of this world for wisdom, for they mostly do not have the keys. They may guide you and inspire you and if I have anointed them, you will know by your spirit and it is pleasing that they share their understanding with you.

Once you have enjoyed the sharing, return to the source for the wisdom that is true. Only My Word contains true wisdom and power. This is the power that you need to be overcomers in this world.

This is the power that will be your fuel as you run this race.

Keep seeking My counsel in all that you do".

Ephesians 5:26
John 13:10

INSTRUCTIONS FOR WARRIORS

"I will make this a time of breakthrough for you. It is a new beginning at a higher level than before. To operate at such a level, you must be prepared to do things at a higher level.

You cannot be content with a worldly religious attitude of a prayer a day and a quick Scripture reading. You must imprint My Word on your heart. Spend more time with Me than you do with the world and I will grant you favor that you cannot find in the world. Their favor pales into insignificance compared to Mine.

Put Me first in all things and seek Me first in all things. Study My Word and hunger after the deeper understanding that is only given to those with clean hearts and eyes to see the truth.

Hear Me well, these are not vain instructions. These are orders for My true soldiers. Let the world see that you are different. Let them see that you are not of their ranks. Let kindness and goodness and the light which comes from My Spirit emanate from your being. This is only possible if you are immersed in Me. Seek earnestly after Me and I will teach you.

Set aside specific amounts of time each day for your activities. Bring the activities to Me before you embark on them. Ask Me about every aspect and I will show you what steps to take. Do not let your own worldly wisdom get in the way of My wisdom. Trust in Me completely and your success will be multiplied says God.

Pray at every opportunity and My Spirit will be with you all the hours of the day, but only if the spiritual atmosphere is maintained. I have no ears for lying tongues or deceptive words and I frown upon disorder and chaos. Keep an orderly place for Me at all times.

Praise Me continually, engage with My Spirit, honor Me and love My presence, then We will work more with you and you can meet all of your deadlines and goals and achieve all your dreams and desires, because through My Spirit everything can be attained."

Ephesians 4:30-32
1 Thessalonians 5:17
Philippians 4:6
Psalms 24:3-4

10

REVIVAL WITH PURPOSE

"I want to separate you from the hooks of this world. You need to cleave to Me ever more closely. Keep your eyes and your heart focused on the only goal that truly matters, the goal of My prize.

Your worldly goals are noble enough but remember My instructions to you: 'seek first the Kingdom and My righteousness all these things shall be added to you'. If you make My kingdom your goal, then everything else will be taken care of.

My people need 'revival with purpose'. It cannot be for the purpose of attaining more worldly possessions, for 'what does it profit a man if he should gain the whole world, but lose his soul'? Many of the saved strive blindly after the things of this world.

You seek after wisdom, but what use is wisdom if it is just for the sake of worldly achievements? The wisdom you attain needs to be My wisdom that will open your eyes to see that you are indeed involved in a vital race. A race for which some of you have not even heard the starter gun, or worse you did hear it, but you think you can start running when it suits you.

Foolishness! I am the only One who knows the length of this race. It could end tomorrow and then each person will be judged on their position at that time in relation to the starting time of their individual race says God.

There is little enough revival in evidence but revival with purpose is virtually nonexistent. I want to see My people stirred up and given a firm direction to move in. I do not want to see them elevated for a few days only to see them plunge back down by the time the messenger has reached the next town.

Hear Me well and take My words to your heart, for I am going to prepare your way, but I want to count on your obedience and your willingness to act on My instructions. When I open the door, you must recognize it and walk through it without hesitation. Be bold and I will deliver to you the desires of your heart according to My will.

Subdue your will and get your own flesh out of the way and there will be no struggle because I am the supplier of all things.

Trust Me in this as I trust that you will grow ever close to Me with your prayers and supplications. My Spirit will abide with you on this journey. Open your heart and focus on Me and My purpose which is the only thing that truly matters and the only thing that is worthy of your attention. This is the only thing that can make a difference to your eternal life. Be strong in Me for I am your strength, I am your path and I am the life that you seek. I will bless you above comprehension in return for your love and diligence".

Philippians 3:14
Matthew 6:33, 16:26
Ephesians 3:17
Psalm 90:12

11

WARNING ABOUT ATTITUDE

"Remember that to please My Spirit, you must provide a pleasant environment. He is easily grieved and responds to your obedience. You must not come before Me out of a sense of guilt, just feeling that you need to appease Me by doing something 'spiritual' before you move onto something that you want to do. Rather that you do not come before Me than to come with an attitude of impatience or even insincerity.

You must sit in My presence and press through for whatever time it takes. We are not working on a timetable to suit you. You are expressing your desire to sit at My feet and learn, you are expressing your desire to hear My voice more clearly and receive instruction. As I told you before, My Spirit is easily offended for He knows the attitude of your heart even before you come before Me says God.

Let go of the world and press in. You are closer now than ever before, but this is not the time to slip back. It would be so easy for you to just slip back into your worldly ways and that is a choice that is open to you. However, if you truly seek the opportunity *to race after My higher calling*, you have to press through to the next level. You must keep pushing the doors until you find the one that is opened for you by My Spirit.

Many people fall short in this respect. They will not even touch upon a door, so they remain as children that make no progress, because they never get to the more challenging levels. I remind you again, seek after Me every hour of every day as truly *abiding with My Spirit* requires this".

Ephesians 4:30
Philippians 3:13
Psalm 139:4
Hebrews 5:13-14

EMPTY BELIEVERS

"No longer for you the occasional effort only when you require a refill from My Spirit. You must be filled with the Spirit at all times for only then will you make the progress you desire says God.

There is much in store for Spirit filled soldiers. There is also much in store for the people of this world who do not know the truth and for the empty believers. The groups though are very different.

For the first group there is a challenging race ahead. It will be very difficult, but you will be chasing unimaginable abundance and untold joy in the coming Kingdom.

For the others, there lies ahead much misery and much torment. Some will say 'I never heard You', when the truth is that they were not partial to Me because the things of this world appeared to be more flavorful and attractive and they hungered only after the lusts of the flesh.

Worse still is to come for the empty believer. Those that express the appearance of being 'religious', but who do not walk in the power of My spoken Word. My people perish through their ignorance. Many will forever lose the opportunity to gain rewards, but others will learn the truth before it is too late.

I will never force or press someone into My service, for an unwilling servant is as disappointing as the roaming cat. He comes to you for food and affection when it suits him and he comes to you for shelter when he senses danger, but the rest of the time he is fiercely independent and roams around seeking after his own life and doing only what pleases him.

The carnally minded believer is the same and I take no pleasure in it. My pleasure comes in seeing believers that are willing to obey Me, for obedience brings great joy.

My pleasure comes from people that ask to hear My voice and then act on My instruction knowing that I would only guide them to what is truly best for them. These are those with the required measure of faith to press forward at My urging without regard for the appearance of worldly circumstance.

I am sovereign. I can do anything I choose and you My children can do anything you choose through Me, for I am your strength. I will go before you; I am your way maker and I am your provider, but you have to get yourselves out of the way so that I can operate the fullness of My anointing in your lives.

I will not remove My hand from you, unless you cause Me to do so.

I only remove My hand from those that shrug Me off and put down My works to indulge themselves with the worries of this world instead. They are a disappointment to Me. Of course, I always know what they are going to choose before they make their choice, but it still grieves Me nonetheless".

Matthew 5:10, 16:27, 13:22
2 Timothy 3:5
Revelation 22:12
1 Corinthians 3:8

13

STAYING IN THE ANOINTING

"See how easily your confidence drops when you slip from My anointing? See how diligent you have to be to enjoy the *fullness* of My presence. At this level, a day out of My presence brings a heaviness of uncertainty and discontent.

These feelings do not come from Me but from the world. The world is the enemy who wants to pull you down at every opportunity. You need to stay in the fullness of My anointing and you can only do that through your obedience.

Meditate upon My word day and night. I give that instruction, because until My word is engrafted into your being, you are still very vulnerable to the wiles of the enemy.

Only My Spirit can defeat the enemy and keep him at bay. My Spirit comes through the Word. Delight in My Word and My Spirit will delight in you.

Let My Words become your words. Speak My Word with power and confidence. I will not forsake you, but you must be open and willing to accept My instruction says God.

There will be no reluctant soldiers in My Kingdom. Only those that made a commitment of the heart to accept My calling. That is why I have told you that many are called but few are chosen, for even some of the chosen will turn and walk away from Me and never enjoy the fullness of the things that could have been possible for them. They will suffer regret.

Do not be counted among them, it is up to you. When you finally let go of this world and embrace Me fully, both in your heart and in your actions, there is much to look forward to. Stop being victims of your own circumstances. The only way to break the cycle is to 'get off the bike'. I will complete that which I have begun, as I always do. Let Me see that you are capable of complete obedience, for that is required for My full anointing to be manifest in your lives.

How foolish! Do you think that if you are half obedient that maybe I will half anoint you? Don't you know that it cannot be for I do not do half measures? Everything I do or give is complete and whole. I expect the same in return from you. I need your complete and wholehearted dedication and obedience.

Uncommon favor will be poured out upon you if you follow My instructions and you meet the requirements that I have set before you. Do not make the mistake of thinking that blessings are given to people because they have some special 'right' to them. Blessings are nothing more than a type of My rewards to come.

Blessings are given as an indication of My pleasure mostly for obedience as through obedience comes the fullness of your relationship with Me. Those seeking only after the blessings but without the relationship, will often receive them, but not from Me. Such blessings are bestowed by the fallen one and at some point, will bring only misery and desolation. Stay in My Spirit and My Word and you will always be able to discern My true blessings".

Luke 11:28
John 6:70
Matthew 22
Deuteronomy 31:6

14

TIME FOR MATURITY

"The time for maturing has come. There is no longer need for you to partake of the pleasures of the children of the world. In My Word and Spirit are all delights. In My instruction and path that I have prepared are all opportunities for a blessed and joyous life.

You will find greater peace, happiness and contentment than from any path you have trodden previously. There is much work to be done, but I will be your strength. Delight in the labors and I will add all joy to you says God.

You will be as a young child again, eager to awake each day and to embrace the work I have prepared for you. Seek more after My wisdom and I will show you the clear way and will not lead you astray into distraction.

Please Me with your offerings of faith and of obedience. In your service and trust I find much delight. Strive towards righteousness in spirit for it overwhelms the world and in it My victory is perfected. The power of true faith is great, but few use it properly for the fears and worries that they allow into their minds weaken the effect.

Strengthen your minds by filling them with My living Spirit through My inspired and infallible Word.

People overlook the importance of My Word and in that lies the power of the enemy. He cannot stand in the presence of My Word.

My Word that is so powerful it can move mountains. Let My Words be your words, speak them out, fill your hearts, minds and your dwelling place constantly with My Word. A mighty time is unfolding and there are many trials ahead for My people. My Spirit filled soldiers will rise above these trials and become a lampstand of example to those that are struggling.

Remove all the hooks of this world, they are your enemy. You cannot go boldly forward in your race with the hooks of the enemy constantly pulling at you and slowing or even stopping your progress.

Wash yourselves in My Word. Speak out My Word and communicate through My Spirit at all times. Speak that which is right to each other for all else is not of Me. Turn every thought over to My Spirit and do not make so much noise that you cannot hear My voice. You must listen carefully".

Ephesians 1:17-23, 4:29
Proverbs 3
2 Corinthians 10:5
Proverbs 23:16-18

15

IMPORTANT WARNINGS

"Do not think I give warnings lightly says God. I put them in My Word so that those with eyes to see can be mindful of the truth. Yes, I love obedience, but I despise those that shrink in the face of My mercy and grace. I will not take kindly to being invited by those that opened the door of their hearts to Me and then slammed it in My face.

There are many warnings in My Word aimed at My children.

These warnings must be understood and feared. My sheep cannot live their earthly lives in ignorance of these truths for if they do, they will not be as fruitful as they should.

Reverent fear is a prerequisite for attaining any rewards. Why else would a servant perform his duties? Would it be because he seeks to reward himself? This should not be. Righteous works should be carried out like a child who is eager to please his loving Father. After I have given that maturing child an important task to carry out with a measure of responsibility, I expect the task to be completed on time and as requested.

If this is not the case, the child should expect to be chastened by his Father out of love. Surely, he will be forgiven if he is mindful of his sin and repents. All sins are covered by the blood and forgiveness is assured but do not be deceived, this does not give license to live as one pleases. Those walking truly hand in hand with Me, will automatically have the reverence I speak of. Even My Spirit is mindful to perform only My will, how much more should My sheep be mindful of Me?

Keep searching Me out and I will reveal more of Myself to you. Wear the mantle of My anointing with humility and I will readily increase your portion. Heighten your reverent fear of Me and I will increase it tenfold. Become one with Me and I will increase it one hundred-fold. You are still as infants.

Mature with Me and the level of My anointing will be such that human words do not have the expression to describe it. Be in eager anticipation for it, crave it and desire it above all else for within this anointing will be the answer to all questions".

Acts 5:32
Exodus 20:20
Deuteronomy 13:4
Proverbs 3:12, 9:10
Hebrews 12:6
1 Corinthians 3:1-3
1 Peter 2:2

16

WARNING AGAINST COMPLACENCY

"You will do well to notice the warnings that I place in My Word. I am a loving Father, but I am also a strict Father, requiring obedience and servanthood from My children. I gave up My only begotten Son so that you might be saved and be My children. I have high expectations of My children. I expect them to honor Me, to worship Me, and to love Me above all else. Anything less diminishes the price I paid and is not pleasing to Me.

Too many of My children are growing complacent in their status of being called by Me. This is foolish; they are blind to their own ignorance. They go about day by day chasing after the things of this world and not being mindful of My instructions. There is much misery ahead in such actions says God.

My Word is life and My Word is Spirit. In My Word there are all of the answers, all the power, all the blessings, all the instructions. My people are lazy; they rely on the interpretations of others to know My Word. There is nothing wrong with hearing the words of an anointed teacher, but how can one know if the teaching is anointed without My Spirit giving the revelation?

You cannot have the Spirit without the Word. My Spirit will not abide where My Word is absent. The greater the abundance of My Word in you, the fuller will be the presence of My Spirit. Fill yourselves with the Word; learn to speak out My Word to one another.

Gird your mind and your lips and your tongue with My Word. In this way you cleanse a path for a filling of My Spirit at a level beyond which your imagination can perceive.

The answer is in the Word; eat it, drink it, and let it live inside of you. The Word is the key to the manifestation of My truth; get it inside you and all around you and My presence, through My Spirit, will be inside of you and all around you and will keep you from deception.

I love you tenderly". Says God

Psalms 19:14
John 1:1
John 14:6
John 11:25

RECOGNIZING YOUR ASSIGNMENT

"I want to refine you. I want to complete in you a more perfect work for which you are not yet qualified. The test of abstinence when a person is fasting shows the weakness of the flesh. If it fails to respond so easily due to the lack of earthly nourishment how much more will it fail for the lack of Spiritual nourishment? You must partake of My Spirit and My Word more regularly than you partake of earthly food and your earthly body will come alive with My Spirit and wisdom and discernment and power will be in your hands says God.

The time is now for you to put into practice the things I have been instructing you on. Be strong and of good courage and work diligently with wisdom on the tasks before you. Do not be afraid and do not shrink back at this hour, the breakthrough is close by and you must press in.

It is true that the worker is worth his wages. If your vision extends greater than wages, then your work and effort must surpass that of the workers. Abundant harvests usually come from abundant seed sowing and lots of diligent effort, rushing to bring in the harvest, so that all will not spoil.

Constantly check the attitude of your heart and your diligence level. Do you recall what I said about working as though I am sitting right by your side, looking over your shoulder, evaluating your efforts? What do you say about the results so far? Would I be nodding My head with approval, would I be patting you on the back? Would I be happy with your production level? What answers does your mouth have for Me or is it too filled with stones to speak?

I have given an assignment to each of My sheep. Their first challenge is to recognize the assignment, the second challenge is to begin it and the third is to complete it. In order to complete these steps, you will need an abundance of these three qualities: Obedience, wisdom and love. Each one leads to the other in truly greater measure. Through your obedience you must work at your assignment more diligently than you would for an earthly master. How much more mindful should you be of your Heavenly Master? For he that honors Me, gets doubly rewarded; here and now with comfort and joy in the earthly time but so much more in the time to come.

Keep putting aside all distractions and focus, focus, focus. The only failure for My people comes when they focus their eyes elsewhere other than the path that leads to Me. Begin each day with new optimism and the knowledge that I am right there with you ordering your every thought, anointing your tongue and your mind. Order your household well and create within it an atmosphere of success and fruit bearing effort. Lift up one another in all things, join hands on the plough and the yoke will be miraculously lighter".

Colossians 2:13
Hebrews 12:2
2 Corinthians 9:13, 10:6
Proverbs 3:13, 4:7, 8:11, 11:2, 23:23
Ephesians 1:17

18

HAVING FAITH FOR THE RACE

"This is the time to press forward says God. Know that I am with you and that I am your strength, your light and your life.

The way ahead is filled with challenges and opportunities and different choices of direction, but My Spirit will be your discerner.

The world will lay snares for your feet, but I will show you the true path. Do not shrink back now for your real race is yet to begin. This is simply a time of preparation. This is like the time of the runner when he runs lap after lap of the training field, improving his time, increasing the condition of his body. Train diligently so that you become great runners.

Don't forget that all great runners were once great walkers. Wear the vest of the righteous, which comes through My Word. That is how the true runners are identified. Tether yourself together for the race, as does the helper with the blind runner; encourage and uplift each other over the rocky ground and the steep hills. In this manner one will not be ahead of the other and one will not be left behind.

Drink from the well of My wisdom and replenish your souls regularly, even daily is not enough for *fullness*. The measure to which I can abide with you reflects the measure to which you can cast out the world from your life.

Make your dreams the true dreams of your heart. Not to please others, not to appear righteous. The true righteous man is the one that follows the desires of his heart with My Spirit power behind him. It is this that gives you the eyes to see the visions of your heart. You must discern them and step forward in faith to attain them, for it will take huge faith before you can see them in the worldly realm.

It takes little faith to believe for today's meal. To believe for the resources to feed 1000 takes more faith. Such faith comes only by My Spirit through My Word".

1 Corinthians 9:24-27, 10:1-13
Psalms 91:3

19

REFRESHING TIMES

"Be careful to use the refreshing times properly says God. They are designed to help you keep filled with the power of My Spirit through the course of the day. It is like leaving home for the day and never again thinking of your beloved until you return home at night. Would you let that happen? Of course not.

What happens in reality is that you stay in communication to check that everything is well, so that you reconnect with your loved one and feel close to them again. You know how it feels to you when you cannot make that connection. You know how it feels when you do not have access to communication. This communication is vital, as it nurtures your love for each other and it shows one that the other one cares for them.

Well My child, so it is with My Spirit. The refreshing times that I speak of are like your phone, you must use them. It is important that these times are used in the correct manner. They are not for fellowship or feeding of the earthly body, they are for nurturing your relationship with My Spirit, getting the answers for the next challenges, refilling the wisdom tanks so that your decisions will be Spirit led and wise. They are for the increase of the anointing, so that you will achieve your goals for the day, even exceed them.

Every day plan your refreshing times first, and then plan everything else around them. I have provided you with the power of My Spirit. It makes no sense to proceed forward with your own fuel when there is so much more available to you".

1 Thessalonians 5:17

20

THE TRUE KEYS

"Discipline and obedience are the true keys to the Spirit filled life. The absence of them leads only to the carnal life where no fruit or rewards are found. It is the natural inclination of the flesh to strive for the reward, yet this should not be the focus. Seek first the righteousness that results from the actions of the Kingdom minded servants, in that way the rewards come later as a matter of course. Again, I repeat the importance of the formula*. This is indeed a hard lesson, but things of eternal consequence are often so says God.

The enemy seeks to blind you to these truths by diminishing their importance with the clutter of this world. Of course, I expect you to operate in the worldly realm, why else would I have you abide there for this season? You need to abide within the structure of My plan and all will be added to you. I have mentioned many times the breakthrough, but you must press through to enter into the fullness and do not shrink back in doubt or fear because you cannot see the fullness of it.

Remember to have a clear picture of your destination, therein lies the importance of the 'written' vision. You ask why I do not visit with you so often. The answer is simple: the guest will not arrive if the host is not present; there is no point in visiting an empty place.

My voice is constantly present to guide and direct those that I have chosen and who are choosing Me. I talk to them all day every day. The question is: are their ears open to hear Me or are their heads filled with the sound of the world? The closer you get to Me, the clearer the words are.

Through unity comes strength and clarity. My blessings are upon My children, be patient and obedient. Focused application of the formula is the final key. You have applied it sporadically and gained some improvement. Now apply it surgically with precision and the floodgates will open," says God.

2 Peter 1:5-11
Proverbs 1:7, 6:23

*See message #1

21

DIFFICULTIES OF DISCIPLINE

"You are witnessing the difficulties of discipline. If it had been easy few would have perished in the past, few would have fallen out of obedience with Me and invoked My displeasure. Perseverance is important; pressing through in difficult times is essential.

I want to bring you encouragement; do not have regard for the difficulties and the challenges, for they are not yours to overcome. I am the true overcomer. Constant contact is greatly important, the inflowing of My Spirit and the special anointing that I have prepared for you will equip you with the wisdom needed to overcome all challenges and to bring forth an abundance of blessings says God.

Now is not the time to shrink back from the edge of the precipice; now is the time to go boldly forward to throw yourself over the edge and to soar like the eagle. The mother of the fledgling pushes him over the edge, confident in his ability to soar. The fledgling has no such knowledge; the only way he could ever know to fly is to be forced into the air in the first place.

Let us continue this journey together; the formula* is your roadmap for the journey, follow it closely and you will not lose your way. What manner of a traveler would set forth on his journey without a map? Remember to have a clear picture of your destination, as again, therein is the importance of the 'written' vision.

What manner of a traveler would have a map that leads to nowhere? Be joyful and be blessed. Be obedient and be blessed, I am with you on every step of the path shown on the map. Take heed not to stray from the path as there are others lying in wait, even devourers lay there. Fear not as they are easily avoided.

The path may be narrow, but it is plain to see for those that have the right map and eyes to watch for it. There is great purpose, strength and power in the things I communicate to you. Seek to surround yourself with the things of which I speak and do not ever underestimate the things that I will achieve as a result of your obedience. Stretch yourselves and increase your faith as I will increase My Faithfulness in you."

1 Corinthians 11:32

Hebrews 12:6-12

John 16:33

1 John 4:4

*See message #1

22

TIME SPENT WITH THE SPIRIT

"As you can see, our communication together reflects the time we get to spend together. It reflects the level of My Spirit abiding within you. The rise of the flesh blocks the flow of communication says God. The Spirit will only overcome the flesh through the sacrifice of praise. I want you to share time with Me out of joy, not out of some enforced kind of religious conviction, for that is more displeasing to Me than no contact. Although it may be a sacrifice to the carnal mind, it should be a duty of the heart, nothing else.

Think intently about the person you want to be; as these thoughts will determine the person you will become. The different outcome will be decided by whether you are thinking with your Spirit anointed mind or your carnal mind. You know how easily My Spirit is offended; yet still, many of you have neglected Me. My Word says, 'My people perish through the lack of knowledge'. Many lack the knowledge about the importance of consistent faithfulness. Sporadic faithfulness will never bring you to the *fullness* of the harvest that I have prepared.

You should focus beyond the immediate situation; focus on your expected outcome beyond the successes as measured by the world. Each step, action or decision needs to be in harmony with that outcome, otherwise do not take it.

Until I return to the earth, the only thing that can give you peace, give you victory, give you wisdom, give you prosperity, is My Spirit. Your only communication channel is My Spirit, there is nothing else. My

Word is life, but as any unbeliever will prove, without My Spirit those words are dead and meaningless, even uninteresting. Through My Spirit they become vibrant, alive, exciting, and full of wisdom and hope to the reader.

What is the message in all this? Well, given the importance of My Spirit, do you want less or more of Me in your life? The closer My Spirit gets to you, the more I abide in every cell of your body, every fiber of your being and the closer you will be to Me. The more you will hear My voice, the easier it will be for Me to guide you, the better you will be at discerning correct decisions during this time on the earth. My Spirit is the 'be all and the end all' of any believer. After all, what is a believer without the Spirit? Sadly, we are often surrounded by the answer to that question. Let us get firmly back on the path I have prepared for you, seek hungrily after My Spirit through My Word and your way will be made easier".

John 14:16-17
John 16:3-13
Titus 2:2

23

WISDOM

"Your sleep will often be troubled if you allow the wiles of the enemy to dislodge you from your path. Stay close to Me and this cannot happen, for My Spirit is your protector and I will keep the enemy from your gates. Grieve My Spirit and I will depart from you. Love Me, praise Me and appreciate Me and I will abide with you day and night. The key to peaceful sleep is to sleep under My precious anointing and the protection of My Spirit who can guard your heart and mind while you rest says God.

Repent for your stubbornness and do not let petty arguments interfere with either your purpose or your relationship with Me. We must move forward as one to accomplish these plans and goals and every distraction simply increases the time required. Celebrate our successes and move forward with the confidence that comes from knowing that you will prevail, because I am with you. I am your strength and through Me you will be able to achieve the desires of your hearts. You must have faith and listen for My voice. Great leaders are always able to display humility first and power last. Wisdom abides in abundance in the mind of a great leader, so seek My counsel and remember My Word contains all wisdom.

Perfect wisdom will cause your love to multiply and this love is the source of living a righteous and rewarding life.

Being a leader comes from your attitude which is forged from either worldly pride, self-elevation or from My anointing. The anointed leaders are easy to detect; 'you will know them by their fruit'. Be strong, press through and seek more after a righteous life.

Keeping these commands between us, amounts to the 'small things' that I require you to be faithful in before I can trust you with everything. My power is with you, use it wisely and stay close to Me.

Be true to your word in all things and expect abundance and success".

Proverbs 6:22, 3:21-26
Psalms 4:8, 127:2
Matthew 25:23

24

FAITH

"Do not be concerned with the past days when your schedule was not properly adhered to. Resolve that the future days will be more fruitful because of your increased obedience says God.

The wise man already knows the entire format of the next day before he even arises from his bed. He has it all planned out and presented to Me the previous evening. He has 'seen' the desired events of the day taking place. He has petitioned before Me for the success of that day and he knows what is going to take place because of his faith.

Without this application the man spends half of his day trying to work out what his day should look like. Then he is easily distracted by this thing or that thing because he was never fixed on a firm determined path, thus he becomes like the fool. He had such good intentions for the day, the problem is that by the time he is finally ready to put the day into action it has already passed, and another opportunity has been foolishly wasted.

Consider the ways of the fool and cause yourself to be far from his actions. Do the opposite of the fool and you will have to be the wise man, there is no other possibility.

Live every moment of every day 'on purpose'. Time spent stumbling on an ill prepared path is time wasted and wasted time is unproductive and can never be recovered.

After your final activity of the day, you need time to reflect, sum up the day, record the outcomes, analyze the progress made in the pursuit of your goals, and calculate what, if any, adjustments need to be made to those goals.

Think, ask My spirit what the next day needs to look like to make further progress, visualize those events, confirm through prayer that they are within My plan for you and pray that day into existence says God.

Give thanks in your morning prayer time, not only thanks for the previous day for that is merely a statement of history a reminder of things past. Give thanks for the things I will be doing for you in the day that is about to happen. That is a great manifestation of your faith. For when you thank Me for the things you have asked Me to do before I actually do them, it is pleasing to know that your faith goes out before you. That is the way it should be.

There is no faith attached to gratitude after the event. Of course, gratitude is significant, but I called you to live by faith, not by gratitude. It is only faith if your thanks are given before it has been done and that you demonstrate the confident expectation that the things that you ask for will be granted to you because My Word says that it is so".

Hebrews 10:38, 11:8-11
Psalms 5:3
Romans 1:17
Galatians 3:11
Habakkuk 2:4

25

RACE RUNNERS

"Shed the cloak of this world utterly and completely. For it is a veil of hypocrisy and lies. The cloak of the world hides the wearer in the shadow of the enemy where My Spirit refuses to dwell. Do not be like the carnal believers and others who remove their cloaks from time to time to 'enjoy' a taste of My Spirit. All they are doing is then replacing the cloak again shortly afterward which denies them the opportunity to be fruitful says God.

If you wear the mantle of humility and My full armor, My Spirit will quicken you. These foul garments of the world; lust, pride, material desires above your needs, these are an offence to My Spirit and will keep believers from the *fullness of My joy*.

Everywhere you look abounds opportunity for you to bear fruit in My name. Just open your eyes, your spiritual eyes and if you also have ears to hear, My instructions will be precise and easy to follow. Most people that do not hear are in that position because they let the noise of this world take precedent in their lives. Shut out the noise of this world by filling your physical bodies with My anointing and the sweet harmony of My Spirit.

Do not look at 'ministry' as some kind of outside entity or association that you need to enter into. A true minister of Mine is evidenced solely by his actions, where he spends his time and by the fruit of these actions. As you know, all race runners will cross the line at the same time. It is not a question of being 'first' in the race; it is a question of running an effective race. Your form and style are all important as they will reflect your true heart and whether you are committed to your own glory or Mine.

Give no thought to the style of other runners. They are not your concern; you should neither seek to emulate them, nor run behind them, nor judge or criticize them. Spend all of your time perfecting your own race. The more attention you give to this, the more effective your race will be. Study the 'runner's guide', which is My Word, therein lies all the answers you will ever need regarding how to qualify to be a runner, equipping yourself for the race, the training you will need to undergo to be able to produce peak performance and of course the skills you will need to recruit and train others.

There are so few runners in this race in comparison to what should be happening. The hooks of this world are strong and relentless, and My people need help. 'Revival with purpose' is required to plant people firmly on the track as race-runners, to equip them with an understanding of the length and difficulty of the course, to equip them through My Word with their 'running shoes' and other equipment.

Develop the mindset of the Spirit filled athlete, one who is determined to run his best race and to never quit regardless of the circumstances and to be an overcomer and a victor in My name. This will not be an easy path, but take comfort in the support and encouragement of My Spirit and the enabling power of My anointing, for this work is precious to Me. I will be your strength, stay ever closer to Me and there are no boundaries that we cannot break through".

Romans 8:18
1 Corinthians 9:24
Galatians 5:7
2 Timothy 4:7
Hebrews 12:1

26

SEED

"How easily we compromise our values to suit to ways of the world. A little untruth here, a small lie there. What then the price of honesty? Maybe protecting the feelings of others is not always the benefit you suppose it to be. Perhaps exposing their error, gently but accurately would be of more benefit. What is our mission, to be pleasing in the sight of people, or to gain My approval? says God.

What treasures do we lay up by allowing another to continue in his own deception? What fruit do we produce by becoming an accessory to the misdirection of another believer? Of course, we can just leave them to go their own way. After all, is that not better than risking that we may cause them some offence? There is no mystery here. The duty of all race runners is to separate themselves from worldly values. Only worldly wisdom operates without correction and in the realm of fear.

Usually this fear stems from the desire not to lose approval. If you are truly seeking after the Kingdom, then every seed planted, either literally from your increase or metaphorically through your words and deeds, must be the finest seed. It must be that which was kept back from the best of the best. Remember the immutable laws of the universe that like has to produce like? If your seed is carefully set aside and skillfully planted, it will produce fruit of unimaginable quality.

Realize the folly of planting seeds of corruption.

Even if you think you can justify your motive, you cannot change the nature of the seed. A seed sown in corruption or with insincerity will produce more of the same and such a vicious cycle of iniquity is difficult to break. Just as one grain of wheat could eventually produce a huge field of amber grain, one corrupt or iniquitous seed can perpetuate itself throughout your race. It will produce copious quantities of wood hay and stubble that will be heaped upon your foundation".

1 Corinthians 3:10-15
Ezekiel 3:20

27

CONTROL THE TONGUE

"Consider that every word you speak is a seed. If you fully understand that every word you speak, being a seed, it has to go forth and sprout, would you change some of the things you say? Make no mistake, this is exactly the case. This is why I give so much instruction about the power of the tongue. An unbridled tongue can scatter a handful of corrupt seed into a field of the finest grain and destroy that whole field in a short space of time. The wise husbandman will choose his seed carefully and with deep understanding of the importance of its quality. The serious Kingdom seeker needs to be of the same heart with not only the seeds of his income, but more importantly with the verbal seeds spoken into existence on a daily basis says God.

Yes, it is very difficult to control the tongue. To do so, you must first control your thoughts, as the tongue only issues forth that which is in your mind. There are often remnants of your old fallen spirit with which you were born, the spirit of this world that is the mind of this world. This is the mind that is willing to accept all possibilities. The mind that constantly nurtures that old carnal spirit by feeding upon the abundance of misdirection offered by the world.

You now live in a world in which murdering unborn children is not only acceptable, a law has been put in place protecting a person's 'right' to commit such murder, a world in which many people live in direct contravention to My Word. These are examples of the fruit of being 'broad minded' or 'open minded'. The teaching of the acceptance of such things has brought and will continue to bring, much destruction and will cause many to stumble.

How can anyone hope to control the tongue, an instrument of the mind without first controlling what they think? You think about what you see, you think about what you hear. Consequently, the more you restrict what you see and hear to things that are consistent with My plan for your life, the more you will think about only these things.

The more you think about these things, the more you will talk of them and speak those seeds into existence says God.

The lesson here is the difficulty of thinking. It has been said that 'thinking is the hardest work in the world'. This is of course true and now you have a clear understanding as to why it is so difficult. It is not the thinking per se that is so hard, it is thinking about the 'right things' that is the key.

Your wisdom should tell you that you that you can only think about the things that you bring into your mind. Although you are bombarded with new information every day, you can choose what information you wish to absorb. You can decide what to present to your mind as food from which it can feed.

There is a simple system that will help you perfect this. Consider your actions before you take them. Why do you think the world has always been so concerned with the encouragement of spontaneity and broad mindedness? Because the enemy knows what havoc it will wreak. Consider then every action and ask yourself 'will planting this seed bear fruit that will be of value in the coming Kingdom?

If the answer is 'no' do not plant that seed. For if you do, you do so at your own peril'".

James 3:5-9
1 Peter 3:10

64

THE POWER OF THINKING

"A race runner that has to spend time every day weeding out the shoots of sprouting 'disasters' that he himself has previously sown; trying to gather up the new seeds before they can multiply, is wasting time and making no progress.

Just the right consideration before talking or acting is incredibly valuable. How often does one 'perfect' thinking? Remove yourself from the pace of this world. Operate at the pace of My Spirit. Practice the skill of thinking. Ask My Spirit to order your mind so that you are not distracted by the constant assault on the senses by the things of the world says God.

Fellowship with like-minded Spirit filled believers. They will converse about the deep meaningful meat of My Word. Fellowship with frivolous people and they will talk frivolously. Those deceived by the riches of this world will talk incessantly about money and deals. It is not an easy place to be, of this there is no doubt. That is why true race runners have to suffer with Me. It is so alien to the carnal mind to consider such drastic withdrawal from the world.

Does this not clearly speak as to why, so few will be chosen? From the start, even the called are relatively few in number, the chosen a tiny percentage of those. What about the faithful? Only those able to conquer the challenge of controlling the 'thinking man' and therefore bridling their tongues and their actions, can even aspire to have hope of being among that number.

I tell you this not to fill you with despair over the difficulty of the path ahead, but to fill you with hope. You know exactly what needs to be done to run the race in the way that you truly want to run it. Difficult? Without doubt. Possible? Of course, because all things are possible through Me says God.

If your thoughts are constantly directed towards the things of Me, My Spirit will keep them in order. Your words and actions will be controlled, and your fruit will be righteous and abundant. This is a powerful revelation for you says God. You should now be more prepared for the real beginning of your journey".

Isaiah 26:3

Romans 8:18

Philippians 4:8

2 Timothy 2:12

James 3:5-9

Revelation 17:14

Matthew 22:14

Acts 14:22

29

KEEPING YOUR MIND CLEAR TO PRODUCE FRUIT

"Look how much clearer your mind becomes when you keep it clear from the nonsense of this world. It will require great effort and diligence to maintain and then build upon this platform, but the outcome will be well worth effort says God. You can increase your efforts in this direction one day at a time. Each day you will grow stronger and more confident that you are on the right path. As the mist and fog of this world clears from your spirit your view of your intended purpose will become clearer and clearer.

One of the wiles of the enemy is to fill a person's mind with 'other stuff' and because of that many of them have never even had a glimpse of their true purpose on this earth. All of the day their thoughts are filled with what they need to do to earn enough money to try and cope with the financial burden they have been placed under; house payments, credit card payments, car payments and so it goes on. The world's sickly system has them buried under these terrible burdens from which many never break free. Then they pass on the acceptance of such a system to their offspring and so it perpetuates.

They may never get to see the incredible possibilities that lay ahead for them if they cannot get the world's clutter out of their heads. Only once you have successfully completed this process yourself, can you begin to help others.

You cannot be holding a cigarette whilst explaining to someone how to quit smoking. Being an example is a powerful testimony.

Just as My Son was an example to the apostles and all of the people that witnessed what was carried out on the earth.

Be fruitful. The fruit says more about what you are doing than any words. Your fruit will stir up the faith of others and cause them to have hope. Wise counsel will help them to put their faith into action and start to produce their own fruit. Their fruit will stir up the faith of still more believers. See how this leads us towards 'revival with purpose'?

It all starts with the fruit and the fruit comes from the actions; the actions are generated by the faith and the faith comes by hearing and the hearing comes by the Word. I am the Word. Stay in Me, around Me, feed your soul and your spirit with Me and in the abundance of your obedience will be the abundance of your success and your reward".

James 3:2
Titus 2:7
Colossians 3:17
Matthew 5:16
1 Corinthians 9:27

30

RIGHTEOUS WORKS

"It is one thing to be mistaken about the meaning of righteous works and getting involved in church programs and law works. However, it is a completely different thing to be fully aware of what correct righteous works are and yet not to be doing any says God.

Opportunities abound all around you and they extend far beyond opportunities to sow financial seed.

Have eyes to see and you will surely discover situations where you can contribute. Righteous works will overflow from the conviction in your heart. You should not be waiting for certain conditions to be met, before you will be able to 'do' something. After all, My laws of giving and receiving dictate that many of the things after which you seek will be released as a consequence of your obedience.

This obedience cannot only be related to things that you find comfort in; it must be complete and relate to all situations. Many people think that running the race should be solely centered around their local church. This could not be further from the truth. This is the same situation as the financial seed; unless it is released into My universe, it has no value; there can be no harvest, it will not produce new seed, it is rendered useless. It is the same with the 'seeds of possibility'. The seeds of things you could be doing in My name, but you are not doing because you are waiting for certain circumstances to fall into place.

Pay heed to the parable of the talents. Not using your seed is really the same as burying it. Would you want Me to return and find all of the seed still in your hands? You know the answer to that question. It is one thing to see the wood, hay and stubble burn up before your eyes at the judgment seat, or perhaps you may think there is something more righteous in a platform with nothing on it in the first place? Be not deceived, they both end up with losses. This is an important issue as time passes quickly and each passing day is a lost opportunity that cannot be reclaimed.

It is one thing to ask Me to restore that which the locust has eaten, but this matter concerns that which you yourselves are destroying. Time waits for no man, so start moving. This does not apply only to your work life as that is concerned mainly with the generation of financial seed, which is necessary but should not be all encompassing. Take heart, you will find nothing more rewarding than this. It will bring joy to you and you will bring joy to others and I will take joy in your obedience," says God.

Matthew 25:14
James 2:18-26
1 Corinthians 3:10-20

31

UNDERSTANDING FAITH

"It is important for you to discover an essential key in the understanding of the manner in which the race runner 'seeking first the kingdom', shall live. Only a life lived by faith can attain the prize says God. Do not be deceived because you know that faith without works is dead. However, faith, is the catalyst for every work.

It is through faith only that you will know that you have heard My voice, that you are doing My will. People who constantly seek confirmation after confirmation of everything they 'think' they hear are just manifesting their lack of faith. Yes, it is true that I instruct that you should test words of knowledge and prophecies against My Word, but this is not the same thing. True faith requires boldness. If you ask for an outcome, you must precisely take the steps that you know will produce that outcome, believing that it will happen before you even take the first step. Just as the faith is sure, the necessary works must be carried out otherwise the end result cannot be as you have desired.

Lack of faith causes falling short of the desired outcome; the Israelites believed, and they were saved out of Egypt, but their faith was sporadic, and they therefore did not complete all of their works in a satisfactory manner, so they were prevented from entering into the fullness of their expectation.

Faith is the unfailing vital ingredient in every aspect of your spiritual life. If your faith is true, you will boldly take the necessary steps and the Spirit filled works will follow. Your faith needs to be constantly fed, it is like a flickering flame, but you need to build it up into a raging fire. When your faith is such, the flame will emanate from you as a bright burning light and you will be as a beacon in the world and people will wonder at your brightness and the joy that accompanies it.

So how do you do that? Oh, it is yet so simple but so many people walk right past the keys because of the simplicity; 'Faith comes by hearing and hearing comes by the Word'.

Immerse yourselves in the understanding of My Word and your faith will be kindled and your fire will burn brighter and brighter.

People think they have faith, but they seldom have even the beginnings of faith. Living by faith in the world is contrary to every inclination of the flesh. The flesh wants to have faith in itself or in some other person, it wants to have faith in something it can feel, touch and see. This is not true faith, it is merely an imitation.

Faith is knowing that everything that you do, is building upon your foundation and that you trust only in Me to provide you with the right material".

1 Corinthians 3:11
Hebrews 10:38, 11
Romans 1:17
Psalms 18:24
1 Corinthians 4:5

32

ACTIONS SPEAK LOUDER THAN WORDS.

"There are many people who talk a good story of being a 'Christian' or a 'believer'. As I have said, 'you will know them by their fruit'. No fruit was ever produced by purely thinking about it. Yes, the thinking is the catalyst, it is the beginning of the process, but still the action required to put those thoughts to proper use has to take place.

Remember again, that faith without works is dead. Likewise, thought without action is dead. Do not fall into the trap of being a 'thinking' believer, for this is a grave error. This is why I call people to be doers of My Word and not just hearers. The thinking believer can become very righteous and effective in his own mind. However, this will have no impact of any positive consequences in the coming Kingdom.

Your thoughts will add nothing to your foundational platform, unless they are accompanied by the necessary actions. The only way that fruit is produced is by action. There will be many on that Day that will swell with pride over their knowledge of My Word, they will be eagerly anticipating their reward for their diligence in studying. A man whose head is full of the wisdom of the Word, that has not put it into action, is no different than the wicked servant who buried his talent. He is no more mature because of his knowledge, as it has profited him nothing says God.

The same can be said of those that study and then teach in error because it is easier or more gainful in the world. In fact, they will be more severely judged, for as teachers they have a greater responsibility.

You must be mindful of the importance of action. Otherwise it will become a limiting factor in your life. Put your faith before you and start 'doing'. You will be in awe of the outcome. It is no good standing in your running clothes, with your new shoes on and then being too fearful to step out on the track. The die is cast, you are now inexorably on this journey of running the race. The days are shortening, and you must constantly ask the question 'where is the fruit?'

If you ask this before every action you will have a clear determination as to the origin of the thoughts that you are contemplating. Beware of the thoughts that try and slip in from the world. You know they are of the enemy. Apply the test: 'where is the fruit' and their deceit will be instantly revealed.

Become more contemplative, more discerning and less impulsive. Take everything under consideration and let My Spirit be your decision maker. Calmness and peacefulness, humility and focus of purpose are the hallmarks of a true race runner. Nurture these qualities and seek after them earnestly. They are all found in My Word and will be of great comfort to you".

Ephesians 5:15-17
Hebrews 12:1
John 15:2-16
Romans 7:4
Colossians1:10
1 Corinthians 3:10
2 Timothy 4:7

33

CREATING THE HEDGE OF JOB

"Playing sweet Spirit inspiring music in your home is pleasing to Me as it creates a fragrant atmosphere. To create the hedge of Job, these things must be in evidence.

Be sure to operate on My timetable and not that of the world. When things 'pop up' to cause you distraction, before acting upon them, you must ask the question, 'where is the fruit'? If it is not clearly evident, then you will discern that it is not My intervention and you can discard it.

The 'sin that so easily besets', is a problem for most believers and is something that you absolutely have to gain victory over, so as not to fall into this snare of the enemy. It is so difficult from a worldly standpoint to resist bowing to the disappointment, the flesh wants to cry out 'oh God why me'? or 'how could You let that happen'? or 'but I thought You said…'

My child, there is so much you cannot understand from your current perspective, rather focus on that which you can understand. The love of the living God is true and all encompassing, it can overcome any disappointment of the flesh.

If My Spirit is abiding with you in fullness nothing will be able to penetrate your hedge. Do not forget, if you leave even the smallest hole, the enemy will come in and he will attack you.

Watch for others that could make holes in your hedge, even inadvertently, with a word, a deed or a distraction. When you leave the protection of your dwelling place, be even more careful that you are wearing the full armor.

Would a soldier at war walk naked into enemy territory with no weapon or protection? As absurd as it sounds, My people do it on a daily basis and wonder why so many are falling".

Ephesians 3:17-19, 6:10-18
Hebrews 12:1-2
Job 1:10
Isaiah 55:9

34

RENEW YOUR FAITH DAILY

"The enemy has a very clear purpose. To disrupt and destroy the lives of the saints. This is not a weekend hobby for him, this is not a game, this is warfare! This is a 24/7 unrelenting battle. This is the most serious fight of your lives on earth.

This enemy has the power to destroy the lives of My children. They must not let down the guard of My protection. They must not underestimate the seriousness of this situation. Running the race of the righteous is a difficult enough proposition but make no mistake, this race track is riddled with landmines, steep hills and false tracks laid right next to the real one, which a runner that loses his focus for even a brief moment, could find himself upon unawares.

It all brings you back again to faith. This faith should be like the manna of old. Renew it every day. Yesterday's faith is not what you need today. Walk in the anointing continually, for the decisions and actions of an anointed man being used of My Spirit will always be perfect. The imperfections only arise when you allow the flesh to participate.

Eat the Word, build the faith, then you will have the strength required to carry the anointing at all times, for therein lies perfection. Strive for it, hunger after it. There are no words that can adequately express the power of the outcome, except to say that those with this level of faith, will be known as the Faith-full and you know who they are. Ask yourself as you read these words, 'am I doing all that has been asked of me"?

1 Peter 5:8
2 John 8

35

TEST EVERYTHING AGAINST THE WORD

"My servant Moses lived among the Egyptians for a season. Even though he enjoyed the fruits of their prosperity, he never lost sight of to whom he belonged. Never forget the example of those that followed Moses, that their wilderness experience was prolonged by their own impatience and disobedience.

Just as Moses had a number of people with advice or suggestions, the Word of God was the only authority. It is the same in the present time. Many will come with this thing and that thing, test them all against My Word and My calling. If the harvest will not resemble the fruit, do not plant that seed," says God.

Hebrews 3:17-19
1 Corinthians 10:1-13

36

DO NOT CONSIDER THE CURRENT CIRCUMSTANCES AS REALITY

"Be careful not to consider the current circumstances as reality. The intensity of the attack from the enemy is simply a reflection of your desire to be pleasing in My sight and to carry out the work I have called you to do. The picture in Ezekiel is a true type of the current situation. My people should take heed against dangerous slothfulness. Those warned have the opportunity to save their souls through this work. What says the enemy of such work? Of course, he does not want this to take place. He seeks to prevent such work and to destroy those that would participate in it.

The enemy will go straight for the weakest point and the easiest thing to affect is your faith, which can so easily waver.

You must remain steadfast through these times, seek even more earnestly after My Spirit and My Anointing. The enemy seeks to embroil you back into the ways of the world where every waking moment is spent in pursuit of the finances needed to exist in the world's system. Escape this system through faithful diligence.

The snare of the world is a wide net, only the wise can avoid it and you know where the wisdom comes from. Resist the devil and he will flee from you. Be careful not to let the circumstances he creates to cause your focus to fail. The smallest hole in the hedge can let in an entire army. You must constantly make repairs. His soldiers are; doubt, uncertainty, faithlessness, unbelief, contention, dismay and resignation. They can all be repelled with your shield of faith and slain completely by the sword of the Spirit.

This is the time to stand, to press through and continue confidently in the assurances of My promise that 'greater is He that is in you than he who is in the world'. Take comfort in My strength and be careful not to feel that you can ever face this adversary alone. There are many that have trod such a path who have either been completely destroyed or who now hold the hand of the enemy in an unwitting and corrupt partnership.

How they will plead on that Day that they never knew; that they were deceived or surprised. Excuses will profit no man. All are given eyes, but not all focus them properly because the deceitfulness of the riches of this world is a great distraction to some of My sheep, even to the destruction of their souls.

Keep Me close, be like the careful warrior, he knows he will gain victory over his adversary, but he is always fully aware of the capability of his foe. Do not let down your guard. Keep the hedges of your camp in good repair.

As you become more skilled in warfare, you will be able to discern the attacks before they will happen and be prepared for them. A well-prepared warrior is free from the emotional trauma of the battle. He directs his armaments with confidence and the assuredness of the Victor.

The enemy will then re-direct his attention to easier prey and will return only occasionally for a hopeful skirmish. Be warned that there must never be a hole in your hedge when he comes back, for this will cause the whole cycle to repeat itself, as is the case for many who are diligent for a season, but then become complacent says God.

The path that you have embarked on is not a 'seasonal vocation'. This has to be a permanent transition. It is the beginning of an eternal journey without end.

Consider the Israelites and the amount of time they circled the same mountain. They kept a very untidy hedge, even one hole would have produced the same situation, so the importance of the matter is clearly evident.

It should not be difficult, but patience and endurance do not come easy to those in the world. Faith is the key, wear it, consume it, nurture it and this victory will be yours," says God.

1 John 4:4 & 5:19
Zechariah 4:6
Ephesians 6:10-18
1 Corinthians 10:1-13
Romans 14:10-12

37

ANOINTING

"The sun goes up and down every day, that you can be sure of. My anointing and My Spirit are equally as certain.

However, some days you cannot actually see the sun because the clouds or the mist is masking its appearance, but it is still there.

It is the same thing with the anointing of My Spirit. It is always there, but sometimes it will be hidden from you by the clouds and the mist of this world and it is up to you to reach through and sweep away those obstructions.

The best way to do this is through speaking My Word, through prayer and direct connection with My Spirit".

Matthew 24:35

38

THE DREAM ABOUT THE LEVELS

"To take a true refreshing time, you must leave the place of your labor, you cannot successfully and fully give your attention to Me if you are surrounded by the environment that has worldly connections in plain view. Detach yourself and put yourself away for that time so that you truly have an opportunity to be refreshed says God.

Consider the dream that you had for I have provided you with the interpretation".

The dream:

I was on a boat, it appeared to be a beautiful luxurious vessel. It did not seem to be particularly large as it was being tossed around in an increasingly stormy sea. I suddenly noticed that I was completely alone on this boat, everyone else had left.

I was in the area where all the controls and navigation equipment are situated. Everything looked incredibly sophisticated and although the sea was rough, it appeared that the boat was able to withstand the storm. Having no idea what to do, I began to search around for some kind of instructions as to how I might steer this boat out of this storm.

In one of the cupboards, I found what appeared to be a handbook.

I started to read, and it said that in these conditions it was best to open one of the hatches and go down to the lower decks. I hadn't even realized that there were lower decks! I looked around and sure enough there was a hatch in the floor. I opened it and proceeded down the stairs. The next level that I got to, resembled part of a huge cruise ship. There was plush carpet and furnishings and I could see the entrance to the casino.

There were lots of people moving around and there seemed to be an air of uncertainty. The carpets were wet and, in some areas, I would see water leaking through quite severely.

I then felt urged to 'go deeper' and so I proceeded down to the next level. This was like a different world. At this level, the boat was completely calm. There was a huge electronic map on the wall and you could clearly see the position of the vessel and exactly where it was going. The people at this level all seemed to be calm and self-assured. The fear and chaos of the other levels were nowhere in evidence.

The interpretation:

The upper level, the first place I found myself to be in, represented the new believer. Here he is having the opportunity to take the helm of his own life and guide it where his will dictates. The fact that he appeared to be safe from the rough sea, mirrors the sense of comfort and assurance we all experience in those early days after conversion.

The handbook that was discovered represents the handbook that every believer has access to, the Word of God. The instruction to go down to a lower level was guiding the reader to start 'descending' into the Word. The first level that I appeared at was representative of where so many people end up.

That the water was leaking in was representative of the fact that even though they are in the Word, there are other things 'leaking in' from the world, dampening the effect of the Word in their lives, hence the wet carpets.

The casino reminds us that these people are still living firmly in the world and to a large degree they are still 'of' the world. The fact that this is a direct contravention of God's instructions who called us to be 'in the world' but not 'of the world' is what is causing the uncertainty and chaos. Sadly, this is a true portrait of the average believer. Yes, he spends time in the Word of God, but he is not deep enough to leave behind the negative and destructive influences of this world.

Then came the instruction to go deeper. Here there was complete calmness and assuredness of direction. This represents what one finds by delving deeply into the Word. This Word is the builder of your faith and the conduit to your relationship with the Spirit. The deeper you go down into the things of the Word, the more you will leave the things of this world behind and your days will have balance, clarity and purpose.

1 John 2:15-17

REMEMBER THE SEED

"Be careful that you do not let your flesh do the things that you do not want it to do. If a student of My wisdom cannot rise above simple worldly imperfections, how can they aspire to teach others to run the race? One cannot 'to and fro' from the track as it suits him. Your eyes need to be firmly fixed on the correct path and gossip and contention between My people is simply a distraction of the enemy designed to subvert your progress says God.

This tactic of his only works if you let the flesh get in the way and start making decisions for you. Anytime you do not like the look of the fruit, remember the nature of the seed that you planted to produce it. Never forget that there is no such thing as fruit which just 'springs up'. Everything has to first be a seed. Identify the seed of your discontent and do not plant it again.

Remember the essence of the faithful believer is love. This is often a most challenging requirement in the context of worldly events. However, the key is that it is an obligation and not a choice. There are no degrees of My love, you either operate from a loving perspective all of the time or you are in danger of falling short. It is precisely these kinds of challenges that make the running of the race so difficult and of course so potentially rewarding".

Romans 7:15 -25
Hebrews 12:2
Galatians 5:6
Titus 2:12

40

KEEPING YOUR HEDGE STRONG

"As you are entering into a time of joy, abundance and prosperity, you must be more careful to build your hedge stronger and check its security more diligently says God. The anointing of My Spirit will give you the ability to keep a strong hedge, but you must be sure to not let your defenses down for even a minute. Never forget that the enemy is like a fox. He just needs one opening and he will often kill all of the chickens just because he can, he does not even need to be hungry.

Use the armor daily, because just a few days passing with no attacks does not mean that the enemy has decided to leave you alone. Be sure of this fact, he will never leave you alone. Sure, he may focus attention elsewhere for a season, but often that is just to lull you into a false sense of security in the hope that you will let your guard down and that you will stop doing the things that provide your protection; that you will return to the world, maybe temporarily.

When you are in the world's influence you are in his domain and your protection is vulnerable; if you lapse back to being of the world you are completely outside of My will and therefore your protection can be penetrated. Stay close to Me, for the fox is ineffective against the Lion. Keep focused with singleness of purpose. Be sure that you are in harmony with your purpose for the blessings fall more easily on you when there is clarity, cooperation and continuity".

James 4:4

Isaiah 5:5

Romans 12:2

Ephesians 2:2

CODE OF THE SEED

"You are still hovering around the edges of the anointing; there is so much more for you if you will just press through to the deeper levels. The building of your faith will bring total commitment, which is what is required. To be anything else, requires you to remain in the world and this is unacceptable.

Pray before every action. Let the Spirit take the lead, get the flesh out of the way. The choices are there for you!

Make sure you understand the importance of sowing and reaping and of naming the seeds. It is clearly evident that all of the seeds that I have provided will produce only that for which they were intended. No other outcome is possible says God.

Through the advent of money, I have given you the same power. You can sow this seed of money into lives, ministries and really anywhere the Spirit leads you. However, money carries no genetic code, it is purely an instrument of transaction.

It is not the money itself that does anything. It is the faith behind the action that bears the fruit. In order for faith to have effect, there has to be action with it. Naming the seed before sowing, embeds the 'code' into that seed, so that the fruit it will produce is predetermined. You already know that nothing is left to chance. Every outcome is the result of a previous action.

Consistent and persistent application out of obedience is what is required of you.

Obedience is difficult, challenging and can be uncomfortable at first. Once it has transcended the flesh, all of those emotions are washed away in a flood of joy that can only be known through the total control of My Spirit and walking each day with Me right there next to you. Strive for the joy for there is nothing that can compare.

Those that I have equipped as leaders, should lead where it is appropriate, follow where it is prudent and be humble and loving at all times. As you grow in wisdom, remember that love, faith and wisdom are inseparable. If one is missing the other two will be diminished to the degree that they are no longer effective".

2 Corinthians 9:10-11
Ephesians 1:17, 3:17-18

42

PURPOSE

"Ask Me to send wisdom upon you says God, the wisdom you need to mingle with your faith and love that you may perform My will. You are called to maturity and must act accordingly. Let love always be the first motivator.

Use the talents I have vested in you. Remember that the flow must be continuous. As it flows forth from you, it will flow back to you multiplied. Your purpose will only fully unfold as you take bold steps forwards. Your overarching vision is to be pleasing in My sight and to perform My will. Better a small step today born out of faith, than a huge leap at some time in the future when it appears that all of the 'conditions' are right.

Faith in action creates its own conditions says God. Learn to let your faith precede you and you will marvel at the outcome.

Create a list of 4 small steps that you can take in the next 30 days. Take one step per week and develop the habit of making progress towards your step each day, then each half of the day, then each hour of the day. Ultimately every action of the day, every thought, every decision, every instruction will be carrying you towards the outcome which you are already confident of because you spoke it into existence under My anointing and you proceed towards it under the teaching of My wisdom and you gain support from others through the application of My love.

There it is then; faith, love and wisdom, the armory of the true soldier of God. With these weapons applied in your life through My Spirit you cannot fail. Your purpose will become self-evident and every day will be filled with joy as the worries of this world will have no room to compete for your attention".

Ephesians 1:17, 5:1, 5:15
1 Corinthians 16:14
Hebrews 5:14

43

FAITH IN ACTION

"Faith in action brings dreams and goals to life. There are many that have dreams and things they would like to achieve with their lives, but they never take the repeated action steps that will bring those things into reality. People say they want to do things in My time and My will, but do they really mean that? Most of the time they hope that the things they desire are going to coincide with My will for their lives so that they can justify having them. Be sure that all actions take you towards the goals we have determined together says God.

Firstly, the small things must be achieved and done properly, then the larger things will be easier to achieve. Then the seemingly impossible things will come clearly into focus and become attainable. As you move towards the attainment of these goals, you will attract attention. Some of the people will look to bless you and some of them will look to hinder you. Be sure to constantly abide with My Spirit so that you can discern who is who. Be a light and a blessing to all. Do not look to undermine any person, for that energy can be better spent uplifting someone else.

You must be consistent in your efforts, as only through this focused effort can any lasting improvement be brought about. Just as you are checking your words with regard to negativity in general, check them with regard to other people. Be diligent in speaking only uplifting things about all people. If there comes a time when you are tempted to speak ill of another, rather say nothing. Never create negative possibilities with your words.

You have witnessed first-hand the importance of the diligence and focus in your life. See how easily the world sucks you in? Right back into an existence of purposelessness.

You must live your lives 'on purpose' for there to be any meaningful significance.

The many hours of watching television has started to creep back into your lives. How will you respond? Rather spend your time, strengthening your spiritual position than filling your heads with the meaningless folly of the world. Remove Jezebel from your environment, she is powerful and destructive. Seek after the anointing of My Spirit. Stay close and see Me as your comforter and protector. This will bring order and authority to your life. My Spirit is your organizer and your planner. Keep Him close through daily communication. Consult Him on every issue. What is the point in having your own personal counselor if you do not seek his advice? Why consult Him only when you have a problem? Rather use His wisdom to prevent the problems from occurring in the first place.

Give Him first place in all things, He is your direct conduit to Me says God and the clearer that communication channel remains, the more clearly you will hear of My direction for your lives.

There is much to be done, but only through obedience can you enter into the abundance of My anointing".

Luke 16:10
Ephesians 4:29
1 John 5:3
Proverbs 16:24
Colossians 4:6
1 Thessalonians 5:11

44

MERCY

"Mercy comes to those who seek it with a pure heart says God. Many repent in words but their hearts are truly revealed with their misdeeds. The mouth overflows with repentance out of a sense of guilt or worse, religious duty. I will not be deceived by such mockery. I can see the true contrite spirit and the repented heart, and My mercy is complete and true. Those that repent in word only but not in heart, let them beware. Rather that they remain silent than open their mouths with insincerity.

Be sure that you are clear on the purpose behind whatever you do. No business exists just for the sake of providing work or just for the sake of being in business, at least not one that will thrive. If a person works 'to make ends meet' that is what they will receive. The vision is nonspecific and inadequate, and the reward will look similar. Make sure that your vision is crystal clear, that you can focus on it daily and seek the wisdom of My Spirit in the steps you must take to bring the vision to reality. Visualize it in your prayers and consolidate its creation through your words. Remember that in the spiritual realm it already exists and you must speak its manifestation into being.

The anointing is something you already possess. You just need to activate it. This takes place through your actions. If you start taking the steps that the good stewards take, you will kindle the anointing within your own life. If you adopt the nature of the good steward, it will become your nature.

Keep records of your stewardship, you will see patterns emerging" says God.

Romans 4:17

Isaiah 29:13

Psalms 19:14, 24:3, 51:10, 51:17

Hebrews 4:16

45

ANGELS AND DEMONS

"My angels abide where there is extreme danger or extreme anointing, which requires the manifest presence of the Spirit says God. Angelic participation is only possible on this basis. The angels are the epitome of the work ethic required to work 'as to The LORD'.

Seek excellence in all that you do, and they will help you every step of the way. You can be sure that every good idea or intention that you think of will immediately generate a response from the demons assigned to subvert your purpose. They are there purely to prevent you from bringing glory to My name. If there is no demonic activity working against you it will only be because you are not doing anything to glorify Me and thus they need not bother with you. Notice how as soon as you start to make progress you meet resistance? This comes from the spiritual realm where the battle is both intense and incessant. The constant presence of My Spirit is therefore necessary in order for you to prevail".

Hebrews 12:2
Ephesians 2:6-7, 6:12
Psalms 103:20
Colossians 3:23-24

46

APPLIED FOCUS

"Excellence is a fruit of diligent persistence, says God.

You will not produce it with erratic attention.

Applied focus is the seed of excellence and prayer will nurture those seeds to produce a glorious bountiful harvest. Now is the time to press through and pursue this power with serious intent. There is no such entity as 'partial focus', it must be full and consistent to bring the desired outcome.

Do not let the distractions of this world hinder your progress. Press through now and move into the abundance I have prepared for you says God.

The table is abundantly laid, come enjoy and together we will perform great exploits and bring hope and relief to many and teach empowerment to others.

Keep our relationship at the forefront of every endeavor, bring all of your decisions before Me for approval or discounting through My Spirit.

Pour out your love upon Me and I will pour Mine out upon you to a degree that you cannot even imagine. Be a blessing in order to be blessed, love in order to be loved and give in order to receive the abundance I am waiting to pour out into your lives. I am your strength and wisdom and I take pleasure in our partnership".

2 Corinthians 8:7
Philippians 4:8
Proverbs 3:6

47

EXCELLENCE

"There is a beauty about excellence which is always self-evident
to everyone that beholds it. Regardless of the field of endeavor,
excellence is always both charismatic and awe-inspiring. It is a state that
every person would secretly love to aspire to, but often they lack the
courage to pursue it for fear of falling short. Excellence requires not
only boldness, but also single-minded focus and determination of the
spirit; a stoic resolution that the prize will be attained and that nothing
will deny the pursuer no matter how challenging the obstacles may
appear. Excellence begins in the mind of the achiever at the precise
moment he makes the decision to settle for nothing less.

Thus begins the journey to a lifetime of fruitfulness and
empowerment of those around us. For an excellent life will always
bring light to the world and illuminate the hope inside those living in
mediocrity. Excellence can only be found through a life that is lived
'on purpose' says God.

Do not settle for anything. Decide right now to strive for excellence
in your life and watch the transformation that occurs. Consider every
thought before you allow it to produce a word or an action. Ask
yourself if it will lead you further along the road to excellence. If it is
not clearly a 'yes' then it is definitely a 'no'.

Now you can go forward with anticipation and expectation; you have
made the decision to pursue excellence in your life. From this moment
forward your life will never be the same as it was before you made this
decision".

1 Corinthians 12:31, 13

48

THE WAR WITH THE FLESH

"To be an instrument of Mine you must remain in constant proximity to the work that you are required to do says God. There are things presented to you as opportunities to spend your time on that will take you away from your purpose and these are to be avoided. There are of course recreational activities that are in harmony with your purpose and My Spirit will be your guide in this respect.

The war with the flesh will never end, but like some enemies, it can be subdued by not giving it opportunities to nurture itself and grow in power. Walk in victory at all times and concentrate your mind on only uplifting, empowering and effective thinking.

This significantly reduces the space available for the flesh to operate in. It will also train your own spirit more effectively to recognize the thoughts that have the ability to empower the flesh. Remember that thoughts have no power until they become either words or actions. Consequently, by controlling your thinking, the flesh will be conquered. It takes consistent focused effort and obedience.

In order to succeed in this arena, you must nourish this anointing through obedience and strengthening of your relationship with the Spirit. He will abide with you at all times, but any promotion of the flesh or inconsiderate actions will lose the continuity. It is like the game of 'snakes and ladders', every time you do one of these things, you slip back to an earlier point. You can end up slipping right back to the start in absence of constant vigilance.

Pray consistently about all things and make a sanctuary for My Spirit by keeping an undefiled mind and body and your days will be long, prosperous and filled with joy beyond your imagination".

1 Peter 4:1
Romans 8:5-9
Psalms 19:14
1 Thessalonians 5:16-18
Jude:23

49

DO NOT DELAY

"The anointing will always manifest far more strongly in an environment of obedience.

I am aware of all of the desires of your heart and everything you seek is already in place at the next level. You have to attain it through wisdom and understanding.

The wisdom of the world will always lead you further away from your purpose and your goals. Your obedience will provide you with the clarity to discern My wisdom which will always guide you on the path that is true says God.

You are hovering around the full implementation of all of the ingredients. You have come this far, got this close, now push through and enter into the realm of joyful abundance. In this realm, you will be able to operate at a level above that of the world, your values are different, your desires are different and your ability to empower others and contribute change to their situations will be at its greatest level of power. To be blessed you must first be a blessing.

Do not delay, for every day lost is a lost opportunity. Make an accurate list of all things required and act upon them immediately. Swift action produces swift results. Do not give your mind time to focus on the draining and wasteful attractions of the world. These distractions hold people captive, they become slaves to the marketing machine of the enemy, bombarding their minds with a constant barrage of meaningless nonsense.

How can they ever focus on the eternal when they are trapped in a world that does not really exist?

Be vigilant in these things I have mentioned and a remarkable transformation is available to you bringing with it a wealth of opportunity and joy".

Psalms 20:4, 37:4-5
Proverbs 16:1-3
Romans 8:28

50

MEEKNESS

"You cannot walk in My anointing wearing the shoes of the world says God. Be sure to cast them aside as they will lead you only to paths of deceit and destruction. Therefore, check your feet before taking even the first step each day. The enemy is cunning, and his path is designed to look very similar to Mine and many of My sheep get led astray in this manner. Some cannot find their way back and I weep for them. The level of anointing around you will increase out of your obedience so consider all of the ingredients and press on. Hold your faith out before you like a banner, be upright, bold and confident.

There is no need for arrogance, but do not misunderstand the term 'meekness'. Even the meek, walking in righteousness, have the self-assuredness of a victorious conqueror. Humility of heart identifies the meek; the lack of desire for promotion of self, but that in no way detracts from the victory.

The enemy cannot defeat the meek for they are the strongest and most powerful of all My children says God. Strive for meekness, as the owners of such a label will wear notable crowns".

Matthew 5:5
Revelation 3:11

51

WALKING IN THE IMAGE OF GOD

"The only way for you to impact the lives of other people in a manner that will be of lasting significance, is by My power working through you says God. In order for this to be effective, you have to be a willing vessel prepared to discard your worldly values for heavenly values and for walking in My image.

Being a true believer is not an attitude, it is a way of being. You cannot 'look' like a believer, you just are.

Be mindful of over-equipping. Many of My children spend too much time getting ready to do something meaningful. They embark on a 'lifetime of preparing'. What are they preparing for? Once they leave this world all the preparations will be meaningless. They will each be called to account for their actions. There is no reward for what you were thinking about doing.

Your daily life, work and business will be transformed by the pursuit of My image. Turn every decision over to Me. This results in far greater success than making your own decisions.

See how much more can be achieved in a day when you walk in obedience? If the things of this world lose their importance to you, the things from My realm will replace them and, in this transition, there is much joy. Every moment that you spend on the wants of this worldly system creates a barrier between you and My Spirit. For some that barrier becomes so effective that it blinds their eyes to the truth and they end up living according to the lies of the enemy".

1 John 2:16
Matthew 6: 23-24
Romans 14:10-12

52

THE NARROW ROAD

"People can give their money to this cause or that project in an attempt to try on a persona of righteousness.

This is not enough says God. I want their hearts, for without the heart the gift is nothing more than a meaningless gesture. There are many sheep living in this ignorance. They think that tossing aside a small part of their worldly blessings is going to build something upon their platform.

This is deception because without the right heart behind it, even the most highly effective gift will still turn to wood, hay and stubble regardless of who is blessed by the action and to what degree.

This has to be true, otherwise it would be possible to 'buy' positions in My kingdom and of course this can never be says God.

It is the soul of the person that is the only currency of any value to Me. The value of each soul will reflect the true heart of each person. Not the one that they showed to their work colleagues or business associates, not the one that they would adorn themselves with on Sundays, not the one that they would quickly get out if they needed something or wanted to impress someone. No, none of these are of interest to Me says God. I am interested in the heart that only you and I know about.

When I gaze upon you, I do not see your sin because of the protection of the Blood of My Son. However, I can see your heart, the deepest depths of the real you. It reveals to Me your every thought, the intention behind every action that you take, every little twist of the truth, every little bending of the rules, every moment of unbelief and fear. I see them all.

Do not think that because in My mercy I leave all of these transgressions unpunished that I am not aware of them. The work of the Cross was complete and final which is good for you. That does not lessen My pain and anguish as I witness so many children living in deceit and those lost ones that just will not listen.

Everything has an opposite, says God and this creates the joy. Just as the Shepherd delights in the return of the lost sheep, I take delight in seeing those who embrace the truth and move themselves in the direction of righteousness. Those who hunger to hear My voice and to gain wisdom and understanding despite the distractions and lies of the world.

This is the narrow road spoken of in the Word. This is the road less traveled that for many will be avoided at all costs. If only they knew the true cost!

Any step in the direction of worldly values will cause you to stray from this path and brings with it the consequences of losing one's way.

My Word is your compass, keep it close at all times.

Those that fail to keep the Word as their compass cannot find their way back to the narrow path and this is a tragedy.

Look at your thoughts and actions, consider the way you are being and reflect on the effect it is having in the spiritual realm. Are you gaining ground or are you losing ground? You cannot stand still, so one or the other is true. Which one is it"?

Hebrews 4:12-13
Psalms 17:3, 33:15, 139:1-4, 24
2Cor 8:12
1 Col 3:10-20
Philippians 4:17
Luke 21:1-4
Psalms 44:21

53

LOVE ME WITH ALL YOUR HEART

"Love me with your whole heart says God. This does not leave room for you to keep a part of your heart where you store the former things. Where you keep the things that you have decided not to give over to Me. Whatever they are; treasured memories, your own secret plans for the future or maybe sins that seemed either so trivial or so tremendous that you decided to 'hide' them from Me. This is foolish says God, for I know every deepest darkest secret. I know of every act however big or small, every indiscretion is stamped in My recollection.

I require you to hand over everything to Me. So much so that you are 'no more', you are completely dead. Only by becoming completely dead to this world and to your fleshly self can you become fully alive in Me. At that point your entire body will run on the power of My Spirit which will multiply the effectiveness of everything that you do. Turn over everything to Me, because as you become completely Mine, I will become completely yours.

Sometimes My children wonder why their prayers are ineffective. It is simple; they have surrounded themselves so much with the noise of the world that they cannot get their communication through. They cannot hear Me because they allow the world to be louder than the Spirit in their lives. The Spirit will never be the one to adjust the volume or the degree to which you can sense My presence. That is completely in the control of the individual. Each person creates their own level of My Spirit presence by their actions.

Repentance removes these 'secret' things from the heart so that there is no longer any need to carry them around. It also makes sure that anything that could grieve or hinder My Spirit is removed which allows the anointing to flow freely through you.

Many make the mistake of thinking that because the Blood of My Son shields them from the penalty of their sins that it is therefore not necessary for them to repent for those sins especially things from long ago, maybe even before they knew Me. This is a great deception. Every transgression must be spoken out and repented for. That is the only way that it gets truly released from a person's soul. Otherwise it sits there, like a bag of stinking garbage which gives off a foul stench which is unpleasant to My Spirit. Some never experience the fullness of My presence because of that.

Even though they are washed by the Blood, their lack of repentance either through fear, ignorance or stubbornness, keeps them from ever entering into the fullness of the relationship I have prepared for them and therefore it becomes impossible for them to fulfill their calling.

Repentance is a form of cleansing, just as fasting can help to cleanse the physical body, so repentance cleanses the soul. A deeper relationship and a clearer channel of communication is the end result and it must be an ongoing daily process to keep the required 'standard of hygiene'. If you take out the trash every day, there will never be a bad odor in your house".

Acts 13:38
Psalms 139:23-24
Ephesians 4:13
1 Peter 2:1-3
James 4:4
John 13:10, 15:3
Titus 2:12
Isaiah 30:15
Jeremiah 15:19
Romans 6:11

54

OBEDIENCE

"Obedience relates to all aspects of your life says God. Spiritual, physical health, business, everything. You should perform every act and every task 'so as to The Lord'. The anointing surrounds you at all times, as it does with every one of My children. It is like the radio; all of the stations are there, all of the time, the ability to hear simply depends on tuning in the receiver.

The anointing is always present, and it is up to you to be 'tuned' in. Increase your productivity through prayer, fasting and focus. Those things will bring success beyond your wildest dreams. In order for everything to fall into place you have to present yourself as a willing and obedient vessel".

1 John:3
Peter 1:2
2 Corinthians 9:13, 10:6

55

THE SPIRIT ANOINTING

"Why not live under the anointing continuously says God? Do you think I provided it for only special occasions? Notice how you feel 'weaker' physically when the anointing envelops you? That is when My Spirit is in total control. That is in fact the time when you are strongest and at your most powerful, when *you* have stepped to one side and allowed Me to be your strength.

Feeling My Spirit surging through your body is one of the most exhilarating experiences possible for a human being. Why then would you want to diminish it by your own thoughts and actions?

Turn yourself completely over to it, bask in it, and revel in it. Be determined that you will enjoy it every day of your life. Why not every minute of every day? What can compare to the anointing of My Spirit, bestowed directly upon you by My own hand?

There is nothing that can equal the joy, the power, the healing that it can bring, the wisdom that it can impart. It is the very essence of true life itself, embrace it! It is My heart's desire that you would desire it above anything else. At first you may feel somewhat incapable of normal activities while under this level of anointing.

This is only because it is so much against the flesh that it has an almost devastating effect at the beginning. However, you will soon find that as you become more at home in your 'new condition', that you can do things, whatever they may be, while still under submission to the power of My Spirit.

Then be ready to witness the miraculous says God. This is where healings will come from. Prophetic words will flow. Extraordinary business success will be generated, and you will be blessed beyond the comprehension of normal understanding. It is challenging to live in this world under such a level of anointing and it has to be replenished on an ongoing basis. The stench of the world tends to diminish the light if complacency is allowed to appear".

Acts 1:8, 5:15, 13 & 14:19-20, 15:12
John 14:16, 16:13

56

ARMOR

"Striving to live every minute of the day in the anointing, literally means living life in another dimension. This is something you can never be complacent about. It is the biggest blessing that I can convey to My earthly children. There is nothing that can surpass either its beauty or its power. The world will constantly try to draw you back into their domain, so be ever vigilant.

The enemy will get extremely nervous when he sees your strength increasing exponentially in the spirit realm. You are now a sword wielding warrior and using the sword of My Spirit you can stand alongside even the noblest of angels and bring destruction upon our enemies.

The words of wisdom issued forth from the tongue under this level of anointing will sear into the hearts of people like a fiery laser. It will lay them open to the truth, as they will be caused to be mindful of your words because of the accuracy of your insight and the humbleness of your heart.

Be sure to use the full armor at all times. You will become prime targets in the spirit realm. Your protection is absolute, but only if there are no holes in your hedges and you are fully armed, fully protected and ready for battle at all times.

I will see to it that you have an abundance of provision so that you will not need to be concerned with that says God. There are very few people that lead this life and you will be required to get into and stay in good physical condition. Spiritual matters use considerable amounts of physical strength and the stronger you are, the better you will be able to sustain your spiritual activities".

Hebrews 4:12

Ephesians 6:10-19

57

MOST POWERFUL WEAPON

"Prayer is the single most powerful weapon available to those on the earth, but it is not being used to anywhere near its potential. The only way to prepare the world for the return of My Son is through prayer. The only way to keep ahead of the onslaught of the enemy is through prayer powered by the Spirit who knows exactly what to ask, when to ask and how to ask for it says God.

This is why the anointing is so vital, for without it the prayers are just largely the ramblings of well-meaning people that are insufficient, because they are petitioning out of their own strength".

1 Corinthians 2:10-16
James 5:16
1 Thessalonians 5:16-18
Ephesians 6:18
Romans 11:33-36

58

IN AND OUT OF THE WORLD

"Spiritual discipline is the highest and most difficult to master of all disciplines because it is the only one that cannot be focused on 'self' says God. Every other discipline can be practiced and developed by anyone without any need to have a relationship with My Spirit.

This is not the case with spiritual discipline. Once you have embarked on the path, to turn away will cause turmoil within your mind or body to the extent that there are only two possible outcomes: return to the world and all the misery that it has to offer or realize the error of your ways. Repent and move forward with a renewed zeal and increased wisdom. Be warned not to spend too much time analyzing what happened. This in itself is a distraction and can cause a person to start analyzing their faith. Faith cannot be analyzed, it must be lived. It is either in evidence or it is not. Little faith is not really any kind of faith, it is almost as ineffective as no faith.

The fact that a person would find it necessary to question how deep their faith extends is the beginning of 'the sin that so easily besets'. You are either a man of faith or not, says God. There is no middle ground.

You can build your faith up but only from the point where you have accepted that it is absolute and applies to everything. As an example; one man may have the capacity to believe for a thousand dollars so that he can bless his family and help the poor. Another may believe for one million to do the same thing. They both have faith of equal measure, it is their positioning within the worldly context which changes their perception of how to employ it".

Hebrews 11:6, 12:1-2

59

NURTURE YOUR SPIRIT

"Understand that living under My anointing is a special and unique experience says God. Once you start to nurture your spirit by bringing it into a loving intimate association with My Spirit, you strengthen the bond beyond measure. To then withdraw your attention is a devastating mistake. It brings such consternation to your own spirit who will not understand what is going on. Your spirit will long to be in the company of the One that loves it and nurtures it, who builds it up and replenishes it.

The withdrawal symptoms start to resemble those of a worldly person endeavoring to escape from an addiction. Their flesh will keep trying to drag them back to their habit.

You will be faced with similar challenges says God, but worse.

On the other hand, your spirit will be grieved and anxious, it will pine for the intimacy to be restored which can leave you feeling disoriented and confused. Additionally, the flesh sensing the possibility of victory, will work overtime encouraging you to participate in more distractions old and new.

The flesh sets up a 'membrane', a barrier around your spirit, which it uses to hinder our communication. The longer you spend in the world, the thicker this membrane will get.

This will help you to understand why there are so many of My children who never get to enter into or enjoy a relationship of any depth with

121

My Spirit. They have cocooned themselves with this 'membrane' and are happily existing within their earthly comfort zone.

For most they even manage to penetrate this 'membrane' for an hour or so on Sunday and get to feel a little better. However, by Monday afternoon, the worries of this world have again overtaken them, and the 'membrane' is once again mending itself.

My Word and the presence of My Spirit are the *only* things that will not only pierce this *membrane* but can in fact dissolve it completely away.

Watch when the revivalist comes to town, especially if he is moving with the power of My Spirit. He comes and in the first meeting he helps people to break through. By the third meeting many have started to experience the joy of entering into an ongoing relationship with the Spirit. They are filled with joy and eager anticipation. They cannot wait to get to the next meeting. Then the revival leaves town and within 48 hours most are right back to where they were. The joy of the relationship starts to fade as the memory of it is suppressed behind the thickening membrane as My children slip back into the world. True, they will emerge again on Wednesday and Sunday, but sadly this peripheral lifestyle will never remove that barrier and it keeps most of My children from entering into the realm of power that I have available for them says God.

For those who have bathed in the river of Living Water there is no going back. You no longer have ignorance as a defense. To even attempt to do so would be folly.

No, for them the only way now is forward and upwards. Press into a deeper relationship with My Spirit and you will be guided how to help others in this situation.

There is a massive spiritual war about to take place says God and only those *constantly* clothed in the full armor will find it possible to stand.

This great battle is imminent and there is little time for preparation. Warriors do not 'go on leave' the day before the battle.

Now is not the time to be dipping your toe into the river of Living Water. No, this is time for full immersion, for swimming 'under water', for 'drinking' it in. You have had all the preliminary instruction and direction that is available".

Hebrews 10:32-39

Ephesians 4:13

1 Timothy 4:15

Romans 7:15-25, 8:5-39

60

IN THE WORLD BUT NOT OF IT

"Restoration does not come through understanding My Word says God, it comes by acting upon it. By living it with your entire being, every hour of every day. You cannot choose to be anointed in certain situations and not in others. You will either live a Spirit filled Christ centered life or not. It cannot be half and half or 'now and then' or 'not in the company of *those* people.'

My anointing is your protection. It is what separates you from the world. How else can you be 'in' the world but not 'of' it says God? You cannot just decide it is so and go your own way. This will never work.

Separation can only be effective when My Spirit transcends the flesh. The very second the flesh is in the ascendancy, you are back in the world and are susceptible to all of the dangers it holds. This is an inner work and not something for show and adornment. The enemy will know of you soon enough but seek the safety of the flock until the time is right. It is by design that at first glance all sheep look exactly the same. To the shepherd they are all different and they all have their unique attributes and he can call upon any of them at any time and they will always respond to his voice.

This is always true unless they have strayed too far and are no longer in earshot. If My actions were not sudden and often overwhelming, they would hardly seem miraculous, and the things surrounding them would not create the impact that is My design.

Maintain a confident expectation that big things are soon going to take place in many aspects of your lives for the time is soon. Only through the eyes of the anointing will you truly be able to recognize the opportunities that are being presented, so maintain the mantle and be vigilant.

Be sure to nurture one another and encourage one another when the burden seems unreasonable as it will feel at times. Remember that My burden is never more than you can bear. Stay in My anointing, dream dreams, hear My Words and live joyously.

There is much work to do and much yet to learn, but the time is now to start being effective in the spiritual realm. Be prepared to find yourself living a new kind of life and finally realizing what it means to be 'in' the world and not 'of' it. My most powerful blessings are available for your fruit says God. Be fruitful and please Me and you will move on to the next level you are seeking".

1 John 2:15-17
John 17:14-18
Rom 12:2
2 Corinthians 5:1-10

61

FAITH FRUIT & DIAMONDS

"There are many different types of fruit says God. Some are desirable, and some are not, but they all serve their purpose. Some are sweet to the taste and are pleasant, some are bitter even poisonous. That is why My Word says, 'by their fruit you shall know them'. It does not mean that *because* they have fruit, you shall know them. It means you shall know them by the *type* of fruit that they produce.

The enemy will try to subvert your calling by casting strange fruit across your path. Do not be tempted to pick it up. You will recognize its type easily and clearly by My Spirit and pondering upon it will only cause you to question yourself in the flesh, which is the beginning of a hole in your hedge, so avoid such action.

An enemy with a smile on its face professing to have a heart for your wellbeing, is still an enemy. There is a simple equation at work here. Would My Spirit cause you to flirt with 'the sin that so easily besets?' This is a simple 'yes' or 'no' question. Well, if the answer is 'no', it is pretty obvious what is taking place here. This is the time to strengthen your resolve says God. It was Daniel's quietness and supreme confidence that kept him from being devoured by the lions. They saw him as an equal, a fellow king among kings.

While it is true that many are called but few chosen, there are also different levels of calling and responsibility in place for My children in the earthly realm. Those at one level cannot truly understand the requirements of those at higher levels. They try to reason and rationalize with the human mind, which of course is foolish says God. They cannot know My ways which is why their faith is their only comfort.

Without faith everything will seem difficult, maybe even impossible. The absence of faith promotes fear and as you know, the spirit of fear does not come through Me, but from the enemy.

I have not taken My eyes off of you for one second.

I hear your cries, your frustrations, your questions even at times your indignations. I hear it all and you should know that it is all part of the process. Look at the work involved in polishing a diamond. It has to be cut and polished then again cut and polished, held up to the light and viewed from every angle. The jeweler will only be happy when every facet gleams with the purest light, when it is 'flawless'.

I am the Master Jeweler, I know where every blemish is, where every imperfection remains, and I am always working on those says God.

Do not focus on the process. Focus on the inevitable outcome, that when you are finally held up to the light you will sparkle like a bright shimmering star and you will emanate a pure light that will bless anyone and everything that gazes upon it or is touched by it and you will be an example of a perfect work crafted by the Perfectionist".

Proverbs 3:5-6
Hebrews 10:35-39, 11:6, 12:1-3
Luke 6:43
Philippians 1:10, 2:15

62

WHAT IS PURPOSE?

"Why do people spend so much time trying to identify their purpose? Most of the time they do not have a genuine interest in knowing what their purpose actually is. No, they want to create a purpose for themselves, which fits easily within their design of how life should be lived. Most only look at the pursuit of this purpose in terms of monetary return, which is a clear sign that they are on the wrong track.

A purpose can only be truly understood in the context of its eternal consequences. If the purpose a person is pursuing is not laying up treasure in heaven for the future, then it is definitely not part of My plan for that person's life says God.

There are only 2 types of activities taking place on the earth at any time. There are the actions powered by My Spirit, carried out by man. Or there are the actions of the enemy, powered by evil, carried out by man. Therein lies a great challenge for the human mind.

Many of the latter actions by the enemy look perfectly innocent. They may even appear to bring benefit to people's lives, but it is all part of the great deception that keeps many from coming to know My voice.

Worse than this is the fact that a lot of the enemy inspired actions are carried out by lost sheep. Some of these have created their own 'purpose' or 'ministry' so effectively that they can no longer hear My voice. Consequently, they exist with a type of godliness but with no power whatsoever.

Life without power is meaningless and without direction. It causes those horrible feelings of living a purposeless existence, which is not a satisfactory way for any person to live. Take all of this into serious consideration.

You can see how important it is that you must have a very clear mandate of what it is that you intend to achieve through your divine purpose. You must be focused on the fruit that it will produce and the eternal consequences of every decision made.

Set your life objectives or goals, having at all times a picture of the precise fruit that they will enable you to produce. Naturally there will still be earthly concerns such as bills to pay and these will be taken care of as a natural consequence of generating the activity necessary to remain in touch with the purpose and achieving the desired results.

There is a natural tendency to want to do this the other way around says God. Be warned, those who put their focus on worldly objectives end up married to the world and a bride cannot have two husbands.

This area needs careful attention and focused faith. To develop a clear picture of the desired fruit you must begin the task with the end already firmly in mind. Once you can do this, it is relatively simple to work backwards and create an action plan to manifest this desired end into your reality.

This way, each day then consists of taking at least the minimum required steps to keep pace. Often these steps will not necessarily produce an immediate, tangible result, this is why it is necessary to have an accurate picture of the end result. Then you can at least sense that progress is being made.

By holding the picture of your intention vividly in your mind the Spirit will cause you to take the necessary actions to create the success. Now of course it is also possible for evil spirits to direct people to success as well. The difference is that these people have no perception of the eternal consequences of their actions.

They do not have to be evil people in any respect. Sadly, many of them are among our brethren that have lost their direction and focus. The enemy will use them to fulfill plans of his that only someone in their position could possibly carry out.

As an example, it could start with a spirit of pride, which could lead a pastor to become so full of his own self-importance that he has to put everyone to work to raise money so that they can build a bigger and better church building. The congregation willingly responds, the money flows in, the church gets built. Now as a consequence of all this, the pastor gets used to hearing people tell him how wonderful he is, what a great thing he has achieved, and his ego and pride often increase.

Then as a result of having this awesome new building, they have room to bring in a full-scale praise and worship team. The pastor receives a recommendation from one of the principal benefactors of the building project, this man tells the pastor about his cousin a wonderfully gifted pianist with a voice like an angel who would be just perfect to lead the praise and worship.

Of course, the pastor is willing to see the woman and hear her play and sing. After all he could not turn down a request from someone who had given so much money. When the pastor meets the woman, she is indeed a gifted pianist and she can sing so beautifully, so he agrees to appoint her to the position of praise and worship leader.

Here is the tragedy. The voices of pride and ego and self-accomplishment are ringing so loud in his ears that he cannot hear My Spirit, who is saying to him 'do not do it', get rid of her now! You see My Spirit knows that the woman is full of the spirit of Jezebel, that within one year, her and this pastor will become embroiled in a love affair that will destroy his marriage and bring down the whole church, dashing the faith of many sheep upon the rocks of disappointment.

So why did this happen?

All because it is so easy for men to put their own purposes ahead of My plans.

The message then is to bring every plan and decision before Me and only when I have sanctioned it should you solicit the help of others to carry out the plan. This is the path that leads to joy, righteousness and the accomplishment of tasks that have true meaning because they are laying up treasures for you in Heaven and not on the earth", says God.

1 John 2:15-17
2 Timothy 4:10
Colossians 3:1-2
Proverbs 3:4
Habakkuk 2:4

63

THE THREE RIVERS

"The course of a man's life runs like a river, says God. Some are straight, some have twists and turns here and there and some are constantly changing direction with many long bends sweeping waterfalls and rapids.

The long straight 'lazy' river is representative of a life lived without any true purpose. It passes by almost without incident. It is admired by the world for its peacefulness and reliability, it can even appear to some to be Godly as they associate the quietness with Godliness.

Those sailing along this river seldom come under attack from the enemy, why would he bother? They are already going in the wrong direction so there is nothing for him to do. These people spend much of their time on the shore, waiting for enough wind to come up to help them continue their journey.

Once they have come out of the river they find themselves completely in the realm of the world. There they can grow fat on earthly delicacies and spend much time indulging in the pleasures of this world. Some of them become so enamored with it that they forget where they are and they get lost and cannot find their way back to the boat.

Before long, it is not possible to tell the difference between them and someone that never knew the truth.

The second category of river dwellers are an entirely different collection of people. Most of the people involved in ministry activities are on this river. The twists and turns serve several purposes. First of all, they create the impression that it is a somewhat more difficult course to take than that of the straight river, which of course it is, plus there are less opportunities to spend time on the shores so it is entirely undesirable to the straight river dwellers.

The twists and turns can be so profound and exhilarating that they encourage a few to *graduate* to the third type of river, which of course was the intention in the first place.

However, they can also cause some to glory in their own navigational skills and get absorbed in their own self-importance. They even receive recognition and reward from those that are not even river dwellers! Some lose their way so completely that they suddenly find themselves adrift in the vast seas of iniquity and deception that the rest of the world are busy reveling in.

These torrid waters feel so comfortable to those that are in them that they are highly resistant to anything that would attempt to remove them. Those that are still on the earth, still on solid ground, there is still hope for them. There is still a chance that they may catch a glimpse of the truth and by giving their heart to Me, they can equip themselves with a vessel of salvation that will set them upon the River of Life.

Even those that end up 'getting lost at sea', like the rest of the world, still have their vessel to save them. When My Son returns He will only be taking this one type of vessel with Him and He will take them all, regardless of what river they are in, what condition they are in, even from the sea of iniquity or deception He will take everyone because they belong to Him and none will remain in this realm.

What of the third river type, who sails upon this?

No one can enter this river if they have not spent some time on each of the others says God. This river requires the highest level of navigational skill. It requires a person to keep sailing in the same direction even though they have no visual perception of where they are going (FAITH)

They have to spend many hours studying *charts and maps* (WORD) to understand the correct course to follow. They must constantly ask Me for favor with the *weather conditions* and for provision (PRAYER)

There will be times where, because of the conditions, they will be required to sustain themselves without basic life nutrients (FASTING) until the course is clearly defined again.

They will have arduous times when they have to combat vicious rapids and weather conditions brought about by the activity of the enemy (SPIRITUAL WARFARE)

The dwellers on this river spend very little time on the shores. Their only purpose there is to provide sustenance and hope to those who may still be able to equip themselves with a vessel.

To aid and encourage those that are already carrying out similar work.

There is need for caution here. You must be able to differentiate those from the ones who only exist on the first two rivers says God. You must avoid these at all costs as they will endeavor to subvert your faith through criticism and accusations, as they fear that otherwise their own mediocrity will be exposed disturbing their 'comfort zone'.

I have called My sheep to dwell in the third river. When the preparation is over, you will have a sound vessel and the knowledge necessary to embark on your journey. You will no longer use a sail, for that can easily be filled out by the winds of the enemy. No! You will then have beautiful twin turbo engines. One is from Faith and one is from Love.

The power from each must be used equally, otherwise you will end up going around in circles and making no progress so be careful of this.

These engines are powered only by My Spirit and it is up to you to constantly refill the tanks as they can run for only a few hours at a time.

For the difficult challenging channels where you have to navigate silently with great care, I will provide you with the oars of Wisdom. This will be particularly important when you have to navigate across enemy waters, as you will have to from time to time.

This will be necessary as the different rivers do intersect in various places. This has to be, in order to give others the opportunity to change direction.

Yes, I did call them enemy waters. Anything that is still attached to the hooks of the worldly realm in some way is a danger to you and you must be as wary of them as of enemies, because they are capable of causing your destruction. Even by just convincing you that you have set your course incorrectly and should be following them.

Be steadfast; follow only the course that we agree upon together says God. Your voyage will not be without incident, but it will be joyous and fruitful. Do not be concerned about spending time ashore. As long as it serves our purpose, I will provide you with the necessary protection. Once the objective has been fulfilled, you must return immediately to the vessel and continue the voyage making sure that all defenses (ARMOR) are in place".

Romans 8:31-39
Hebrews 13:5-6
2 Corinthians 6
1 Corinthians 13:13

64

THE IMPORTANCE OF THE LITTLE THINGS.

"It is the small things that really make a difference says God. When all added up together, the small things that slipped past your attention or did not seem to really matter, these can amass to be something of incredible significance.

This is particularly important from two very different perspectives. The small things that you *do* and the small things that you *do not do*.

In the former case they can produce a sudden and unexpected blessing, they will also have laid up some treasure for you in Heaven. In the latter case, not only have you heaped some unnecessary 'wood, hay and stubble' upon your platform in heaven, but also you have deprived yourself of an earthly blessing.

There is an important lesson here. People do not realize that in the act of 'not' doing something, that they are still adding to their platform. It is therefore as bad to *not* take an action that you know that you should be doing, as it is to *take* an action that you know that you should not be doing.

It is easy enough to not take a refreshing time or to not go through with a fast or something else that we had agreed upon. You must therefore understand that all actions or inactions have a consequence.

Imagine you are hanging over the edge of a cliff on a rope. Every righteous thought that you have adds on a tiny strand to the rope.

Every action that you take in accordance with My will for your life causes you to be pulled up one tiny measure towards the top.

In contrast, every action that you should take but do not, causes you to be lowered one measure. Every unrighteous thought that you allow into your soul destroys one strand of your rope.

Where are you? Are you going up or are you going down? Is your rope getting thinner? Realize that it is also not satisfactory to just remain stationary and increase the thickness of the rope. Be careful that it does not get so thick that you can no longer hold unto it.

Let us consider what a righteous life looks like says God. This will enable you to see how closely you are walking in relation to the desired path. You will now know the importance of having a structured life. Without this, your daily walk will be subject to the whims of the flesh and you need only be interested in a Spirit led life".

Matthew 6:19-21, 25:45
Luke 16:10
1 Corinthians 3:10-20

65

SPIRIT OF SELF DESTRUCTION

"The spirit of self-destruction is one that it will serve you well to know about and to be able to easily discern says God. This is one of the most sinister of the enemy spirits because there are large numbers of them and they operate at different levels in many different ways.

Only at the extreme do they have the power to get someone to end their own life on earth. However, there are many other subtler forms of destruction that they practice which will bring about the same consequences. They are able to stop some of My children from entering into the fullness of the relationship that I desire to have with them.

These spirits can often cause a person to constantly repeat one action that brings something else undesirable into their life, such as guilt or shame or feelings of unworthiness, which hold them back in their spiritual walk.

The reason that the spirit of self-destruction is so sinister is that it can change its angle of attack at will. One day it can cause a person to do one wrong thing, the next day another. Its presence can account for why many people, having been delivered from a particular affliction, seemingly return to their old ways from time to time, particularly during periods of stress or turmoil.

What happens is that once a person's overall spiritual defenses are down, this spirit will often 'mimic' the behavior of something that the individual had previously been delivered from. Subsequently this can lead to doubt, even unbelief, which of course can set the person concerned on a spiral of self-destructing actions and confessions.

This is one of the main factors behind the words of the apostle Paul when he talked of not doing what he knew he should be doing and doing what he knew he should not. Without overcoming this spirit, a race runner can easily reduce his chances of running an effective race. If a race is not run with the keen expectation of victory and the receipt of the winner's garland it is without power or reason.

Understand then how to discern the presence of this spirit says God. At the extreme it will be someone under a great cloud of depression, in its subtler form it will be a person repeating an action from which they have previously been delivered or someone who is continuously repeating the same behavior which is keeping them from running a good race.

Remember this spirit has the ability to *mimic* other spirits as well as his tendency to *partner* with other spirits. As an example; you may obviously witness the spirit of pride at work in someone's life which is seriously holding them back. What is not evident to those without this knowledge is that the spirit of self-destruction has formed a partnership with pride and is goading and encouraging him.

If the individual will come to understand that this pride is hurting his spiritual race, he can repent for it and pray that ugly spirit out of his life. Unbeknown to him though, self-destruction can still be lurking nearby, just biding his time, waiting for just a tiny hole in the hedge and he will slip back in.

This is where he can be at his most dangerous. You see, if he is merely 'mimicking' a spirit, a deliverer can call upon the name of the spirit being mimicked, but it will be to no avail. He must be specifically named to be removed, so be constantly watchful of him in his various guises", says God.

Romans 7:15-25

2 Peter 1:8-9

SPIRITUAL WARFARE IS REAL

"You must not take spiritual warfare lightly says God. There will be an intensity developing in the spiritual realm around you and it is vital that not only are you aware of it, but also, that you are prepared to do battle at all times.

The attacks can come at any time and will often be from areas that you would least expect to be attacked in. Build up your strength in the Spirit by prayer and making sure that you are under the protection of My Spirit and pray in the Spirit at all times to keep your plans secret from the enemy, says God.

Make proclamations of victory and confound the wicked ones by surrounding yourselves with My Spirit and Light. Process your thoughts carefully and with diligent focus. Be sure that you capture anything unseemly and turn it over to Me.

Keep My Word on your lips and dress yourself in My armor, especially in the night. This is a vulnerable time for you and it is crucially important that you do not sleep without your armor.

Remember, during wartime you could be called to defend yourselves or even to attack at any time. The enemy will not be saying 'ok, well, we'll just wait while you get ready'

They will immediately seek to gain advantage from such a situation and would want to inflict wounds upon you or worse. It is within your own control to make sure that this does not happen. Keep your equipment clean and in tiptop condition and realize that now, as a spiritual warrior, it must become a permanent part of you. To spend any time not wearing it is highly dangerous. It is like a person who drives a vehicle without wearing a seatbelt; they are flirting with danger in an unnecessary manner.

As you will recall from My Word, the names of these evil spirits are so numerous they are called 'legion'. In fact, they are constantly being re-assigned and given new names in an attempt to gain the upper hand in the battle.

There is an important principle to understand here, which can save you a tremendous amount of wasted time and effort in seeking names or natures of those evil ones.

Firstly, you already have total victory and dominion over any and all of them, you just have to learn to *walk* in that victory. When you are in your own domain and *walking in righteousness,* they cannot touch you.

This is true regardless of whether you are walking in the earthly realm, in the spiritual realm or in the heavenlies.

This righteousness is so pure that it will completely overwhelm and overpower any demon. Consider this analogy; It is completely impossible for a germ to exist in a sterile environment.

I have given you the tools with which to keep your environment and your earthly body in a completely sterilized condition. Just use these tools on an ongoing basis and this whole situation with spirits is taken care of".

Luke 8:30
Colossians 2:15
2 Timothy 2:22
2 Corinthians 10:5
I Thessalonians 5:17
1 Corinthians 14:2, 14-15
Ephesians 2:6-7, 6:10-18

67

YOUR ADVERSARY

"Once you have attained even an elementary level of being set-apart from the world, no evil can exist anywhere near you. Even the 'aroma' that you give off will repulse them. Any that are foolish enough to enter your domain will be beheaded by your sword of the Spirit, speaking out My Word will bring destruction upon them. The light emanating from your eyes as you capture them in your gaze in the spirit realm will incinerate others.

How is this level of righteousness obtained? By diligent focus, by bringing the mind and body under control and by nourishing it with the Word and the Spirit. Encapsulate your entire body with My anointing at all times says God.

Make regular checks not only on your own armor but also to that of those close to you. A blunt sword is of no use in this battle; pay careful attention to the condition of all equipment.

The tongue is still your greatest adversary. It can almost be like 'the enemy within'. You must be so vigilant regarding what you confess into being says God. Even talking of any challenging spiritual activities taking place in your lives can be dangerous, as it is often giving unnecessary energy to the enemy ranks.

Debating the nature of these spirits can create internal fear however small. This is fuel for their existence, the trigger that empowers them to start operating their destructive ways.

So be extremely careful with what is allowed to leave your tongue.

Take immediate action to cleanse your house and put on your armor, then drape yourself in the mantle of the anointing and you will present a formidable stature.

Remember that in doing these things you will draw attention to yourselves in the spirit realm and as such there will be no going back for you.

Having walked into the fray, you must now be warriors. You know that you are called to be more than conquerors, an assignment that in no way will resemble your old life.

If you seek any understanding of what has taken place before in your life, just know that it was all either part of the preparation for this time or part of the enemies attempt to make sure that you never made it to this point.

There are new horizons ahead for you says God. New challenges, new destinations and new environments. They will all be part of this new spiritual assignment. The battle lines have been drawn in the sand. You have your armor and you have your weapons. The entire battle plan cannot yet be revealed as it is so secret that only I know the full plan says God.

My people will be made aware of each new step as the time arrives for them to take it. If I were to reveal it all now, it would seem as though the odds against success were too great and so for now, each person will only see the part they can cope with."

Philippians 1:6
Ephesians 6:10-18
James 3:2-12
Romans 8:37
Proverbs 3:5-6

68

MAKING DECISIONS

"Breaking old habits and introducing new ones is as easy as *making the decision* that it is going to happen says God. The problem for many is that they do not have a proper understanding of what it means to *decide* to do something.

A *decision* means to 'cut off' the possibility of any other outcome and this is the missing ingredient for most.

You have to decide that you are going to live your life in the way that we have been discussing and then it will happen because no other possibility exists. Never make the mistake of saying you are going to 'try' to do something. That is foolish.

A decision has to be made and then adhered to. 'Let your yes be yes and your no be no'. Once we have created a new plan together, it will provide a perfect opportunity to show what progress is being made over time. To implement this plan effectively will require more diligence and focus than anything that has been asked of you before says God.

It will push you to new levels of obedience. This is the way that will lead you through the door into the fullness of My abundance".

Matthew 5:37
Titus 2:12-14

ARMOR

"Understand the importance of maintaining the intimacy and consistency of our relationship says God. Depleting the level of your anointing can make you feel tired and listless. You begin to feel as though you have lost your connection. Remember that I will not cause this to happen. It is a self-inflicted malady that is easily prevented. A day without the protection of My armor makes you vulnerable to enemy attack.

You have experienced this in the past and the absence of the proper protection has allowed the enemy to wound you. The outcome is feelings of anger, disappointment, self-doubt and fear and these are all fleshly emotions which would be entirely avoidable under the mantle of the anointing, so you can see the importance of that armor" says God.

Ephesians 6:10-18

70

DOUBTS AND FEARS

"Doubts, fears and apprehension are not My way says God. If you find such things coming against you, recognize them for what they are; spiritual warfare is to be waged and seek to repair the hole in your hedge that made you vulnerable to such an attack.

Never forget that the shield of faith can quench ALL the fiery darts of the enemy. Which brings you back to 'the sin that so easily besets'.

If you look at every challenge through natural eyes, of course the situation will often seem difficult maybe even impossible and because your viewpoint is from the flesh, you will be operating outside the protection of the anointing.

You have effectively 'removed' your armor and those fiery darts will start striking home and wounding you. Because there is no sword for you to strike back with you end up having to retreat. It is natural for those in the flesh to now spend time brooding about the defeat, wondering why their armor had suddenly become ineffective!

All the time this is taking place you will make yourself open to even more attacks in greater measure says God, as the enemy will press for the opportunity to create a foothold by attaching himself to you through one of his demonic spirits who will dwell in your environment seeking an opportunity.

Depression, fear, lack, apprehension, double-mindedness, uncertainty, lowliness, unworthiness, victim syndrome, unbelief, hopelessness, undeserving, anxiety, nervousness. This list can go on and on. As I have said, their names are 'legion' and they all seek to nullify your effectiveness.

Now this may all sound intimidating to some. However, you know the truth and therefore the solution is simple. None of these can operate in the presence of the anointing of My Spirit.

None of them can even stand against the proclamation of the name of My Son. None of them can have any effect against the protection of the full armor.

Remember recently how just by being obedient and speaking the truth to a business colleague, by confessing the power of My Son to them over the phone, all the things that were seemingly coming against you were immediately removed?

What happened was, in the course of that conversation you picked up your shield of Faith, which immediately started to quench those darts. Then as you begin to speak out My Word, that spiritual sword began wreaking havoc through the enemy ranks sending them scampering away.

There is an important lesson through all of this. For one of My chosen warriors to walk in victory *all* of the time, it is essential that battle readiness is maintained. Be alert to even the slightest sting of an enemy dart. If you so much as feel something, you will know that your defenses need attention and you can attend to it immediately.

There is of course another level to move to here.

As you know the best method of defense is attack.

The sword is not designed to be a defensive weapon says God. It is time to realize that we cannot be content with 'standing our ground'.

No, we must go forward and regain ground that has previously been lost. We must make inroads into the enemy territory and start creating casualties in their ranks. Get them on the back foot and win victories in My name.

It is time to show them that they are no match for My forces, we are the most powerful beings in the fray. Human bodies being driven by the anointing of My Spirit dwelling within them, equipped with My unstoppable weapons of warfare.

If I am with you nothing can stand against you in the spiritual or in the natural. Remember you must take your victories in the spiritual realm first. If you take them only in the natural, they will only be temporary and of no eternal significance.

It is the same with everything that you do. Achieve victory at the supernatural level and you will make huge strides along the path I have prepared. This is what I am calling you to do and your strength and your blessings will be multiplied".

Psalms 91:7

1 Peter 5:8

Romans 8:31

Ephesians 6:12

Hebrews 12:1

1 John 4:4

71

HE SEES EVERYTHING

"As you can see there are no new answers says God. That which you have known for some time is the key to living a righteous and effective life. It starts with getting fully in touch with My Spirit, being centered in the anointing at all times. This will equip you with the discernment to know if the actions that you contemplate are properly in tune with My will for your life.

Look at your surroundings and ask yourself this question: Is this a place that I would invite the King of Kings to abide in, to work with me in?

If you knew that My Son was about to knock on the door for a visit, is there anything that you would want to hurriedly change? Maybe the things you are thinking about, maybe the way your surroundings look? Supposing He wants to go out with you in your car somewhere. How would that be?

What if He wanted to look in your garage, or open your doors, look in your closet or check your hidden drawers or even your shoes? You see, 'surface attention', providing a façade of excellence for the benefit of the world is one thing, but in My eyes, it is not enough. I can see everything at all times says God. I know where everything is and how everything looks. Just because I do not comment does not mean I have overlooked it.

Remember that the condition of your surroundings is often a reflection of your thinking and 'As a man thinks in his heart, so is he'. What is your attention to excellence saying about you at the moment? Consider this carefully and make the necessary corrections. These again are some of the 'small things' that will benefit from your attention".

Proverbs 23:7
2 Chronicles 16:9

72

SPIRITUAL INTIMACY

"Intimacy is the highest form of communication; the deeper the level of intimacy, the more effective that the communication will be says God. I have called you to a new level of intimacy, to a time when we are in a constant state of communion and communication.

To make this possible you have to be a willing instrument.

You must submit to cleansing and purging so that there is nothing that can block the flow of My Spirit. If the level of the anointing upon you is considerably more than you have experienced before, it is because you are prepared and ready to accept it and also to be obedient in the sacrifice of your own will.

This preparation creates a level of intimate joy between us that the human mind cannot rationalize or perceive. It is a passion above which there is only spiritual existence. It is the highest level of intimate communication available in the earthly realm. Here you will hear My voice more clearly, receive My direction and have the opportunity to stay at My feet.

Any angelic activity around you is there for your protection. My Spirit is there for your education and equipping. My anointing is the fuel that will drive your progress on the path I have chosen for your feet. The further you get from the ways of the world, the more joyful I become.

Now that you have a sense of My love from a Spiritual rather than a physical perspective, you can see why we have to spend all of our time together. This is a fire that does not consume, it simply keeps refueling itself and you are going to see that your earthly mind cannot even perceive the level of intensity at which it will burn".

Hebrews 12:4-6
1 Corinthians 2:9
Acts 17:28
Psalms 42:7

73

THE SOURCE OF LIFE

"Keep pressing through to new levels and you will be involved in more activity in the supernatural realm says God. Do not forget that your only weapon in that realm is the sword of the Spirit which is My Word. Keep your sword honed and sharpened at all times. A dull blunt blade is of no use. Remember that the shield you are holding is the shield of Faith. Now where does that come from? That's right, it comes by 'hearing' and 'hearing' comes from the Word. You must give attention to this every day.

It is the only way to keep these parts of the armor in pristine condition. The helmet of salvation I gave to you as a gift. Not so the breastplate of righteousness. This is empowered by your actions.

Your actions performed in accordance with My will, which of course brings you back to the same source, the Word. And what of the sandals of the gospel? The gospel is of course the Good News, the truth of which can only be revealed through the Word.

As you can see, daily life in the absence of total immersion in My Word is worthless and without purpose.

A deeper level of the anointing will cry out to be fed.

It can only be fed by direct communication with My Spirit and through the Word. Nurture it in these ways and it will increase in power even more. Remember that this is a power that can move mountains, that can heal the sick, that can provide a word of prophecy so accurate and insightful that the hearer will be in awe. A power that can raise the dead!

You have not seen the fullness of what is possible at this level.

It is one thing to be here and to feel the might of My presence says God. To experience it in action requires you to fuel that fire with the Word. Consume it, nourish your spirit with it, pursue its secrets and everything will be revealed.

The Word is the belt of truth and every answer is found within it. This is the source of life itself".

Ephesians 1: 18-22, 6
Hebrews 4:12
Psalms 18:30, 119:11 & 105
Proverbs 30:5
Matthew 4:4

74

CLEAR THINKING AND FOCUS

"Be diligent in your pursuit of ordered and controlled thinking says God. Allow yourself to think only righteous uplifting thoughts and let those thoughts lead to good works. The nature of these works will give a good indication of who is doing the thinking.

Is it the anointed mind which is methodical, calm and sees the solution immediately? Or is it the unfocused ramblings of the flesh? Obviously, fleshly thinking will lead only to fleshly words or fleshly actions and there is no profit in either.

Actions that bear good fruit will create the addition of gold, silver and precious stones to your foundation. You must seek the integrity in everything that you do and be in control of your thinking when making decisions that have an effect on other people".

Psalms 19:14

Philippians 4:18

1 Corinthians 3:11-12

75

THE STORY OF THE HORSES AND LEADERSHIP

"A man had a beautiful horse which he had spent a lot of time training and feeding and grooming so that it could perform for him in an excellent way. One day he acquired a new horse. Although this one was young and unruly, it was obvious to the man that it had as much or maybe even greater potential than his first horse.

The man gave much attention to getting the new horse ready to perform and, in his zeal, he forgot about the first horse.

When he realized this, he went to look at the first horse and saw the error of his ways. The horse's coat had no luster, it looked dull and mangy and could not run properly because it was undernourished as the man has neglected to feed it.

The man repented and gave immediate attention to the first horse. He bathed it and fed it and saw it quickly restored to full health. Now the man had a dilemma, how could he make sure that this scenario did not repeat itself? What if along the way he was happened upon another fine horse and then another and another?

Well, does one man maintain a stable of fine horses alone? says God. Does he groom them all, exercise them all, feed them all? Of course not. He selects a team of people that are willing and able to work with him to take care of the necessary tasks. There are many tasks that any willing helper can perform and there are some tasks that can only be performed by the one with the vision and the anointing.

If the one with the vision and the anointing is spending time completing tasks that could easily be carried out by another then time is not being maximized.

Understanding how this man would behave in order to create a stable of pristine and powerful horses will be a lamp to your feet says God.

A leader should not necessarily have the same mindset as the follower. The leader must delegate the application of as many ideas as possible to those willing and able to follow, those who are not yet ready to lead.

As you know, the hours in the day cannot be extended and optimization of time is extremely important.

Procrastination prevents seeds from being sown and must be avoided.

Stop *waiting* for something to happen or for your business to perform in a certain way before you start taking leadership decisions. You have to be that leader person first before you can *perform* as that leader.

There are many things that need the attention of a leader and there is no way to perform all of these tasks and still have time to give personal attention to others and spend adequate time with Me seeking vision and direction says God. Prayerful delegation will produce the fruit.

Visualize what areas can be covered by others and plan accordingly. Do not wait for the circumstances to be right. As a leader you are responsible for *creating* the circumstances. Whatever you are currently surrounded by, whatever challenges are being faced, are a consequence of what you have allowed to happen. You have the victory, you just have to walk in it.

Your armor and My anointing can see you past *any* obstacle, but you have to remember to use them and stop imagining that you will accomplish anything in your own strength.

You have to see the value that your labors can add to others and change the way you think about what you do. You are creating a life for yourselves not just a job or a business. You are creating something that will provide an enormous amount of financial seed which can bring great blessings to many that need them.

Believers are called to live unconventional lives that cannot be lived in a conventional way or conformed to the thinking of the people in the world.

If your work and your life are intertwined because they are both in the total pursuit of My glory, you will not think that you have to stop doing one before you can start being involved in the other.

On earth My Son was the Christ everyday all of the time. He did not hang up His anointing on the weekend. He did not keep His eye on the clock so that He could start to have fun or be someone or something else at a certain time or on a certain day.

Use every minute wisely for you cannot reuse it if you are not happy with the result. You get one chance to use each second, each minute, each hour, each day. If you look back at the day's end and see wasted, unproductive time, you cannot reach back for it as it is now a part of history.

If someone read your history from yesterday, what would they think? What contribution did it make? Did it create any treasure?

What if you thought I was watching what you did, every minute of every day? What would I think?

We have had such discussions before says God and you have been slow to learn. The Israelites went around the same mountain, so you know that I have the patience.

Why repeat that foolishness when you have the clear path laid out right before your eyes?

Just open your eyes and start walking and do not deviate from the path".

Hebrews 12:2

76

SEEK FIRST THE KINGDOM

"Remember to 'seek first the Kingdom' says God.

This is the way to ensure that everything that you are looking forward to will in fact be added unto you. It is by now obvious to you that you have been traipsing around the proverbial mountain, producing a good comparison to the Israelites.

Is the path to success not yet obvious to you?

How else would you like Me to illustrate it to you? says God.

We could continue on and on, but it is not necessary. You have understood that through both righteousness and obedience everything will fall into place. These two are inextricably entwined and you cannot have one in the absence of the other.

You must stand up and be that person, but it is only possible through righteousness and obedience. Your 'no' must be 'no' and your 'yes' must be 'yes'.

Show your righteousness and obedience by your actions and not your words only.

We have previously talked about structure, attitude and focus regarding your work endeavors but you have yet to respond fully to My requests.

For this reason, you will sometimes feel that forces are at work that slow you down and give you the appearance of still moving but maybe only at the pace of a snail.

If you have been wondering how to change that situation, it is quite simple says God. Constant focused obedience will provoke righteousness and true righteousness will always move at the correct speed. Never too slow, never too fast, because it will always achieve the desired result.

A righteous man walking in obedience could never be unfruitful as that would be a direct contradiction of My promises. If you would be consistent in your obedience, there would be no waiting for a breakthrough and your 'stable of horses' would be ready for you.

The ones for business endeavors, the ones for ministry activities and those that you ride into battle in the spiritual realm.

Never forget that you can only ride one horse at a time, so be sure to be on the right horse at the right time to create the desired result.

Each 'horse' requires the same food which is *My Word*. This is the sustenance that will set them apart from all others and keep them in glowing pristine condition. It is the source of all food for all things and cannot be replaced by any substitute. The time that you spend in My presence and in My Word will strengthen you for maximum effectiveness in everything that you do.

Help others understand that is it 'ok' to be a *successful* believer. That you can thrive in this world without sharing its values. That you can bring glory to My Name in anything that you put your hand to.

Show people that ministry is not about segregation, rules or buildings. It is about righteousness and love for your fellow man and refusing to compromise your integrity for anything. It is about standing up for who you are, wherever you are and demonstrating the faith you have in knowing that I will prosper My obedient children in any situation I choose, because I can and because I want those I have *called* to have the opportunity to be *chosen* through their obedience.

I long for you to have the desires of your heart and as long as those desires do not threaten the perfection of our love for one another, I will happily grant them to you, for your happiness is the source of My joy. There is no joy for Me in seeing one of My children in a state of confusion, sadness or doubt or unbelief as that grieves Me greatly. That is why My patience is unending and My forgiveness unlimited and complete.

I love to see My children achieving the desires of their hearts. After all, didn't I give them the hearts and the desires in the first place? If you can grasp this you will unearth a huge revelation, one so big that most cannot perceive its reality. This knowledge transcends the ability of the fleshly mind to assimilate.

If I gave you the heart and the desires in the first place, then your receipt of the desires brings the whole process to perfection.

I am *using you to do the things that I love to do*. Did I not do signs, miracles, wonders and demonstrations of My love *through* people? I am the same yesterday, today and tomorrow and nothing has changed. Human successes are always a great joy to Me and if they give Me the glory, it is a double joy because then I see righteousness perfected in them. They not only understand the reason for the success they have, but also the true source of it. Did I not say that 'We will make man after our own image'? It should be obvious then that man walking in righteousness would act in the very way that We would act" says God.

Hebrews 13:8, 12:10-11
Psalms 20:4, 37:4
1 Corinthians 10:11-13

163

Matthew 6:33
2 Timothy 1:7
Revelation 3:19
Job 5:17-18
Romans 8:38-39

77

THE POWER OF THE SPOKEN WORD

"See the power of My spoken Word. It brings a conviction and cleansing that cannot be equaled by the words of men. My word truly is that 'two-edged sword'. It can cleave your enemy in two with one blow, it can cut right to the heart of a matter and remove all obstacles. This is why I have continually focused you back to the source, to the Word, to the I AM. It is the source of all wisdom, all knowledge and all power says God.

Learning to love the way I want you to love, is a vital key says God.

For this reason, you must learn to see with My eyes and to think with My understanding. This can only be accomplished by My Spirit. When are you going to learn that the only way you can accomplish anything is by My Spirit? That is why I told you, 'It is not by might, nor by power, but by My spirit'. You may get people's attention by might and power, but it is when the Spirit operates through you that you will get results.

Beware of compromise, there is never a justification for it. You can never compromise who you are being to protect the feelings of the people in the world. You must never dim your light so that it will not dazzle people that are coming towards you. If it causes them to swerve off of the road they are on, so be it. That will ultimately be a blessing for them. Hold fast to your spiritual principles at all times. They are what separate you from the world".

Ephesians 3:18-19
Hebrews 4:12
Zechariah 4:6

78

RIGHTEOUSNESS IS REQUIRED

"Revelation requires you to develop a gradual understanding of the full picture says God. If your human eyes tried to take in the entire picture in one sitting, it would appear to be both overwhelming and meaningless at the same time. You would be crying out 'what is this?' and 'what does that mean?'

This is why I have only revealed things at a certain pace and in a certain order. It was important not to give you too much information at once for you have to be *made ready* to accept it.

For this reason, discipline and obedience have been stressed so strongly. The life of a righteous man requires much of each.

Otherwise there is a tendency to operate from outside of My righteousness. Obviously if a person is outside of My righteousness, they must be outside of My will, how else could it be? Would it be My will for a child of mine to walk in unrighteousness? Of course not. This is why obedience is so vital.

Attaining to righteousness while still living in the world is a tremendously difficult task. I call it a 'task' because it is a requirement says God. You have to work at it every minute of every day.

You are either walking in righteousness or you are walking in unbelief. There is no 'in-between'. You cannot be a 'bit' righteous or 'nearly' righteous; it is a state of being.

Remember the 'be-do-have' equation? If you are 'being' righteous you will naturally 'do' the things that righteous children do and as a consequence you will 'have' the things that the righteous deserve.

You know from My Word that My righteous children never lack anything.

To operate in the fullness of your calling you have to be overcomers. You have to walk in righteousness so that others will see the light in you and desire the same. You have to walk in righteousness, because it is the only way that My Spirit can work freely through you. In the absence of My Spirit you will be operating in the flesh which of course can produce a *type* of righteousness but without power.

There are many examples of this today and you must avoid this error at all costs. You cannot expect to fulfill your commission and have a life that looks even remotely similar those living in unrighteousness. You cannot make comparisons between your lives and theirs, it will only frustrate you, because there is no commonality. If they were walking the same path as you, it would be clearly evident. You would never have to enquire. If they are walking in a different direction to you, how could it lead to righteousness?

There is only one path that leads to righteousness. That path is only found in the footsteps of My Son. It is often overlooked that the only way to properly walk in His footsteps is to be carrying your burden in the same way that He carried it.

The flesh will never be willing, so you have to remove it from the equation through submission and obedience".

Psalms 7:8, 11:5, 15:1-2
Hebrews 12:11
Galatians 5:16
Philippians 1:9-11
2 Timothy 2:22
1 John 2:6

79

I WILL BLESS YOU WHERE YOU ARE

"Most have not managed to separate righteousness from religion says God. Righteousness in your life does not need a 'religious veil' added to do it. Having Christ at the core of your life is manifested in the choices that you make; in the way that you choose to be. It is not about church buildings and religious paraphernalia.

I will bless My children wherever they are, not because they go to church or leave their jobs to join the ministry. No! I will bless them because they enter into righteous obedience which allows My relationship with them to be perfected.

If you are to be an ambassador for My love, grace and power, you must be prepared to be excellent in all things at all times. Nothing else will do justice. Nothing else can be acceptable. My children are called to be the best of the best in everything says God. Anything but that is a lie and a manifestation of unbelief.

Why would I want you to settle for second best? So that people could say that My love for My children is less than perfect? Of course, you can see this trick of the enemy working with those not built up in the faith. He fools them to believe that My path leads to lack and his to abundance. We all know where his path leads. Be a light for as many as will see it. This will always be your purpose and you can manifest it in many different ways. Stay true to your resolutions and your path will be brighter and your burden lighter".

Matthew 5:6
Psalms 63
Psalms 106:3

80

INTEGRITY & RIGHTEOUSNESS

"Your success will be determined only by your actions, never by your intentions, however noble they may be. Let the old things pass away and begin again with serious intent. A person that questions his own integrity cannot walk in righteousness as these two have to be in harmony with each other. If someone has compromised their integrity they can in no way call themselves righteous.

If you question your own integrity through your actions, how much more will other people question it?

Integrity is the right hand of righteousness and honor is the left. Obedience leads to it and faith works through it. Meditate on this truth. You therefore must never compromise it. Let your repentance be made manifest by your actions.

I am your only provider. It is I that will make the way for you and if there seems to be no way, I will still make the way for you says God.

The fear of loss is a powerful emotion. It is also a great manifestation of doubt and unbelief and consequently an unhealthy emotion. You can never lose anything by following only My Word for your direction and My will for your life".

Psalms 7:8, 25:21
Proverbs 13:6
Matthew 22:16
1Kings 9:4
Nehemiah 7:2
Job 27:5

169

81

THE DECEPTION OF UNWORTHINESS

"People hunger for prophetic words because they want to believe that I would actually take the time to speak to them says God. Many are convicted by the spirit of unworthiness that their sins have in some way blocked their relationship with Me. They desperately want to hear something from Me, if only to know that I know that they exist. Others know at some level that they are saved and that they will have the opportunity to spend eternity in heaven. They sadly miss the true reality of the situation.

I abide in the heart and the soul of every sheep says God. I long to have a deep personal loving relationship with every one of them. I am constantly talking to them all of the time. Unfortunately, most of them never hear even one word that I say unless I say it to them through someone else. Even then they are often skeptical because of their feelings of unworthiness.

This is the enemy's great lie; that My children are unworthy. Even in unbelief they are still worthy says God. However desperate their circumstances are, they are still worthy. However great their sin may seem through worldly eyes, they are still worthy.

A child of mine can never be unworthy, else My promises could not be relied upon.

Unworthiness is therefore a lie of the enemy and a deception. It can be easily revealed. Once revealed it can be overcome.

The only way to overcome unworthiness is through love. Education cannot do it, criticism cannot do it, nor reason, nor logic, only love which transcends everything can relieve the heavy burden.

It must be communicated that unworthiness is a spirit. No evil spirit can abide in the presence of true unconditional love. Now you see that the easiest way to deliver people from unworthiness is to love them.

The Book of Ruth demonstrates how her unconditional love of Naomi, despite circumstances and unfathomable difficulty, restored her to fullness and vanquished that unworthy spirit from their lives. A deeper study reveals the full significance of this. At first glance, it would appear that Ruth and Naomi are the main issue, but this is not the case says God. Naomi's feelings of unworthiness could have destroyed the most significant bloodline of all time were it not for the love of Ruth.

This same pattern is repeated constantly today and I am grieved that people do not realize the significance of it. You see, Ruth's simple acts of unconditional love for her mother-in-law, and obedience in doing everything she was asked to do without question, changed the course of the known world forever!

How many people come across your path for whom the simple act of your unconditional love could change the course of the known world? Of course, you have no idea says God. If you knew the answer to this question you would be overwhelmed

My children have the right and the ability to hear My voice any time they choose. They just have to get all of the other noises out of their head first. Demonstrate unconditional love, then coupling that with simple obedience, you too can change the course of the world".

Psalms 103:11-13
Ephesians 3:18
Romans 8:1
Ruth

171

82

HEARING GOD'S VOICE

"Only in the quietness can you hear My voice says God. You must understand the importance of listening. Many when they pray are practicing a one-sided conversation because they are so intent on letting Me know what they require from Me that they never get the chance to hear My instructions to them.

In most examples of My answers to prayer, the person requesting My help is asked to do something or not to do something in order to receive the blessings. For many today they do not get the chance to see the blessings unfold, because they surround themselves with so much noise they cannot hear the instructions.

Consistent focus on time periods and activities without being distracted is a very challenging task. The flesh will always rebel. It will attempt to fill your mind with distractions which you must resist to move in victory.

The keys you are seeking are contained in the decision itself says God. If you are truly decided, truly of single-minded focus and your 'quietness within' has confirmed that what you are seeking is within My will for your life, then your victory is assured. I cannot contradict My own promises says God. I told you that the desires of you heart would be given to you and so it is.

If your decision is firm, you will be focused on the one track that leads to your objective. Beware of the temptation to travel on other tracks.

No matter how similar they appear, there can only be one track for each journey and every detour will simply hold you back from entering into the fullness of the blessings.

It is seldom what a person does that gets them the reward they are seeking, it is more a question of the fact that it is the little details that they *overlook* that hold them back from the prize. The little details usually represent the simple acts of obedience that would effectively get the flesh out of the way and let the Spirit take control of the situation.

People are so concerned with being able to say 'look what I did' rather than 'look what God has used me to accomplish'. If you become an *instrument* rather than looking to find new tools or other people that have them, you can accomplish much more in a much shorter time frame.

Do not measure time in the traditional worldly sense, as this will keep you conformed to the ways of this world. For this reason, it requires you to make a supreme effort to control the flesh as it is only the flesh that can prevent you from succeeding. The greater your success in controlling the flesh, the bigger your victory will be.

So how do you win the battle? By keeping the Spirit and the anointing in the ascendancy at all times. Where obedience exists, there is no room for the flesh to operate.

Think about that. You could never say of a person 'well he operates mainly in the flesh, but he is always obedient to God' It is not possible!

Obedience subdues the flesh and it is the key to victory. This is why I have focused and re-focused on this point. You will see an obvious pattern emerging. The more obedient you become, the weaker your flesh will be.

Think on that! The weaker your flesh is, the stronger you will be and the greater your victory. The concept is just so simple, it can be explained in just a short sentence; the greater your obedience to Me, the greater your rewards here and now, and for eternity".

Psalms 37:4, 131:2
1 Corinthians 9:27
Galatians 5:16
1 John 5:3
Romans 8:5-17, 13:14
Philippians 3:14

83

STRUGGLE WITH THE FLESH

"The endless struggle between flesh and spirit continues on and on. You may have a hope that one day this battle will be over. This may be the case but not in the way that you would like says God. All the time that you remain on the earth dwelling in the earthly body that you now possess, the struggle will continue at some level. The desires of the flesh can either be a slight irritation to you, or if you allow, they can be a major stumbling block for you. It is all about choice.

The choice is in your own hands and the actions that you take will clearly show which of the paths you have chosen to take. There is no way to just ignore the flesh and hope that it will not cause you any problems. In periods of seemingly innocent quietness, it is busy making plans and scheming your downfall. The enemy seeks to render you 'ineffective'. He wants to see you either constantly engaged in warfare or walking in complacency where he can attack you directly. The key is to be so filled with My anointing that you can instantly recognize any work of the enemy and you will not be deceived.

The only way to stay in tune with My anointing is by following the action steps that I have already called you to take. Meaningless words are easy to speak, but it is only actions that produce fruit says God. I said, 'you will know them by their fruit' not 'you will know them by their words'. The outcome of your lives is going to be determined only by what you do. Never by what you say you are going to do".

1 Peter 4:1
John 6:63
Galatians 5:16
Matthew 3:18, 7:16
Romans 7:4-6

84

PURSUING HOLINESS

"Being holy begins with a decision says God. You cannot stumble upon it or suddenly awaken one day feeling set apart to Me. You first have to be called. Unless you are in that category the concept of holiness would not even be apparent to you.

Once you know that you have been called, it is not as though holiness is handed to you on a plate. Rather, that you have to make a conscious decision to pursue it. Once the decision is made the quest begins to strive for the attainment of it. This goal can only be reached through obedience and consistent focused effort and it can vanish as swiftly as it arrives if the consistency is not maintained.

The flesh is the enemy of your effort to be holy and if it is allowed any input into your life, holiness is immediately removed, as it will not share a stage with the flesh. As you can see therefore, constant subjugation of the flesh is necessary to perfect being set apart.

Physical intimacy within the sanctity of marriage can be enjoyed without compromising your quest for holiness. It however does not add anything to your holiness, but neither does it detract from it.

Being set apart is a condition that can be both sensed and measured says God. You will soon know if the measure of holiness in your life has dropped. When such things happen, you have to make extra effort to restore it. The longer it is left the more difficult it becomes to get back where you were before.

Look at how people get obsessed about the things of this world. Whether it be a sport, a hobby, television shows, their cars or other material possessions. To what end? These things are all so temporary. There is nothing wrong with having the nicest things, but they should come as a result of your obsession with 'seeking first the Kingdom' and living a life of holiness. There are some that would argue that if you are living in holiness, it is somehow wrong to have nice things. This is incorrect; people will recognize holiness in you by the actions you take, nothing else.

Make sure that everything that you do is performed in the manner that I would expect you to do it says God. You will know that if I would be pleased by it, you have carried out that task satisfactorily.

Now you can see the foolishness of compromising to suit other people. In fact, it is a double loss. First you get tainted by their worldliness and second, there is no opportunity for them to benefit from your holiness if you are not walking in obedience".

Hebrews 12:14
Romans 6:19-22, 12:1-2
2 Timothy 1:9
1 Cor 1:2, 1:30
2Cor 7:1
2 Peter 3:10-13
1 Peter 1:15-16

85

LOVE

"Let love be the most prominent emotion in your life says God. It is the most powerful of all emotions and is your greatest weapon against the flesh. This may sound confusing, but if you think of all of the bad things that the flesh would want to involve you in, you could not carry out any of those actions in the presence of love.

You must learn to operate under the 'influence' of love. It is highly contagious, but it is the opposite of disease. When under the influence of love, you will always be at ease and be able to put others at ease at the same time. If love is your example, who could fail to be impacted?

Remember that love has to be unceasing and unconditional. The flesh is looking for an opening to discredit love, to prove that it is not true. Love is the truth, but you have to literally *be* that love, before you can do loving things. Otherwise they become actions created by the mind and not the Spirit and this opens the door to carnality.

Carnal love is fallible because it allows the flesh to participate. Real Godly love is a function of the Spirit and therefore the flesh cannot be allowed to participate. Learn to love the *act of loving*. Every person has something about them that is loveable. Seek after that thing and focus only on that thing until you see the love creating a breakthrough in your communication with that person.

There is a tendency from a worldly perspective to attempt to help people through their problems by focusing on the problem itself and helping them to manage and understand the problem.

This will at best produce a temporary solution, but more often than not it just leads to deeper frustration. It is in part why many people that enter into therapy either remain in it or keep returning for more.

Most of the 'so called problems' are nothing more than the absence of love in the individual's life in an area that has not been satisfactorily dealt with. What is abuse after all? It is the antithesis of love. People suffering rejection or lack of self-esteem, really only need their perception of love transformed so that they can experience it again.

There is no love that can even compare to the love of their Heavenly Father. Let people see that My love is available to all. Be the manifestation of Godly love and they will seek after it for themselves. This is the only therapy they need".

Ephesians 3:17-19, 4:13-16
1 Peter 4:8
1 Corinthians 13:13
1 Thessalonians 5:8
1 Timothy 1:4-5, 14
2 Timothy 1:7, 2:22
Hebrews 10:24
1 John 4:7-21
Romans 8:37-39

86

SEPARATION BEGINS IN THE HEART

"Separation begins in the heart. When your love for Me overwhelms your love for anything else it is then easy to make the decision as to what side of the line you are going to live.

Once you establish yourself *firmly* on the supernatural side, you will flourish. Everything that previously seemed difficult and confusing will be simple. Choices that you have previously wrestled with will be obvious. There will be no uncertainty in your life, ever. Your faith will go before you like a banner, confounding the wisdom of the world and you will rise above all challenges.

The difference between the worldly life and the spiritual life is like the difference between night and day, black and white. It is an obvious difference. If you look at your life and it looks very similar to that of people that live *in the world*, you are missing something!

If you spend most of your time doing the things they do in the way that they do them, you are fooling yourself.

You can still do the work I require of you in the world and maintain your separation. This 'separateness' is essential. It is the flag that waves to the lost and helps them to realize that there is another way to live their lives.

In both your spiritual health, which is found through your obedience to living a separate life and your physical health, without which I cannot use you effectively in the natural realm, I have given you the wisdom, the knowledge and the tools to maintain peak condition. It is now up to you to use them with consistent focus.

If these two ingredients are maintained properly everything will automatically fall into place says God.

Your business will flourish at a level beyond your perception when you realize that you are nothing more than an instrument and that all forms of commerce are operated on supernatural principals. This will remove any requirement to spend endless hours in connection with financial matters."

John 17:16
2 Corinthians 6:17
1 Corinthians 5:9-10

87

FAITH FOR THE RUNNING OF THE RACE

"You are capable of tremendous faith, but you have to walk in it not just talk about it. Back to the basics 'faith without works is dead'. In other words; only *action* leads to righteousness and rewards.

You cannot *think* or *talk* your way to the end of the race. You have to get up, put on your shoes and run, run, run.

Remember this is not a relay race where the racers hand over the baton to the others. It is true that this can reduce the time that the race takes, but there is only one person in each team that can cross the line and finish.

No, this race is like a marathon says God. First of all, only the bravest, strongest and most committed will even enter a marathon. It is a long and arduous race that causes pain and frustration along the way as well as joy and elation. Runners form groups to help each other along the way and provide support. It is the same thing with your spiritual race. Look for opportunities to both give and receive support along the way.

You have done your basic training, you have your 'running suit' and your 'shoes', you have your 'fitness plan' and you have 'walked the course' so you know the direction you have to go in. There will be many detours along the way; routes that will take you completely in the wrong direction. These must be avoided at all costs as it can be extremely difficult to find your way back from some of them.

The pistol is loaded and ready to fire. This can be the end of your old life and the beginning of a new one, but you have to claim that for yourself.

I give you possibilities in the earthly realm, but it is your actions that determine the choices. You cannot choose a new life in the supernatural realm and then continue to live your old life in the worldly realm, as there is no way for you to be in two places at once.

You know through My Word that everything that was ever accomplished on this earth was made possible through love and faith. These two are the primary ingredients in the miracles that are happening every day.

Be blessed My children. If you could even fathom the depth of My love for you, your physical body would die from the power of it. Receive My love through My Spirit anointing. I am looking forward to seeing the difference that you will make" says God.

Hebrews 12:1-3
1 Corinthians 9:24-27
2 Timothy 4:7
Colossians 3:10
Ephesians 3: 16-17

88

FAITH FOR VICTORY IN THE SPIRITUAL REALM

"Walking in faith requires constant interaction with My Spirit says God. Therein lies the strength of your faith.

Faith in the absence of the Spirit is nothing more than self-belief. However noble that may be, it will ultimately lead only to destruction. If this were not the case, Faith would be irrelevant. People would just need to believe in themselves and their race would run true.

To believe in yourself is to believe in the power of the flesh. While it is true that the flesh has a 'type' of power, it is an illusion. It is a lie laid closely to the truth by the enemy and it leads many to destruction.

This false impression of power is prevalent in the world and you must be on your guard against it. 'Look what I have done' and 'look what God has done through me' are not far apart in words, but they are an incalculable distance apart in the context of eternity.

In the coming years things will be moving at what appears to be an incredible speed. This is why your planning and preparations must be accurate and consistent. There will not be time to work out your days as you go along. You must be able to see each day unfolding before you begin and begin it in *faith* with the outcome of the day held in your mind with righteous confidence.

Be sure to continue to feed your spirit and soul with the Word. They crave this, their only sustenance. The more nurtured and developed they are in the Word, the more effective they are in both the natural and the supernatural.

You must develop the habit of winning your victories in the supernatural realm first, then victories in the natural will seem effortless. Nothing happens in the natural realm that does not first begin in the supernatural. After all, the spiritual realm is where eternity in its true sense is being played out.

The natural is only a temporal mirror image of some aspects of the supernatural. Those with eyes to see and ears to hear, those that can transcend the world and the flesh here and now, are already able to have an effect in the supernatural realm. Just look at the power of simple prayers spoken with faith. This is just one example. Give focus to this issue of separation from worldly desires. The more evident it is, the easier it will become for you to spend time in the supernatural, which is where the truth is".

John 6:63
Matthew 17:20

89

TITHES & CHOICES

"Consider prayerfully every opportunity and situation that you are faced with. The reason that your spirit is concerned with issues of tithes and offerings is that you know that something is not correct in that area says God.

If a person ties My hands in any area of their lives, it makes it impossible for Me to bless them in the way that I would like, unless I contradict My own spiritual laws which of course is also impossible.

You should seek wisdom in these matters as correct understanding and application will not only bring unfathomable blessings into your own lives but will equip you with a much needed and powerful example through which you will be able to demonstrate the effectiveness of it and not just talk about it.

Study and prayer will bring you to the obvious conclusion in this matter. Seek the counsel of My Spirit, as He is the final authority in spiritual matters on the earth. The worldly affairs of mortgages and expenses are easily taken care of through faith, obedience and a correct understanding and application of the spiritual principles concerning financial matters.

The quest that you are facing need not be difficult in any respect. If your faith goes before you and you have a confident expectation of the blessings to come, there is nothing to be concerned or apprehensive about.

This will be a blessed and joyous time for you that will also provide the breakthrough to the next spiritual level that you are seeking. There is no more time for pretense or imagination. Now is the time for action. You have to start *being* who you are, who you desire to be and who I have called and anointed you to be.

Ask yourselves: do you want to be a person that is approved of by other people, bending this way or that in an attempt to be all things to all people, giving whatever answers you calculate will keep you in the best light with them and doing the things that they want you to do in the way that they want you to do them? Do you want to diminish your true identity in the spiritual realm just to maintain the status quo in the natural?

Or do you want to walk in the supernatural, blessed and anointed by the power of My Spirit, being a shining light to the people you interact with using the fullness of your gifts to expose the lie? The lie that says My children must live lesser, or less effective lives than the people of the world.

The choice is right in front of you and is in your hands only.

You are the only one that can make the choice for yourself. The opinions of people will never work, because they will consider the situation from the perspective of their flesh.

No one can consider something from the perspective of My Spirit operating inside you except you and you alone.

Spontaneous prayer in any situation is always a positive step. The flesh will resist and that is to be expected because this is a manifestation of My Spirit taking control of your life.

The more you control the flesh by subduing it, the more you will accomplish and the more you will see in the supernatural. It is difficult to see anything in the supernatural when your eyes are only ever confronted by the things of the world".

1Corinthians 2:10-16
John 14:26
Luke 12:12
Romans 13:14
Galatians 5:16
1John 2:20
John 6:63

90

MOVING AWAY FROM THE THINGS OF THE WORLD

"A man can only move towards the great things I have for him when he moves away from the things of the world says God.

You must pursue the things consistent with your purpose and vision only. Any other pursuit is only the unnecessary passing of time.

Always consider the eternal consequences of your idea or action. If there are no eternal consequences or only negative consequences, then it is obviously not a desired idea or action.

Every choice that you make will lead you one way or the other. Remember that taking too many wrong turns is what causes people to get lost.

That is why you must constantly check your position relative to My Spirit. If the Spirit is guiding you, it is impossible for you to get lost. If you are guiding yourself, it is inevitable that you will get lost at some point. With that being so obvious, why even take the chance?

To operate at the level of holiness appropriate to the calling I bestow upon you will require great diligence and focus says God. Holiness must be your trademark, it must be stamped upon every aspect of your life. If there is an erratic element showing up it will keep you from the fullness of both the power and the blessings.

There is also a warning to be heeded here. To walk in the supernatural realm in the absence of holiness is highly dangerous. Letting your guard down, even for a brief moment will leave you susceptible to attack from the enemy.

Self-doubt, fear, struggling to pray, feelings of unworthiness, unbelief, these are all examples of conditions that will easily fall upon a chosen warrior who drops the mantle of holiness even for a short time. Understand that the enemy and his cohorts do not take vacations, they do not even take 'lunch breaks'. They are on mission 24/7 and so it has to be with you".

Isaiah 30:21, 58:11
John 14:26
1 Peter 5:8

91

LOOK CAREFULLY AT EVERY PLAN

"This journey is continuous and will continue until it is time to leave this earth at which point it will change direction. For this season, the die is already cast. The battle between good and evil is underway and will never be interrupted by the whims of man.

Consider this; all the ways of the world ultimately lead only to death. There is no other possible outcome. If they are not bringing glory to My Name, what purpose is there to their endeavors? says God. If they do not exalt Me in their actions or their triumphs, then who are they exalting? Well it can only be themselves, another person or the enemy.

Either way it can lead only to destruction. The message here is crystal clear. Look very closely at every plan, idea and direction and pinpoint the righteousness within it. If there is none to be found, you will know not to proceed in that particular direction.

Remember to continuously be feeding both mind and body with nutritious sustenance and building fuel. Just as it takes several glasses of water to flush out one glass of soda, every piece of negative 'garbage' that you put into either your mind or your body takes a similar amount of extra effort to remove before you can again begin to make progress.

This makes your journey far more difficult than it should be. If you just learn that lesson enough to not put the garbage in there in the first place, it will be far easier to make the progress you are seeking.

Imagine the power behind carrying out the daily actions of your work under the anointing of My Spirit? If this was available to you, would you want to do that? To be directed only by My Spirit in every aspect of your daily life. Can you imagine the results that could be achieved if that was available to you?

Well it is not only available, but it is right here in your hands to pick up and use!

Stop trying to create success in your own strength, your efforts will produce some results but that is true for many people. What we are interested in are supernatural results says God. The results that bring glory to My name and provide an abundance of seed for the tasks that we are set upon carrying out".

Proverbs 16:9
Psalms 32:8
John 16:13
1 Thessalonians 5:16-18

92

LIVING WITH JOY AND WALKING WITH THE SPIRIT

"Learning to live with joy is an important component of walking in the supernatural says God. There is an opportunity to find joy in every activity that you participate in. Obviously, prayer should be a joyous experience and in the same manner so should everything else that you do.

How else can you expect to reflect My love and My light to the world if your countenance is not full of joy and delight.

Walking continuously in My anointing will bring that joyfulness to your spirit which will have a positive effect on everyone and everything around you.

Remember how wonderful you felt on days when you completely resisted the enemy and subdued the flesh and your day was blessed and filled with joy?

This is how separation from the world looks. You are still there, you are still doing things that have to be done and being in places that you have to be, but you are insulated and protected by the anointing so that your spirit can be directed by My Spirit.

Choosing to nourish your mind with uplifting and health enhancing food brings its own instant rewards. Notice how your clarity of thinking improves? You can see the same difference with just one day of walking in the supernatural realm and giving more attention to our relationship than to a relationship with worldly matters.

Your task now is to add *consistency* to your efforts. Without this there is a danger that you would be the double minded man spoken of in James. Like a wave being blown this way and that by the wind.

This is not acceptable for a supernatural warrior. You must be resolute and determined. Let your yes be yes and your no be no. If you say that you are going to live supernaturally anointed lives, then you must do that every day. If this were not the case, you are choosing to forget the man in the mirror who boldly declared that he would do these things".

Romans 14:17, 15:13,
Proverbs 10:28
Nehemiah 8:10
Psalms 28:7-8
James 1:6, 1:23
Matthew 5:37
Colossians 1:12

93

TAKING JOY IN YOUR VICTORIES

"Taking joy in your victories and your labors will make your burden so much lighter says God. Soak yourself in the joy of My anointing at every possible opportunity. You have stated how wonderful it would be to live every day under the joy of the anointing. The only thing that has stopped that from happening is you and your reluctance to *enter in* because the issues of the world appeared to be more pressing.

This is a great error, because the issues of this world would be so much easier to navigate under the guidance of My Spirit. It is like deciding to rent a car and then trying to find your way around without using the navigation device. Operating under the anointing gives you permanent access to the greatest and most powerful 'navigation device' ever, My Spirit. Why would you want to attempt anything without My Spirit which is always available to you?

The flesh wants to make things difficult for you, or even to see you fail! That is exactly the function of the flesh; constantly warring against the Spirit inside of you, trying to cause its destruction and to place you in the hands of the enemy. Remember the enemy never drops the ball, never gives up and is always seeking opportunity. Therefore, you must demonstrate even greater vigilance. Never make the mistake of complacency. You have seen many that have carried out great exploits in My name suddenly fall from grace for this reason. They make the mistake of lowering their defenses. When this happens, the damage may not appear immediately, but it will appear if it is not addressed and repaired, so always be aware of any mistakes that you have made and repent for them and repair any holes in your hedge".

Romans 8:5-8

195

94

THE ART OF RESET

"It is time to learn the art of *reset* says God. Your focus has to be on *allowing* things to happen rather than using force to make them happen. You cannot force something to flow, as once you stop applying the force, the flow will immediately stop.

Flow can only be achieved and maintained by allowing. You do your part, take the necessary action steps and then allow the Spirit to flow freely through you and the result you are seeking will happen.

The key to allowing, is to focus on the power of My Spirit and setting aside any notion of your own strength. Yes, you have talents, yes you have gifts, but whose are they? They work best in conjunction with their Creator and this requires the vehicle which is you, to step to one side and allow the production of the fruit to take place.

Such righteous fruit is nectar to Me says God. Let us go forward together and create a bountiful harvest.

Proper planning is essential because it allows you to structure your activities in the Spiritual realm before you embark upon them in the natural realm. Without planning, how can people know what to pray and ask for?

So many people use their prayer life as a crisis management tool. They are always asking for help with things that have gone wrong. Many never come to the realization that if they planned their lives properly, consulted Me about things before they did them, they would not be having these things going wrong in the first place.

Together we will create the blueprint. You will walk in diligent obedience, taking the action steps and sticking to the plan. Then you will rest and watch the miraculous outcome unfold.

Pressure can create coal or diamonds and fortunately for you there is a choice. The outcome is decided by the choices you make. Keep focusing on the action steps that you know will produce the results that you are looking for.

Stay in the flow and the good success that you deserve will come naturally to you. Maintain a confident, disciplined, obedient attitude and you will be able to attain any goal with My Spirit working through you.

You can achieve everything through Me for I am your strength says God. Look only to Me and beware not to fall into the 'Look what I can do' mindset. It leads only to self-destruction. 'Look what God has done' should be your banner. Wave it proudly.

For people to succeed, there are certain basic daily actions that they have to be taking. If they miss out on any of these actions their results are going to suffer. If you can so easily understand that principle in the natural realm, it should be even more understandable in the Supernatural realm.

You cannot expect to get supernatural results without supernatural effort. Prayer and the sword of the Spirit are the key weapons which you are currently under employing. Just as people say in business to 'hit the reset button', it is time for you to 'hit the Supernatural reset button.' Do not let times and circumstances hinder you in any way".

Zechariah 4:6
Philippians 4:13
197

95

THE IMPORTANCE OF FOCUSED FAITH AND OBEDIENCE

"Every setback or period of inertia has followed a loss of focused Faith. Hold your purpose in the forefront of your mind and measure the consistency and congruency of your actions with your purpose. This will allow you to constantly correct your course.

You should not be operating in accordance with the world's concept of timing. At the supernatural level you just have to follow the formula* that we have discussed, and your flow will be continuous.

Like many prophetic declarations, the degree of the manifestation of the prophecy is contingent on your obedience. Miracles are birthed out of obedience. If you desire to live in the flow of the miraculous, simply learn to flow in obedience. Once you get a correct perception of what that means, it will become easier to maintain. It can never be without challenge, because the flesh is forever in conflict with the Spirit. Through obedience and discipline it is of course possible to keep the flesh subdued and increase the flow of joy.

Obedience brings all the positive things that you desire in your life. Disobedience of course brings the opposite. Therefore, there is nothing to discuss; there is a choice to be made, it is that simple.

At the end of a year, people are always looking for a 'magic button'. They want something to press or do that is going to make the new year better than the old one. They busy themselves making their resolutions and declarations about how, through their own strength, they are going to make great changes. At the first sight of a challenge, their fleshly resolve literally folds up and leaves them disappointed. I have not called you to live this way. You have your unique and perfect blueprint, all you have to do is apply it consistently and with focus.

Know also that this path can only be walked in a spirit of love and joy. Attempting to pursue this life out of a sense of religious obedience is as bad as not doing it at all. Celebrate every successful step on the path with joy, praise, peace and thanksgiving.

Observe any shortfall briefly and move on immediately and stay in the flow. Do not give any energy to any incidents of missing the mark. Observe them, repent and move on without looking back. Giving them energy gives them life and invites the spirits accompanying them to hang around or return later.

Giving them energy brings condemnation and you already know that there is no condemnation in Me says God. Stay in My flow and keep making forward progress. It is impossible for the enemy to defeat you when you are flowing forward in the Spirit says God. Only when you are standing still, or in inertia, or when you are reaching back into the past and going backwards, do you become vulnerable. Use the formula* to ensure continuous forward progress and watch the flow of miracles break through in your life".

Philippians 3:13-14
Romans 8:1, 8:7
Colossians 1:10-11
2 Corinthians 10:5
Revelation 14:12
1Peter 1:14
Isaiah 43:18-19
1John 2:1-29

*See message #1

96

ANOTHER OPPORTUNITY

"Today is another gift, another opportunity for you to make a difference in the lives of other people. What value is a man's life if he contributes only to his own wellbeing? Note that anything you do solely for yourself never bears any fruit. That is why servants and leaders in the true sense of the word, are the same people. It is impossible to lead without being a servant at heart and a true servant will naturally demonstrate leadership, just by his example. Be a person of total integrity and let your word always be true says God

To start a day relying on the strength of your own flesh is foolish. We all know where those days lead. When the things of this world grow so big in your life that you cannot see past them to focus your eyes on Me, you are going to continue to struggle.

It is true that My patience knows no depths or limitations. Any such notion is a lie from the enemy who is busy trying to convince you that you have reached the end of the line, that if you have not got it right by now, you will never get it right. Do not listen to these lies, just be diligent and obedient and keep your eyes focused on Me.

Everything is interconnected says God. Your faithfulness with small things will provide the opportunity for stewardship over things that are so big, right now you cannot even perceive them. Do not let yourself be engulfed by the worries of this world, they are only there to distract you from the Truth. Stay in step with the Truth and nothing can prevent our progress".

Philippians 2:3
Ephesians 4:29

97

NOTHING WILL TAKE YOU OUT OF MY HAND

"Imagine that life is like the pages of an unwritten book says God. Each day you are given 24 blank pages and it is entirely your choice what is written on them. How would your book look? Would there be endless wasted pages that have nothing written on them? Would there be the same stories repeated over and over again? Would there be things so awful that you would not want anyone to see your book? I can tell you that all of these things apply to all people says God. The human nature guarantees it. The enemy wants you to think that I spend all of My time reading the bad stuff or shaking My head at the blank pages. This is a lie. I am not interested in the blank pages and neither should you be. They are gone and forgotten and require no further attention. I do not even see the bad stuff to read it. The words are washed away by the blood of My Son, all I see are the possibilities in you. Once you know that this is how I see you, why would you look at yourself in any other way?

Why spend time anguishing over what might have been? Why wish that you could just go back a few pages and re write something when it is neither possible nor necessary? What you write on today's pages can only affect today and even then, you can only affect the moment you are in by the actions you take in the moment.

If you want to create momentum in your life, concentrate on being *consistently effective* in the moment. Talking about what you are going to do can be therapeutic, even inspirational. However, one moment of *doing* is worth a lifetime of talking. That is why I tell people to be doers of the Word, not just hearers.

Measure your days in moments of focused action and you will create momentous breakthroughs. There is no spiritual barrier for you to break through, just a fleshly reluctance to overcome. Staying in 'moment mode' will also help you to control and subdue the flesh. Focused thinking and definiteness of purpose are key points for each moment. Consistency is a skill; it has to be practiced before it becomes natural.

Remember that anxiety, fear and depression are tools of the enemy. I told you to be anxious for nothing and that means nothing. When these feelings take hold of you, just shake them off like the dust from your feet. Neither dwell on nor discuss them. Recognize them instantly for what you know they are; the fallen nature of the flesh trying to drag you away from your place of spiritual security.

There is nothing on this earth powerful enough to take you out of My hand says God, so change those moments into moments of joyful realization that you are a hand selected child of the living God and no weapon formed against you shall prosper because My Word is the truth."

Isaiah 43:18, 54:17
John 10:28
Philippians 3:13-14, 4:6-8

98

CAUSE & EFFECT.

"Life is a constant cycle of cause and effect. Most of the time you are too busy worrying about the effects rather than the causes says God. The life that you have today is the one that you have designed for yourself. I put the brush in your hand initially, but it was you that made the decisions about what to paint. Then came the time that we were painting together, and look how much better that became? Sure, we still went off the canvas a few times when the flesh was permitted to participate, but overall you see a far more pleasant picture than when you were painting by yourself, all alone.

Now it is time for you to become the brush and let me do the painting. There is still plenty of room on your canvas and together we will create a masterpiece. That means that there is no time to spend analyzing previous pictures; a wrong color here, too much shadow there. It is a pointless exercise, unless you intend to keep on doing your own painting.

It is much easier to start with a clean piece of canvas and see what you truly desire appear on it, than it would be to change something you had previously worked on so that it only appears different. It has to be different from the first stroke. It is the same with the things that challenge you. It is necessary for you to be different on a consistent basis in these areas. To plan out a day of activity is one thing, but if those activities are not carried out, what was the point?

Excellence begins in the heart, not in the head. It is something that you have to *be*, before you will consistently *do* excellent things. If you are not being excellent in your heart it is impossible to maintain a mindset of excellence says God.

Make progress today by revisiting the principles of excellence and deciding that you are not going to settle for anything else".

Psalms 90:12

GODLY THINKING

"To think as My Son thinks and to act as He would act should be the goal of all men. Just as there are places and times for certain things to take place, there are certain people selected for certain purposes says God.

It is a lie from the enemy that the achievements of one person, can diminish the significance of the life of another.

It would appear that brother Yun* has been thrown into prison and beaten for My sake more times than anyone mentioned in My Word. Does this make him better or greater than others? Of course not. Comparing yourself to others is pointless, it is the work of the enemy trying to place discouragement in your path. The only person you should have any interest in emulating is My Son. Learning to think as He thinks and to act as He acts should be the goal of all men.

Living in this way, in the context of what I have called you to do, is the key says God. You should not look to create your own calling into an area that you think will look more honorable or impressive.

Pursue My will for your life and there will be no time for making comparisons with the lives of others. Take courage that you can also be like many others who are living out the plan that I have placed in their hearts and are doing valuable work in this preparation time".

(* A well-known Christian missionary in China mentioned in the book 'The Heavenly man')

1 John 2:6, 5:11-12

100

WHO'S CAMP ARE YOU IN?

"One who seeks the council and approval of men will always find himself in a dry place. The path of the righteous can only be ordained by Me says God. Of course, there are many paths to choose from, but only one leads to righteousness and to sanctification.

You have let yourselves be blown around like a leaf in the wind. As you let one perceived 'source' dwindle you started to scurry about like a squirrel with no store for the winter crying 'is this my source?' Maybe it's here, maybe it is this thing or maybe it is that. Perhaps I should do several things at once and then one of them is bound to turn out to be the source.

Foolish man, surely if you have learned nothing else over these years you would at least have a rock-solid understanding of the fact that I am your only source. All other things that manifest as a source or supply may meet your needs for a season, but they will then disappear as suddenly as they arrived leaving you bewildered, disoriented and confused. Just as you have found yourself in recent times says God.

The enemy invites you to wear the crown of disobedience. It is usually cleverly disguised as some other type of crown that fits well and feels really good. It could be the crown of self-importance or independence or self-righteousness or superiority and there are many others.

Unbeknown to the wearer, these crowns have a more sinister power that is not immediately evident. They have the ability to dull the senses.

Consequently the wearers find it more and more difficult to hear My voice or to see My face or to read My Word and they are gradually sucked into an abyss of wrong thinking and lies from which many sheep can never escape.

It is time to make sure that your head is bare says God. Cast off any false crowns and turn your attention fully to Me in humility and love and you will once again hear My voice without effort. Clarity will be restored to your thinking and you can continue making progress on the right path".

1 Corinthians 2:5
Psalms 16:11, 25:4, 119:35
Jeremiah 6:16
2 Peter 1:3
Acts 17:28

101

TAKING CONTROL

"It is time to 'take control' says God, but you have to realize that the only effective way to take control is to give it up. Let My Spirit be in control and your steps will be well ordered. To attempt to keep the control for yourself is pointless, because the enemy will ultimately wrestle it away from you.

The only thing worse than being out of control is being controlled by someone else that has your suffering as his goal.

Did I not tell you that transformation comes through the renewing of your mind? Well, to re-new something literally means to 'make it like new again'. This can only be accomplished by completely eradicating the old mind. If this is not done, that little piece of old thinking will ultimately have a negative impact on the new mind and hinder its proper focus.

In your position now, everything is a spiritual matter that requires Godly counsel and Spiritual consideration. You cannot interject worldly thinking into these matters, as that is like trying to mix water with oil.

See how easily the heaviness lifts with the clarity of understanding that comes from a yielded heart and a Spirit directed soul? The more you fill your spaces with My things the less likely it is that the things of the world can interfere with your progress.

Follow through is a practice that should be more important in your life. An unfinished task or project need not have been started in the first place. There is more to obedience than just beginning something, it has to be pursued to completion. You must follow through.

If I give one of My children the mantles of Obedience, Focus and Follow-Through, they should be sure to wear them every moment of every day. Be warned though; they are only effective if worn together with the mantle of Humility. Without this they look like pride, arrogance and self-gratification or greed, so always make sure that the mantle of Humility is in place.

Remember that many hands make light work. If you overload yourself with things to do, you will not do any of them in an excellent manner. I again point you towards excellence says God. Look around you and discern if your environment and habits reflect excellence. Back to the renewing of the mind again.

The life of a righteous man is simple, but it will never be easy. Those that delight in the challenge will always find more joy than those that struggle against it. Those that choose not to walk in obedience have at the same time chosen to be disobedient and cast themselves into the camp of the enemy.

There is no middle ground here. Your choices will define whose camp you are spending your time in, so choose wisely. Choices are best made in an atmosphere of Spiritual deliberation as choices made in the flesh will always be wrong, however correct they appear at the time.

The flesh is incapable of making a choice that leads to righteousness as it is unrighteous by its very nature and is at enmity with the Spirit within you. This then is a major key. Never make choices in the absence of My Spirit, and every choice you make will be right and proper".

Romans 12:2
Matthew 9:17
Hebrews 12:11
Romans 8:5-9

102

STRUGGLES WITH THE FLESH

"Circles, circles, nothing but circles. Around and around you go on the same old merry-go-round. Nothing changes except your level of frustration and dissatisfaction which varies depending on the current financial situation.

This is a mess that needs clearing up. It all comes back to being 'on purpose' with your lives. A minute spent 'off purpose' is a minute wasted; an hour causes consternation and a day? A day 'off purpose' is a shame, because in that day no progress is made and days are few enough as it is. This is not about condemnation and guilt says God, it is about direction.

Even the greatest of efforts are truly fruitless if they are misdirected. One minute of prayer in harmony with your purpose is greater than hours of vain babbling. The reason that you feel anxious and disjointed is that you have no focus and that has been diminished due to your own lack of obedience and diligence.

Only by constant communication with My Spirit will you receive the mentorship you are seeking. You are double-minded in the issue of stewardship of financial recourses. We discussed the right way and then you do differently and justify it with your excuses about debts. Who created the debts in the first place? And now others must suffer while you scramble to retrieve the situation. Surely you grow weary of the 'just in time' syndrome?

Life should not be centered around harvesting the necessary dollars in the last few days of each month just so that you can repeat the process the next month. That does not even resemble abundant living. That is lack to the highest degree.

It is time for a new game plan says God. These old plays are not working for you. I repeat again; there are no new answers, you have them all. You have everything required to go forward, you just have to pick up the right tools and use them properly. You have to stop getting in your own way by trying to do everything yourself.

I have illustrated the way to you over and over. My patience never runs out, but yours is long gone and now that is obscuring your vision for the future. Remember what you learned regarding the importance of repentance?

Change the way you are thinking about all of these things and start taking immediate action. Be faithful in all things as I am always faithful says God. Be forthright, organized and of the highest level of integrity. Be focused, diligent and obedient and take joy in your labors. These are the qualities of a righteous man and will always produce an abundant harvest of the most succulent fruit".

Revelation 3:14
2 Peter 3:9
Exodus 34:6
Psalms 103:8
Joel 2:13
John 6:63, 15:16

103

SPIRIT OF INERTIA

"Questions, questions always questions! It makes Me smile says God how people always have more questions in the hope that eventually, they will hear the answer that fits into the life they are creating for themselves to match their own preferences.

Sometimes people are so busy asking questions that they cannot hear clearly to discern the answers that are being provided. Sometimes they just do not like the answers they hear, so they ask another question. If you were to consider the answers that I have given you through the pages of My Word, you have all the answers necessary to live a divinely appointed supernatural existence in My perfect will for your lives.

There are no better answers, only the truth or the path of the enemy, so the choice should be easy. The flesh will keep you second guessing; the flesh will keep you walking in fear and the flesh will continually pull you back to the spirit of mammon.

You have all of the tools to not only overcome in this arena, but to also bless others with the example of being overcomers. Inertia is a cursed spirit that holds back many from being overcomers. They incorrectly perceive that because they are not losing ground, things are on track and they are maintaining the status quo. That is a lie and a deception. It is impossible to not be moving in one direction or the other. Consequently, a person is either moving towards Me or towards the enemy. Inertia is an illusion. It is like the 'frog in the cooking pot'. The water warms so gradually he does not realize that he is being cooked until it is too late. It is time to jump out of the pot says God. Shake off the slumber of complacency and hit the road running".

2 Peter 1:3

104

OVERCOMING ENEMY SPIRITS

"There is not much evidence of 'crushing the flesh' taking place in your household. The spirit of jezebel is a dangerous enemy and only through your strength at the supernatural level can she be defeated. If one puts to flight a 1000, then that is 2000 between you.

The Word clearly states that two together will put to flight 10,000, but know this, that two that I have handpicked to operate as one, can vanquish a 100,000 and more says God.

This should not be a difficult message to unravel. You should anticipate your prayer time together with excitement and relish.

It should be your joy of joys, your best time of the day. This is the time that you can wage your most powerful battles in the supernatural realm. You can also build each other up by releasing the flow of the anointing, which will flow far more strongly when you agree. This will provide you with extra protection for the times that you must enter separately.

You have placed yourselves firmly in the midst of the fray says God. As I have told you before there is now no going back, the opportunity for retreat is long past as you are now operating behind enemy lines. You are an insurgent. As such you have to remain one step ahead of the enemy which is only possible through the Mind of Christ and the Tongue of Truth.

We are seeking to take back ground which requires the pulling down of strongholds and vanquishing of principalities and powers. For this to be possible you have to *identify* them and make war against them specifically.

On your own, you cannot make war against a principality or power that has a foothold, however small, in your life. This fact has rendered many of My soldiers ineffective says God.

'Dabbling' in the supernatural is a very dangerous pursuit and will lead only to the destruction of the dabblers. It is vital that you take this very seriously. Once your positioning in this realm is significantly elevated, you have to be fully prepared.

If you were in a fight for your survival and your *only* weapon was prayer, how much praying would you do? If worship is the key to unleashing an abundant flow of My supernatural anointing, how often should there be worship taking place in your home?

Beware of believing the lie that 'once we move away from *this* place or *that* situation things will be better'. This is a deception. What we are talking about here is an attitude of the heart, it should be manifesting in any location you are at. *Every thought, every word, every action should have a Kingdom purpose powering it.* If not, what is the point?

The time for idle gossip is past. You need to be builders of lives, not contributing to the stumbling blocks that the world constantly produces.

You know about 'planks in eyes' etc., but what use is all of this knowledge if it is not acted upon. It does not matter how much water is in the well if you do not put your bucket on the end of the rope.

Even so, you have to consistently return to the well to replenish your supply. If this is not done you will become thirsty and ultimately the body will cease to function properly and die.

There are so many sheep that are currently not functioning properly. They need to return to the well says God, or their days on the earth will be cut short. Do not identify yourselves with them by behaving in the same manner. Support them through prayer and example at all times.

Look at the Spirit influence of everything you do and say. Remember that all things not led by the Spirit are therefore led by the flesh by default.

You must only speak out of the wisdom of My anointing which requires the constant removal of worldly obstacles blocking its flow. The further removed from the world you become, the greater the depth and the power of that flow will be.

Increase your diligence in the area of physical health. The more intense your spiritual battles become, the more draining it will be on your physical body so you should optimize your strength and energy.

Lay out your battle plan. Remember to focus on that plan until it has been successfully executed. Do not let other distractions sway you from your goal.

The enemy will often present you with an easier target and if you make the mistake of shifting your focus for even an instant, the principality or power that was your *primary* target is able to escape. They will then launch a major assault against you for revenge. The enemy never walks in forgiveness. This is why you see so many sheep under attack immediately after what appeared to be a major breakthrough in their lives.

A righteous husband has to be effective in his marriage before he can be truly effective in the Kingdom. If he cannot steward and lead one willing sheep, what success would he expect to have with others to whom he is unconnected in the physical sense? A wife must follow the

217

path determined by the husband, so he should always carry the map, or they can both stray from the true path and become lost. A sheep that is not on the path is therefore of the world and cannot attain to holiness," says God.

1 Corinthians 2:14-16
1 Thessalonians 5:16-18
Proverbs 21:31
Psalms 91:7
Joshua 23:10-11
Deuteronomy 32:30
Hebrews 4:12
Ephesians 6:10-18
Philippians 2:5-14

105

MAMMON

"What you see behind you is the consequence of years spent mainly serving the spirit of mammon says God. Although you have not even realized it, the effects are highly evident. It is a pattern experienced by so many, but you cannot help them until you are truly walking in the other direction yourself.

You have to bring money into servitude. It has to be a 'tool', a means to an end over which you have total control. For that to be the case any money that literally leaves your hand has to be your own money or money that has been placed in your control.

If you use money before you have the 'legal' right to use it, you will be placing yourself in the hands of the spirit of mammon. Any debt puts you under the control of the spirit of mammon. Those that have consumer debt are in the clutches of the spirit of mammon and must be set free. There is a simple logic to this. Do not have store cards and other types of credit cards for the purpose of buying things that you cannot afford. Buy things that you already have the money for. Buy them only when you have the money in your hands. Not when it is 'on the way' or when the deal is 'nearly through' or because someone said they will 'definitely be giving you the money'.

That which is Mine should be immediately set to one side says God, as should that which is for investment.

Only those who understand that they have to be part of the 'flow' of money can escape the service of mammon. They should use their talents to generate money, use some for their own needs, some to help create more flow and let the rest flow to others in greater need.

Those with incorrect thinking see the money itself as the end. This is a great error as it promotes fear of loss.

This in turn places that person back into the service of mammon.

Developing a high level of skill in using money as a servant and acquiring significant assets will keep a person free from consumer debt and provide enough overflow to sow into the lives of others.

Be warned though, from this height the fall is the greatest. The adoration of the world combined with their perception of the significance of riches can cause the achiever to start considering the magnitude of his own accomplishments. This will inevitably lead to pride and we all know where that leads. The watchword here is humility says God.

The lack of humility has rendered so many potentially great leaders totally ineffective. Prayerful obedience added to diligent financial stewardship can unlock the gates to a consistent flow of abundant grace and blessings. However, humility is the valve that controls the flow. Without it, the gates will either be slammed shut and the flow cut off, or they will be thrust open and the ensuing tidal wave just crushes everything in its path.

You have witnessed people that have risen and fallen like shooting stars. It is often the lack of humility that caused their demise".

Proverbs 11:2, 18:12, 22:4

1 Peter 5:6-7

Matthew 6:24

106

STRIVE FOR SPIRITUAL EXCELLENCE

"If your life in the supernatural realm still looks and feels too much like your old life, it shows you that there is still much to do. Keep pressing forward and embrace the differences. More prayer brings more anointing. More anointing increases the flow of the Spirit in your life, which elevates your standing in the supernatural.

Strive for spiritual excellence, for only through that door can you expect it to manifest in the natural realm. Continuously revisit the concept of excellence in everything from your thoughts to your speech and actions.

Regardless of any challenges you may face, envision a life where you always strive for excellence where you allow only excellent thoughts to dwell in your mind. Where you speak only excellent words and do only excellent things and carry them out in the most excellent manner.

This is a picture of what it truly means to be 'Christ-like'.

These were the exact attributes made manifest in My time among men says God.

What do you want for yourself during the next year as it unfolds from this moment? When you reflect again in 12 months' time, what do you want to see? Will it be another 12 months of 'if only' or 'I wish I had' or 'why didn't we?' Or will it be 12 months of awe inspiring progress? A year of victory upon victory, breakthrough upon breakthrough, miracle upon miracle? A year of supernatural living in the spiritual realm, stepping forward as a leader and mighty warrior, claiming back territory for My coming Kingdom?

The answer lies purely in your own hands. You can crush the flesh and become Spirit focused and Spirit led or continue on a path of mediocrity and inconsistency. My *love* remains the same either way says God. The only thing at stake here is your love for Me and how much you choose to demonstrate it. There is a tremendous revelatory truth in that last sentence which has the power to set many people free.

In order for excellence to be an effective key in your hands you have to understand it, embrace it and then insert it into the lock of your own life. As you throw open that door, you will be engulfed by a supernatural anointing which has such a brilliant light attached to it that it will empower you to lead many, many sheep out of the spiritual darkness that has overtaken them. Just start taking the steps and My Spirit will guide your feet".

Romans 8:38-39

2 Corinthians 5:9, 8:7, 13:11

Psalms 73:25-26

Daniel 6:3

Philippians 4:18

107

THE KEY TO THE GREAT DOORS

"Discipline and obedience, discipline and obedience, discipline and obedience. The world talks about 'D.M.O', their 'daily method of operation'. Even they have a picture of the importance of this issue although the truth is missing from their understanding.

You can still use a 'DMO' but with a far more powerful interpretation. *Discipline Manifests Obedience.* These two qualities are very important to your *focus* and *progress.* That is why they are so elusive.

The flesh naturally resists any pressure to be aligned in this matter. The reason should be obvious. Successful application of these qualities will lead a person to righteousness and the flesh abhors righteousness. Once you are walking in righteousness you become effective in *both* the natural and the supernatural realm says God.

This is a simple to understand, yet much overlooked key. A believer stranded in the mire of unrighteousness becomes totally ineffective in the battle, worse still he becomes a stumbling block to those around him. Not only is he not contributing, he negates the efforts of others who are striving to make progress but have to waste precious time and resources in rescuing the undisciplined disobedient sheep who demand constant attention because of his iniquity.

Imagine the power that will be unleashed upon the earth when all of My chosen anointed warriors focus all of their time and effort winning the lost and bringing prophecy and healings through praise and worship. Imagine the outpouring of My Spirit that this will produce says God. It will cause changes in this world that will astonish even the most righteous among you and confound the enemy.

Looking upon this picture it is simple to see why the flesh so vehemently resists any move towards discipline and obedience. They are the lifeblood of spiritual development. Such development is impossible without these qualities and these qualities will considerably accelerate your spiritual development which exponentially increases their value.

These insights are part of the beginnings of wisdom; the knowledge of joy to be found within the intimate sanctuary of praise and worship, the power of walking in the world under the anointing of My Spirit, the joy of constantly hearing My voice and having a true personal relationship with Me, the sheer exhilaration of seeing the power of prayer manifest in your life, the peace that comes through the hope of a better world to strive for in the age to come, the overwhelming love that you feel for others when you are able to see them through My eyes, the honor of being selected as one of My chosen warriors called to do battle for My glory in these last days.

Reflect on all of these revelations. Let the power of them permeate every cell in your body. These are the precious gifts says God. The things that the flesh hates and the world cannot fathom or understand because they are so blinded to them by the lies of the enemy.

What keeps you from the blissful existence of enjoying all of the gifts all day every day? Lack of discipline and lack of obedience!

Therefore, the lesson here is very simple. If the lack of these two qualities is keeping you from the blessings you deserve, it is obvious what has to be done to change the situation. With the solution being so obvious, why then does it seem so difficult to implement? It is of course a lie perpetuated by the enemy *who uses the resistance of the flesh to* place a veil over your eyes so that you cannot perceive the straight easy path that answers the question:

'Almighty loving Father, God of all creation, from where do I get the strength to live every moment of every day in a state of disciplined obedience'?

The door that obscures the answer to this question looks like a huge foreboding fortified gate in the natural. The kind of door you would imagine would be required to keep people out of somewhere of great importance. The kind of vault-like doors shielding and protecting a great treasure. What is the key that unlocks these great doors? I hear you ask. That key is simply your prayer. Your fervent prayers yielded out of the joy we share in communing together says God.

Now it all comes together. My Word says that it is the *'effectual fervent prayer of a righteous man that availeth much'*.

Discipline and obedience are the eternal companions of righteousness. A person can never attain righteousness in the absence of these two. Can you imagine a righteous man that lacks discipline, or a disobedient, yet righteous man? It is not possible to have righteousness without these companions, so they have to be put in place first. Can you put discipline and focus into your own being and will that produce the obedience that you need? Well, if it was that simple the world would look like a very different place and would be ready for My Kingdom. It is obvious that no man can achieve this transplant in his own strength. This is spiritual surgery that can only be performed in the prayer rooms of Heaven. Just as prayer releases My power to be effective on the earth, prayer also conditions and positions My people to be effective in their calling. Prayer will transition people from the called to the chosen and even to the faithful. Prayer will instill the discipline and obedience as the fuel to attain unto righteousness.

The analytical among you will now have another question: 'so from where do we get the initial discipline and obedience to pray consistently enough so that true discipline and obedience is engrafted in us?' Well that is one of the many wonders of grace says God. The grace gifted to you through your faith which prompted you to seek something that although you could not see it you knew it was there and you knew that if you followed that faith it would lead you to the truth.

Grace never leaves, you just forget to walk in it. Let this grace, through your faith lead you easily and effortlessly into the realm of supernatural prayer through which the Spirit of Discipline and Obedience will be engrafted into your soul, which will cause your flesh to fall into subjugation allowing righteousness to burst forth in your life like a dazzling rainbow of light, fueling your 'effective fervent prayers' which can only be spoken by righteous lips.

This will cause every day to be a Spirit filled anointed opportunity to offer praise and worship to Me and to see lives touched and changed and miracles to be performed in abundance. Never forget that when you live a supernatural existence, 'everything is spiritual' so you must pursue Discipline and Obedience at the spiritual level" says God.

Proverbs 10:17
Romans 6:16
1 Peter 4:18-19
James 5:16
Revelation 17:14
2 Corinthians 12:8-10

108

THE GREAT AWAKENING

"See how man seeks after the glorification of man? The more ardently they seek to glorify each other, the further they are from Me says God. They are glorious in their own eyes, they keep their own books and records of greatness, and they give awards and prizes to esteem each other. For what purpose? How does such behavior permit any obedience to My instructions?

Where is the righteous fruitfulness of such an existence? What will such people present to Me at the judgment seat? All of the awards and rewards that have been bestowed on this earth will burn up in a second in the fire. In the blink of an eye they will become just a puff of smoke, gone and forgotten. What will remain after that? Only the works completed out of the fullness of an obedient heart; the unselfish exploits carried out in My name for the good of others.

There are many finger pointers among you says God. Those that although they do not share in the stage and the spotlight share the same vain iniquities in their hearts, whom in a second would put on the fine garments of fame and fortune and marry themselves to the deception of riches and worldly adoration.

There are no rewards for finger pointing and condemnation, especially when one's own heart carries affection for the things condemned. This is the worst kind of double-mindedness. Learn to place your confidence only in Me. The source of all your increase is in your faith. There can be no increase without faith and greater faith can create greater increase.

Look at what is happening around you. Reality television is now the biggest form of entertainment available. What kind of 'reality' does this portray? A reality of lost confused people looking for their brief moment of fame; looking to win the recognition of the world. They have become the epitome of 'the blind leading the blind'.

Look how people so willingly displace their integrity to have the opportunity for a moment of glory. There are so many mockers who would cease their mocking and willingly grab any hand offering to pull them up to the same place. How many of you would say 'I will only participate if you allow Me to glorify My Savior with My words. I will only participate if I can give Him all of the glory for every success. I will only participate if I can say look what God has done'? They will tell you that this is not possible, because they do not want to make the program too 'religious'. See how religion separates people from the truth of My love? See how the power of the media can alienate people from the truth?

Imagine there was a television show called 'Look what God has done!'. That it played continuously and showed people all the wondrous things that are taking place in My name, all day every day. Just imagine how powerful that would be. Until such a time, the responsibility falls upon the believers to become that voice. I am calling My people together to create a great company of witnesses here on earth. The predecessors of the cloud in thought, words and actions.

You should be My ambassadors and send up a great cry 'look what God has done'! Together we will claim back the territory; in the workplace, in the entertainment industry, in the so called 'religious' world. We will initiate a great transformation says God. We will bring people to a point where they are forced by the weight of the evidence before them to refocus, to turn their attention away from the glorification of man and all his ambitions and put it onto the love and greatness offered through Me, their Heavenly Father.

There is an urgency in this instruction says God. Being critical of the world and its ways or even refusing to encourage or support them will only alienate My people from their task.

You must become a living testimony to the fact that there is a better way, a higher choice, a more pleasant path to follow.

Now you will see the importance of having your own house in order. Your fruit has to be attractive and beautiful so that others will want to get some for themselves. Be extremely cautious therefore as to what seeds you are planting now, because when the harvest comes the result will be carried in your basket for all to see. With everything you involve yourself in, be sure that you can see the consistency with this commission. If it is hard to find you will understand the message.

Are you 'all in' says God? Are you truly committed to this cause? Are you like the people in Luke 21 that gave out of their abundance or are you like the widow who with her 2 mites gave everything she had? Are you ready to give Me your everything? Or are you happy to carry out this task and at the same time retain your seat in the world so as not to disrupt your positioning in the minds of men?

There can be no bit players on My team says God. Only full out on fire warriors can walk this walk, otherwise they will bury themselves under their own hypocrisy.

Compliment your armor with the Mind of Christ and the Tongue of Truth and equip others in the same manner and there will be a great shaking taking place on the earth.

People will once again tremble with a reverent fear and adoration of their Creator. They will be restored to a natural balance in their lives where I am their provision, their mentor, their delight. The burdens of the world will be cast off from the backs of My sheep so that they in turn may spread the joy of the good news of freedom.

Hold this picture firmly in your heart; a mighty army of truth filled believers walking in righteous abundance bearing witness to My Truth and becoming gatherers of kindred souls in preparation for the great battle to come.

The symbol and sound of the Shofar will be a sign to the people, a sign that the great gathering together and separation has begun. This will be a signal to those with eyes to see and ears to hear that the time to stand up and be counted has arisen. That the line in the sand has been struck for the last time. It will also be a rallying cry for those that do not know the truth. A revelation that there is a dimension to knowing Me that was not previously evident. A new way of life out of which springs hope and a joyful existence free from the shackles of the world.

The collective actions of those obedient to My call will produce supernatural activity at an unprecedented level. The outpouring of miracles and manifestations of My Spirit power at work on the earth will be so powerful that the hearts of many will be transformed. Many followers of the enemy will be redeemed. The powerful blast from this horn will quicken the slothful servants and strike fear into the hearts of the enemy.

Our ranks will swell and the barrier between those that know the fullness of My love and those living in the deception of man's version of the truth will be removed.

Only through obedience will all this transpire when those that are called are not found wanting or searching for excuses for their unwillingness or unreadiness, when their view of the world no longer obscures their view of the truth.

Sound the horns! The eagles are in sight and a great victory cry is about to go up which will shake the very foundation of heaven. My people are ready to stand up. The awakening is beginning, the dawn of

My glory is pushing at the horizon and the perfume of faithfulness is in the air. A cloud of blessings will descend upon this army and rain down an abundance of joy upon them", says God.

1 Corinthians 3:13-15, 2:5
2 Corinthians 4:16-18, 5:10
Hebrews 2:4, 11:1
Romans 1:17
Galatians 3:11
Hebrews 10:35-39
Matthew 21:22
Mark 9:23, 11:22-24
Philippians 4:13

109

BEWARE OF THE SPIRIT OF HYPOCRISY

"Hypocrisy is a very dangerous and debilitating spirit. It affects so many people who say one thing and do another. Most do not understand this to be a spirit. This is curious, as every inclination of the human mind is spiritually driven, either by My Spirit or by an evil spirit. There are no 3rd type of spirits says God. Therefore, if a character trait in a person is not a manifestation of My Spirit at work in their lives, then it has to be the enemy at work in their lives.

This is black and white. It therefore becomes very easy to discern what is happening with both your own behavior and that of people that you interact with. The spirit of hypocrisy is rampant in this world today. Think about things you say that should not be done and then even the same day you find yourself doing precisely that thing. The greatest evil about this spirit is not just that it weakens your own position in the supernatural realm, more importantly it invariably causes others to stumble and therefore weakens their position which causes still more to stumble and on and on. Just one act of hypocrisy can create a huge domino effect causing major damage in both the natural and supernatural realm.

The direct opposite of this spirit is Righteousness. When you are truly walking in righteousness the spirit of hypocrisy will be unable to stand in your presence. A righteous man will send the hypocrites scurrying away unable to withstand the presence of My Spirit which overcomes all evil.

How do I protect myself from the spirit of hypocrisy I hear you ask?

'Seek first the Kingdom' and 'wear the full armor'. If your every action is in pursuit of My Kingdom and you are under the protection of My full armor, you will keep yourself safe from the spirit of hypocrisy says God.

This lesson gives you a perception as to how relentless the enemy is with his intention to attack and defeat you. Evil knows no boundaries. He will not suddenly 'give up' and let you alone. This is an ongoing and never-ending battle which is why you require a 24/7 strategy to keep the ascendancy. Understanding this, it is easy to see why the lives of sheep whose spiritual involvement amounts to 10 minutes a day and an hour on Sundays are in such turmoil. The best they can expect is to get a band aid on their wounds once per week. This leads to unfulfilled lives of misery and confusion for so many of My children says God.

They keep wondering where I am in their lives. Why I am not manifesting in their lives. They cry out to Me on the one side while completely sabotaging themselves on the other. They are busy serving the spirit of mammon and nurturing the spirit of hypocrisy through their actions. They then fall into unbelief and that is followed by the spirit of unworthiness taking a firm grip on them. Consequently, they come wandering back the next Sunday, lifting up their wounded hearts at the church and then returning for another week of action.

Most do not even realize that there is a battle going on. This brings a whole new perspective to the concept of 'equipping the saints'. The task is literally to get them to understand the nature of the battle they are engaged in, the magnitude of which it is about to escalate and how they can participate in it as a Warrior rather than as cannon fodder for the enemy.

The righteousness, truth and humility that accompany you will keep the evil one from your domain. *You have to first win your victories in the supernatural realm before they will manifest in the physical.*

It appeared that My Son had been defeated by the crucifixion, but after winning the victory in the supernatural and setting free the captives, the victory manifested in the natural through the Resurrection. This created the 'blueprint' for victorious living. Wage war in the supernatural and enjoy the spoils of victory in the natural. It also serves as a typological example of what needs to be achieved in these last days. You must strive through supernatural means, with the guidance of My Spirit, to 'set the captives free'; the captives that are all around you, every day. Fellow spiritual believers that are trapped by their own lack of knowledge of the situation they are in.

Everything required for this mission is already available in the Sword of the Spirit. You must exhort others to pick up their swords and start using them again".

Romans 2:1-5

Psalms 149:6

Hebrews 4:12

Ephesians 4:1-32, 6:10-18

2 Corinthians 10:3-6

Titus 1:16

James 1:21-26

Matthew 7:21-23

110

PROTECTION CHECK LIST

"Just like the engine of a motor car there are certain components in your life that require to be maintained at a certain level. If this is not done, like the vehicle, you will still be able to perform, but not at the maximum possible performance level. With what you are called to do, it is essential that all levels are kept 'topped up' and you should check them each day. Consider the pilot of a small plane, cruising along at 15,000 ft would not be a good time to discover that the oil level in the engine or the fuel in the tank was low!

Check list

Anointing

Are you operating in the power of the Spirit or are you relying on your own strength?

Protection

Are you wearing the full armor? *Do not just reel off the words.* Check each component thoroughly. The helmet of salvation should be like a beacon to the world. This strange and beautiful helmet should make you stand out from the crowd. It also protects your ears and eyes from the lies of the world.

The breastplate of righteousness protects your heart and is most effective when you are walking in the opposite direction to the world.

The sword of the Spirit must be kept clean and sharp. Use the Word daily sharpening the sword.

Your shield of faith must be held boldly in front of you to be effective. If you let it drop even for a second you are susceptible to an attack from the enemy.

Is your belt of truth secure? Check it daily, for discernment of truth will keep you from unbelief.

Never be without your sandals, the readiness to preach the gospel. They will ensure that you feel balanced on any type of ground and you will walk with confidence.

Preparation

Are you working on a structured plan or are you blindly stumbling into each day hoping to end up in the right direction? Plan and prepare, it is far easier to get somewhere when you know where you are going.

Planning

Planning your days, if done correctly will enable you to prophesy your day producing the results that you desire. Give more attention and detail to the time that you devote to preparation and consulting with Me for ideas says God. You must seek the counsel of My Spirit on all decisions.

You should pray over the content of the coming day after you have completed your strategy session. In your planning you can set appointments to spend time in the serious diligent pursuit of the breakthroughs you are seeking in the spiritual realm.

There is a formula you can use here:

Is it God's will and part of my purpose?

Have I confidently prophesied it into existence?

Is my armor in place?

Have I thanked God for what He is about to do for me?

Discipline and obedience

If your discipline and obedience level is anything but the maximum, you will lose effectiveness. The one small thing in which you are undisciplined and disobedient will be the one that throws you completely off course. Pay special attention to this.

Excellence

Where is your excellence level? Ask that about everything you are doing.

Anointing, Protection, Preparation, Planning, Discipline and Obedience and Excellence.

These are your reservoirs that should be continuously monitored. Provided they are properly maintained there are no limits to what we can achieve together." says God.

Ephesians 6:10-18

111

THE WORDS THAT YOU SPEAK

"The prophet can only speak My words after he has heard My voice says God. The prophet can only hear My voice if he inclines his ear to Me and *deliberately* shuts out the noise of the world.

You are responsible for creating your own reality through the words that you speak into existence. Thoughts, words and actions, when combined together are the substance of creation.

Look at an artist. He will hold the picture in his mind, he will describe what his picture is going to look like and then act to create it. If you take one of the ingredients away, the process is more difficult and less effective.

As the challenges presented by daily life appear to get bigger and more difficult, it is a clear sign that you are *focusing on the process and not the outcome*. The true prophet of God will always focus on the outcome if he is letting the Spirit flow through him in the proper manner.

Focusing on the process blocks the Spirit as it leads to letting the flesh take control and that will immediately make tasks appear to be more difficult. Pay careful attention to thoughts and words.

You can prophesy the things into your life that are the desires of your heart when they are in accordance with My perfect will and they will happen at incredible speed says God. Stop limiting yourselves by using worldly standards to create your expectations. My ability to supply and increase is limitless. My ability to expand your territory is limitless. The limits are coming from you.

You hold yourself back by stifling the development of your gift with your lack of consistent obedience. This causes you to doubt both your own capacity for achievement and My willingness to let you expand. These are deceptions. You can achieve whatever you can believe for and act upon.

Thinking, talking, doing. These 3 activities should be more evident in your daily progress. Take bigger bolder steps and act upon your ideas, that is why I give them to you. The greatest idea will produce no fruit until it is put into action.

Learn to speak things out with prophetic confidence and watch how quickly they manifest in your life. Manifest the Godly confidence that I have ordained for you and your impact for Me will dramatically increase," says God.

James 3:1-13
Matthew 12:37

112

FOOD MUST BE FUEL

"The healthier you are able to keep your physical body the easier you will find it to stay under the anointing and be effective in the supernatural realm. Often, physical weakness causes your attention to be focused inwardly on yourself which lets the flesh get control of your thinking.

You are also much more susceptible to attack from the enemy as he knows that physical weakness will cause you to drop your guard. His forces are always lurking in the shadows waiting for their opportunity to pounce. Be sure not to give them such an opportunity. Especially when you have crossed over into the supernatural realm, that makes you more of a target, so you must increase your vigilance and attention in this regard.

'Food must be Fuel'. Make that your mantra and strive to look at it that way and your health will dramatically improve.

'Exercise brings life'. The human frame was designed to operate in a physical environment which on a daily basis would use all of the components keeping them honed and in pristine condition. The lifestyle into which mankind has evolved is almost the exact opposite and so the effect has been disastrous upon the body's ability to function normally. Man's answer has been to create chemicals that will hide or claim to repair the effects of the abuse, but which ultimately replaces one problem with another.

Take 'food must be fuel' and 'exercise is life' and you can add to it daily fresh air and sunlight, plus one hour more sleep than you think you require and you have the recipe for a correctly functioning human body says God.

Now take the body and continuously fill it with My Spirit and concentrate the mind to think on the things that I have ordained for your life. Focus the eyes on the living Word which I am and the path to your own dreams will be clearly illuminated.

When will you be this person says God? Are you waiting for some great sign? For there will be none.

Now is the hour, every day lost is another that can never be regained. A single day without these ingredients weakens the body, a day with them strengthens it. The choice is yours.

Every time you look to put something in your mouth ask the question 'is this just *food* or is it *fuel*'? Your body has to go through unnecessary stress to process any item of 'just food'.

Fuel on the other hand is nutrient dense and builds strength and energy so the choice should be obvious.

The time you spend building strength and life in the physical body is vitally important so give it due attention".

1 Peter 5:8-11
Hebrews 12:2

113

A WARNING

"Today holds an important warning for you says God. A warning regarding the importance for you to stay under the anointing regardless of the circumstances. I have made it clear to you how vigilant believers have to be, particularly those with some level of experience regarding spiritual matters. You felt today what it was like to suddenly find yourself back fully in the flesh. See how stepping away from the supernatural even for a brief moment transforms you from a warrior to a target. None of them can even come close to you if your weapons go before you with confidence and the power of My Spirit.

Just as a person cannot hold a negative and positive vibration at the same time, a person cannot operate under the flesh and the Spirit at the same time.

You must heed this warning. You may have myriad excuses as to why you slipped out from the anointing. However, I have no interest in excuses, only in action. Stop focusing on amounts of money and 'deals', just keep your eye on your spiritual attitude and your obedience and the outcome will greatly exceed your expectations.

You have also seen the frustrations of slipping in and out of the anointing to fraternize with the world. Even though they have nothing to offer you at the spiritual level, the flesh is weak and easily 'hooked back in'. The television is a great example. How easy it is to find a valid reason to sit for hours on end allowing things into your mind that contribute absolutely nothing to your life or the lives of anyone else.

This subject will continue to come up until you are able to understand the way that it acts as a snare for you.

There is a fine line in front of you; it is easy to be on one side or the other, but you must make the choice and step deliberately into the realm that you are going to operate in. Will it be the worldly realm, occasionally brightened by a dose of the spiritual? Or will it be the spiritual realm where life is lived at the supernatural level and the world is illuminated by your presence?

The choice is yours and yours alone, but you have to choose. You cannot continue to walk along the line or to jump from one side to the other. I will not permit that", says God.

Hebrews 6:1-3
Romans 12:2
Galatians 5:16

114

THE WORRIES OF THIS WORLD

"The enemy has launched an assault against you and this has only been possible because of your lack of obedience. I have told you previously that the enemy will lurk waiting for a momentary opportunity and then he will pounce. Let us look at the area of finances because this has been the major stumbling block.

I stressed the importance of correctly allocating money as it comes in. However, you have not done it on a consistent basis.

Every time we discuss the stewardship of finances you are repentant and willing to do things differently and then you slip back into your old ways. You yourself teach 'tomorrow will be exactly the same as today unless *you* do something to make it different'.

Why is it then that you do *nothing* to make tomorrow different for yourself? You keep on making the same errors.

Credit cards are not to be used to create debt in your lives. You must not spend money that you do not yet have.

How do you ever expect to make financial progress when you start every month from behind? Why are you surprised when there is a blockage in the flow of your finances when you are the ones that have created the blockage through your disobedience.

There is no gentle way to put it. I cannot bless you abundantly if you do not adhere to the simple basic principles of financial stewardship.

I do not care how it looks in your accounts, what matters is how it looks in Mine! You cannot even profess to walk in righteousness if you are not upright in your dealings with that which belongs to Me.

Get this financial house in order immediately and things will start flowing in the true measure of abundance. Pay Caesar what is due him and follow through with the instructions I gave regarding finances.

I am ready to send many opportunities and financial blessings in your direction, but you have to prove yourselves worthy through obedience. Let's get this right once and for all says God. You know what is required so just do it!

With regard to the spiritual oppression you are feeling, this is also self-inflicted. You have removed yourself from the flow of the anointing and the presence of My Spirit and the 'worries of this world' have turned their ranks towards you. These are very dangerous demons because they can affect your physical health as well as your psychological well-being.

However powerful they may be, they are no match for the sword of the Spirit and your shield of Faith can easily deflect their arrows and spears. Like all weapons, yours can only be effective if you use them".

Revelation 3:19
Proverbs 3:12, 6:23
Hebrews 12:5-11
Mark 4:19

115

THE CROSSROADS OF DECISION

"Build up your strength by focusing on your successes says God. Take note of their roots and duplicate the implementation into areas that still require attention.

In the physical realm you have made considerable progress, exercising regularly and eating correctly will serve you well.

Keeping your physical body in good order is essential for the Journey is long and arduous. The spiritual realm is the area that needs most attention. Your ability to perform at the supernatural level is predicated on your willingness to die to the world. This is not a situation where you can wear both hats. Those kinds of positions are abundantly available and there are many sheep that are lost in that way as you have been.

You cannot keep running over to slip into your armor and pick up your weapons every time there is a crisis, only to take them off and to return to the world dressed in more 'acceptable' clothes.

No, this is not only unbecoming of My children who are called and chosen, it is also highly dangerous. If the enemy comes upon a person in the middle of that transition, they could suffer terrible consequences.

You have reached a crossroads of decision and the decision required is of vital importance. You can no longer be in a 'changing' mode, people either smoke or they don't, there is no 'middle' category. It is the same in this instance. You either live for Me or you live for yourself and the world, says God. You have the license and the right to make either choice, but you must choose.

Once you are clear about *who* you are living for, the way that you are required to be, will not only be more obvious but far more natural.

Learn to be bold in your supernatural existence. When people ask, 'what you do', give them the answer in supernatural terms, instead of looking for the best way to make them feel most comfortable.

It is time to leave behind the comfort zones of man's approval and recognition for human achievement. Leave all that for those that seek to glory in their own glory. You have broken the yoke of the television and that is a major breakthrough. You are exercising regularly and eating properly and now you need to apply the same discipline that you give to these matters to other things that need attention. However, these things can also be carried out in the same way by any person, regardless as to whether they are in the world, of the world or both.

Therefore, you must choose to move everything to a supernatural level. I know that you have made the decision at the *head* level says God. However, decisions at the level of the soul are only made apparent by the *actions that accompany the thoughts and words*. Faith without works is dead!

You do not have to see this as a dilemma, rather as an enormous blessing. Never forget, many never even get to make such a choice. You see in other people that are at the same place as you, the hunger they have for the separation from the world.

That is how it is for the leaders in this battle. Just as the apostle Paul knew it would be better to leave the world and be with Me, he also knew that he had a huge supernatural task to carry out on the earth.

Imagine that the only way for you to represent Me was to wear a hat that had a big 'S' on it at all times and that this would separate you out as a person that was known to 'live for God', who makes all of their decisions through prayer and that hears directly from Me through dreams, prophetic words and divinely inspired writings. A person that would never involve themselves in anything unless they knew it was part of My perfect will for their lives. Would you wear that hat, all day every day?

Those that can sincerely answer 'yes' to this question are those after My own heart. These are the ones that become the chosen. I will choose them, because they have chosen Me says God. Once the choice is made, it is not necessary to wear 'the hat', because the distinction is obvious. The people of the world, believers and the lost, all look the same and to the large part act the same.

As I said, 'you will know them by their fruit'

If the fruit does not have eternal value its production is pointless. Fruit that contains no seed just withers and dies.

My chosen warriors are obvious through everything they do. The way that they think, the words that they speak, the plans that they make, the actions that they take. Look at your own performance in these categories and you will instantly know why I am calling you to choose once again. There are new levels for you to move onto right now, but you cannot move to them dressed in the clothing of this world".

1 Peter 4:1-2
Galatians 20:2
Philippians 1:23-24
Matthew 7:16
Ephesians 4:22 -24
Colossians 3:5
1 Timothy 6:12

116

PRAYER IS THE KEY

"You are witnessing the discomfort of flipping back and forth from living at the supernatural level to the natural level. In and out of the anointing of the Spirit. You gain some ground and then you lapse and lose some back. Sometimes you lose more ground than you gained because you fall into a period of fear which is another disguise used by unbelief.

You have to draw a line in the sand and refuse to retreat past it. This is the only way to end this roller coaster existence.

When praying is as natural to you as talking; when prophesying is as natural to you as asking for things, you will start to make much faster progress.

Ask yourself 'what is prayer?'

It is: you talking to Me. There is nothing complicated about it. It is you talking to Me.

If you find yourself doing a lot of thinking and talking and not a lot of praying, then who are you talking to?

It would seem far more advantageous for you to spend as much time as possible talking to Me says God.

You are wise to take seriously the warnings I sent to you. I have warned you previously that stepping into the supernatural has serious consequences and you must never forget that. Not only do you have the ability to do far more in less time but also, you have exposed yourself to the forces of evil that seek to subvert My work.

You must be constantly aware of this fact and be vigilant at all times. The enemy can never harm you if you are fully equipped in your armor moving boldly in his direction. He will flee from you like the coward he is.

A believer can only be vulnerable to him when their back is exposed. Either by walking in the same direction as the world or by entering unprepared into the supernatural realm.

Concentrate more time and focus into the perfection of your prayer life. It should be obvious to you why you have found this so difficult; why the flesh resists against it so vehemently. Why the enemy attempts to use it to create enmity between you.

It is the final most powerful piece of the puzzle. You see, all of the knowledge, systems and formulae I have given to you, have to be 'fueled' to make them work properly.

Hence, 'The effectual fervent prayer of a righteous man availeth much'

When you try to power those systems in your own strength you are wasting their supernatural perspective. You are taking a Spirit conceived plan and translating it into a manmade plan.

The plans of men often fail or produce mediocre results. My plans never fail, that is why I am all power at all times in all things.

You have made requests to Me regarding certain periods of time. You see once again you are putting things into the context of man's timing. In other words, you are tying My hands by creating a box for My Spirit to operate in and that is not the way that We work.

Consider the prayer that Jabez offered.

He did not ask for a certain blessing in a certain way at a certain time. No. He did not want to limit the things that I could do for him says God.

You are still thinking about expanding your territory in the context of what you already have. Do not do that because it limits your potential. Do not focus on amounts of money. The spirit of mammon thrives on such focus. That gives him license to control your thoughts and actions as is the case with so many of My sheep.

Again, consistent prayer about everything at all times is the key that you have to turn. This will unlock the door to the throne room. It will unlock the vaults of supernatural provision beyond your comprehension. It will unlock the arsenal of supernatural weaponry which will equip you to launch an all-out assault against the enemy. It will unlock the doors to the library of wisdom which is beyond the earthly perception of wisdom. It will unlock the gates to the Kingdom of heaven", says God.

James 5:16
1 Chronicles 4:9-10
1 Thessalonians 5:17
Isaiah 55:8-10

117

PRAYER IS THE FUEL

"As it feels natural to put one foot in front of the other, so it should feel natural to pray. Once you apply this consistently your flesh will be subdued, and you will see things with your supernatural eyes and not your worldly eyes. The engine of a fine car is useless unless you are going to put fuel in it and drive it.

All of the wisdom that has been shared with you is equally useless if you do not put it into daily operation. There is little point in sharing these wonders with other people if you are not living them yourself.

You do not have time to make a gradual transition or build yourself up to this. The enemy will see you as easy prey if you are not walking in righteous obedience. The enemy's plan is always to ensnare the righteous for his own ends. You have the clear directions as to how to avoid this so be sure that you follow them.

Again, I caution you about times. You must stop operating on the time table of the world or worldly values. For example, if prayer is the fuel that drives everything that you do in the supernatural, how can you even contemplate doing anything in the absence of prayer first?

Develop P.F.S. 'Prayer First Syndrome'

This is why planning your days is so important.

You can literally determine the outcome of meetings before you even attend them. You can pre-determine outcomes before doing actions.

You can start attracting the right people into your environment. If people can utilize tactics like 'law of attraction' and 'positive thinking' to get results in the absence of My Spirit anointing, you should know how much more can be achieved through your obedience.

Those people have to be consistent and focused to make it work and so do you. It is just that the focus is different. Your focus is on getting the flesh out of the way through prayer. Then the Spirit can flow unrestricted. Not by might, nor by power, but by My Spirit", says God.

1 Thessalonians 5:17
Zechariah 4:6
James 1:22

118

CONSIDER MY INSTRUCTIONS REGARDING LOVE

"I called believers to love each other as brothers and sisters. I called husbands to love their wives with the same love that My Son loves you. Easy words to read, but how ready are you to implement them?

As a believer, are you ready to consider how decisions you make and actions you take are going to affect your fellow believers, *before* you think about how it affects you? How many people do you know that give that level of consideration to others? Do you think and act that way?

Would the world look different if people behaved that way? Just think about that for a moment. We talk about helping others to develop the 'mind of Christ'. What does that really mean? Let us look at adopting the mind of Christ for just one full day and consider the implications:

You awake in the morning and like any child you have a yearning to get into the presence of your Father. You crave to hear His voice, to be comforted by His loving arms, to see Him gazing lovingly and approvingly at you. You long to hear what exciting things He has planned for you today (there is a powerful message here)

Once you have fed upon the strength of your Father, you are ready to face the day. Now remember, every thought that you permit to be formed into a word and be spoken out, has to be something that will be of benefit to someone or something other than you.

Every thought that you allow within you to produce an action has to be carried out in a way that will be a blessing to someone else and bring glory to My name only.

How easy is this sounding?

Maybe do not attempt a whole day at the beginning, try half a day or even just an hour. This is the true path to righteousness, or 'enlightenment' as the new age people would like to call it.

True enlightenment can only come through knowing My mind and My plan for your life first and then through diligent effort and sacrifice, pursuing the application of it in your own life.

Only through applying the 'Christ mindset' can one ever fulfill the instructions regarding love that I gave says God.

To attempt to love someone that you do not even like through your rational human mind is foolish. The human mind is inextricably married to the flesh and always will be. That is why it is so important to learn how to quiet that part of yourself.

By doing so, it becomes possible to start thinking through the Spirit that I have placed within you. The Spirit that can communicate directly with the mind of Christ, the Risen One, who after all, left it with you for that purpose.

If we follow through the implications of this, it is a perfect illumination of the path to righteousness. You must first quiet and control the natural mind.

This will allow your spirit mind to have a direct channel of communication. At this point your thinking will be pure, anointed and Spirit powered. This alone will give you the capacity for the love that I call every person to demonstrate.

Can you now see the true power in that commandment regarding love? If My sheep follow just that one thing properly, the entire world would be a completely different place and My Son could return tomorrow.

When you ask yourself the question 'How can I love people in the way God wants?' You know that it is impossible to do with a worldly mindset. The answer therefore is only by developing the mind of Christ can you learn to love like We love.

It is likely that as a child you spent hours listening to your earthly father, watching the way that he did things. What effect did that have on you? Do you think that you have developed a similar mindset to him? How would any other outcome be possible other than you thinking and doing many things in exactly the same way that your father does.

The Wisdom in My Word has an even more profound and lasting effect. I know that should be obvious but if it is so obvious why is it not taught in schools and churches? It seems that they have overlooked the significance of My wisdom.

People talk about attaining to righteousness but have missed the point that true righteousness is impossible in the absence of the mind of Christ. You cannot win the heart of the Father, except through the Son. The objective is to develop the 'Mind of Christ', the new mind placed in you by the anointing of the Spirit.

Every new believer receives this gift, it is up to each of you to develop it. Just like the natural carnal mind, it can only be developed by using it consistently and effectively.

The error for most is that they try in vain to change their earthly carnal mind and make it into the mind of Christ. This is not going to happen.

The correct path is to subdue the carnal mind, to keep the flesh under and allow the Spirit in you to gain the ascendancy. This then makes it possible for you to walk in the worldly realm and at the same time, to think with the mind of Christ at a supernatural level.

Once you embark on this path, you have to 'burn the boats', there can be no going back to the old way. If you think that maybe you would like to 'give it a try', you should not even start. This is the very 'narrow way' spoken of in the Word.

This is more than a 'what would Jesus do' bracelet and then living no different to before. Just one person pursuing this path would have a positive impact on the lives of thousands of others. It is a life work, a race that never ends. Those that pursue this righteousness will see the world as never before. The perfections will override the imperfections.

Learn to see the truth, speak the truth and be the truth in every situation. If you do not instantly love someone you meet, whose mind are you thinking with? Or worse are you thinking at all?

Is it possible for anyone to completely develop the mind of Christ? Of course not, for this would make that person the same as Christ which is of course impossible. It is however both possible and acceptable to become 'Christ-like'.

Our overall objective is therefore both simple and very challenging. To empower a vast army to prepare the earth for the return of Christ, to make His transition from the heir-apparent to the King of Kings.

It has not proven possible to do this by shepherding people along as they stumble around hoping to find good in an evil world. It has not proven possible through developing man's wisdom and preaching messages of prosperity as though more material success will bring someone closer to Me.

It has not proven possible by the development of so many religious groups who cannot agree with each other on major issues and minor issues alike. When people start learning directly through My Spirit and hearing My voice clearly through My prophets, calling them to be accountable for their own reality, there will be a great shaking in this world and a transformation will take place among the believers that will herald the completion of the preparation of the Bride".

1 Corinthians 2:10-16
Revelation 1:4-6, 19:11-16
1 Timothy 6:14-16
John 16:13
Philippians 2:5, 4:8
Ephesians 1:17-20, 5:25
Matthew 7:13-14
1 Corinthians 2:16

119

WATCH WHO YOU ASSOCIATE WITH

"You have seen firsthand how 'the worries of this world and the deceitfulness of riches' so easily impact people's lives. The situation is not that these are bad people or even that they do not know Me. No, the problem for them is that they think that they and their abilities are the source of their supply.

They are focusing on trusting themselves or worse, trusting in other men to provide them with opportunity and with increase.

There are only 2 sources of supply available on earth says God. That which I supply and that which is being provided by the enemy which is always a counterfeit of the truth.

This illuminates a very simple yet profoundly important issue.

If I am not the provider of what you have because you have not been diligent in seeking My counsel and involving Me in the process, to whom do you belong?

Be warned, a man cannot take his bread from one camp and then claim that his heart is in another. Those that feed you will be able to exercise the greatest influence over you. So be careful with whom you are eating.

A cat may return to your house to sleep but refuse to eat the food that you offer because the cat has been eating elsewhere. Someone else is feeding and nurturing the cat, even though he spends time in your house, to whom does he really belong?

Consider therefore people that you spend time with. Where and from whom do they 'get their food'? The answer to such questions will bring you much wisdom and discernment in dealing with people and their ways says God.

How does a person truly escape from the 'worries of this world and the deceitfulness of riches' and yet remain on the earth? The answer is to while you remain on the earth literally in your physical bodies, to remove yourselves from this earth spiritually and exist from a supernatural perspective.

As an example, you are looking at establish a business. You should consider if that will be a 'natural' company with all of the usual worldly stuff that goes on with business. Or will it be a 'supernatural' company that does things purely under the anointing of My Spirit? A person that chooses the first scenario would have great difficulty in being able to separate themselves from the world.

It is far easier to start a company on a supernatural basis than it is to try and change into one at some point in the future. The foundation that any business is built upon is the key factor. Once the 'house' is erected, you can never change the foundation without tearing down the house and starting all over again.

Just as it is with those in the parable of the sower. Those that do not have the Rock as the foundation cannot survive the course. It is the same with personal relationships and with business and everything else. If it is not based on My truth and My Rock, it will not stand.

Everything is temporal except that which is eternal. Only the Truth can be eternal, for anything that is not the Truth and therefore a lie, must lead to destruction. You may think that this sounds ridiculously simple, even childlike, but it is the most profound wisdom and you will do well to embrace its message wholeheartedly.

You cannot wear the belt of truth and have lies on your tongue. Any lies will impair the effectiveness of your belt causing it to be removed. This is very serious. You see, the breastplate of righteousness clips onto your belt to help keep it secure. If the belt is removed, your righteousness will automatically become unstable and that will then require you to hold it in place with your hand in order to make progress at any rate of speed.

Think about what that causes! You have to put down either the sword of the Spirit or the shield of faith in order to be able to hold your righteousness in place and move forward.

You become both ineffective and vulnerable at the same time. In addition, you will become a stumbling block to many because the truth is no longer within you. This is the critical condition that so many find themselves in today says God.

Back to a familiar subject then. Think carefully about what you are going to say and let the mind of Christ, not the carnal mind, do the thinking.

That way, the words that you use will be truthful, anointed and powerful and that should always be your primary objective; to use the creative power of anointed Spirit words to bring truth to the hearts of others. Spontaneous answers usually originate in the flesh. Discern the thought. Is this the mind of Christ or the mind of man? Say only what needs to be said. Do not add anything as this will simply introduce the flesh into the picture and cause confusion. Before answering or asking important questions, pause and pray;

'Grant me the mind of Christ and the tongue of truth'. You will immediately see an incredible difference in the things that you say and the way that you communicate with and relate to others"

1 Corinthians 2:16
Mark 4:19
Matthew 7:24-27

120

FOLLOW THROUGH

"Follow through on everything that you have been shown, says God. Each step will lead to the next step so complete the first steps first. There is much excitement ahead and great blessings, but they can only be found through focus and harvested with gratitude.

A man who writes down his goals and then does not fervently measure his progress will never know how close he is. The Israelites could have known where they were if they had focused on their ultimate goal instead of complaining about the circumstances of the day. Keep moving forward at all times and convey to others that this will be what you will continue to do, with them or without them.

If you are always sure to be on a Kingdom assignment you will not be concerned with the earthly passengers. Just give them the invitation and the right ones will get on board with you. Keep on in the pursuit of excellence in all that you do as it will not only bring the results you desire, but it will also empower you to attract others of an excellent nature.

Watch out for the time stealing distractions! A little here, a little there, the chatter in your head grows louder and louder; 'maybe I could do this as well' and on and on.

All that happens is you get moved away from your goals because you cease to make forward progress towards them. You have to attain excellence in one thing before you embark on something else. If you have witnessed others getting far higher levels of success doing the same thing as you, the difference between them and you is simply belief, commitment and focus. Their level of belief in what they are doing is so high that their commitment is total. Their focus is one hundred percent.

If you think about it, if something is less than 100% focused, even if it is 98% focused, it is actually out of focus. You cannot achieve at the level you desire if you are out of focus. Being out of focus means that you are out of integrity and that is not acceptable. Imagine trying to drive a car and being 50% focused on that task and 50% on something else. Stand up for who you have committed to be and do not be swayed here and there. If other people confront you with their distractions, move on forwards, do not embrace them as your own. Your mission is to be adhered to at all costs. Keep moving forward doing what is required on a daily basis. We are together on this journey; just make sure that you do not go off on your own.

It is time to stop living on the edge, says God. Uncertainty brings with it stress and apprehension that carries through into everything that you do. That is why it is so important that you have planned properly and are acting upon your plan. This removes uncertainty from the picture.

It is far better to embark upon each day with clear goals for the day. Goals that are in harmony with your purpose and that you can easily measure to make sure that you are on track. Accountability is vitally important as that will help you keep on the track. Once you have successfully used an accountability system for the first month, it will become second nature for you to use it on an ongoing basis".

Hebrews 12:2

121

EVERYTHING ORIGINATES IN THE THOUGHT PROCESS

"Everything originates in the thought process says God. Your ability to be creative is part of your being, your willingness to be creative is the real key. Each person has the ability, but not necessarily the will. Most people have the desire, but not necessarily the will. Some people use their creative abilities to manifest situations through which they can control, manipulate or subjugate others. These people are mixing their creative ability with the carnality of the flesh. Others use the creative ability to produce abundance and opportunity for advancement that can flow through to others.

This is a sign of co-creativity where working together with My Spirit, you can unleash the sudden impact of abundant blessings on yourself and on others. Therefore, when a person makes the transition from the competitive mindset to the creative mindset, it is vitally important that they take the final step which requires them to push aside the flesh and be in a co-creativity attitude, consulting with My Spirit on every action and decision. This promotes right thinking and in turn takes the person further on their pursuit of righteousness.

When a man has a number of plans and goals which he needs to implement, he should begin immediately with what he has in his hands. Waiting for every condition to be perfect before beginning is not a wise tactic. There are countless wonderful ideas waiting to be co-created which will never see the light of day, because those concerned will not take the first steps of faith to start the project.

Begin, and I will work with you to completion says God. Hold the expected outcome firmly in your mind, have the faith to know that my Word is true and act. Notice that the book of Acts was not called 'the thoughts' or 'good intentions' of the apostles. Certainly, everything they did started as a thought, but taking the action is what produced the fruit.

In order for the spiritual attraction of prosperity to manifest in people's lives, they have to be living out these instructions, says God. They have to be physically involved in the process, as well as spiritually involved. All the scriptural knowledge in the world is to no avail if it is not put into action. Likewise, all the action in the world is of no eternal consequence if the motivation behind the action is not righteous.

The measure to which My Word is ingrained into the spiritual heart of a person will be directly reflected in the quality of their life, provided that they are acting daily in congruence with that knowledge. Let the truths of Scripture be your guide and your chief mentor. All other teachings are invalid if they contradict My Word. Test and measure everything before you impart it to others".

Philippians 1:6

122

BEING AN OVERCOMER

"The joy of being an overcomer will far exceed the heaviness of missing the mark, says God. See how a simple tool like an accountability sheet can have such a profound impact!

When you are confronted by your lack of consistency on a daily basis, it creates one of two scenarios; either a person enters into denial, discontinues using the accountability system and reverts to the old way of doing things, or are they wake up and apply themselves more diligently and press on to a new level of excellence. It is decided by the response.

The flesh, that old wineskin, will scream its protests and cling desperately to any glimmer of an opportunity to revert to the old system. It is therefore essential to take dominion over the flesh at the spiritual level, discard that old wineskin and fill the new one with new habits, new levels of faith and obedience and a new zeal for excellence. It is essential that you do it this way, because you cannot stretch that old skin any further, it will tear and split forcing you to start over.

Do not succumb to the worries of this world. Be confident in your faith and keep striving for excellence in all you do. You cannot live a supernatural life unless you have a faithful expectation that things will happen for you in a supernatural way. Why do people pray for miracles and then act totally surprised when they happen?

You are having discussions regarding your purpose again. It is important for you to get a clear picture of it so that you can measure everything you do to make sure it is congruent with that purpose before embarking upon the action. If an idea or action was to take you away from your purpose to any degree, why would you even waste time considering it?

Write out a definition of your purpose so that you can feel connected to it and you can burn the image of it into your soul so that you become that purpose.

Be focused and be sure to be like minded and work together, your only hope is as a focused team.

If unity were unimportant, it would be easy to attain. The enemy's greatest fear is to see My chosen children unified in spirit and soul and walking in righteousness, with clarity of purpose, their faith going before them, crushing any obstacle! That is why he constantly strives to subvert your unity and you have to be alert to these plans and be overcomers.

Trust in Me, says God, stand on the Rock of your Faith and be confident in My Truth".

Matthew 9:14
Mark 2:18-22, 3:25

123

LEADERSHIP

"Make sure that you understand all of the characteristics of leadership and that you are *being* those things on a daily basis. You cannot talk like a leader and then act in a different manner and still expect to reap a leader's reward. The leader is fully aware of his responsibilities and is careful to take care of challenges as and when they arise.

Develop a reputation as a leader with integrity and people will be happy to follow you and support you. Strive always to allow others to develop their own leadership qualities. Surround yourself with leaders and your own abilities and gifts will develop further. Remember that the primary requisite of leadership is service. The greater your level of service, the better chance you will have to develop other leaders. The more leaders you develop, the more you will achieve as a leader.

To be a great leader you must understand that all great leaders are first great followers. Those that follow Me, will be the greatest leaders ever says God, for they will embrace leadership with humility and that is the combination that promotes greatness and creates legacy.

There has never been a humble leader who did not leave a powerful legacy on the earth. These will be honored people in the Kingdom. Leaders lacking in humility are always remembered more for their arrogance and worldliness and material achievements. Many will not even attain the Kingdom. This is a powerful lesson for aspiring leaders. You cannot teach it through instruction, you can only teach it by example".

Mark 10:43-45

124

SEEK FIRST THE KINGDOM

"Building your eternal future is a series of *choices* says God. Every day, you have the opportunity to choose in which direction you are going to focus your time and talents. You are going to choose the materials that you will use to build on the *foundation* of your salvation.

What will it be today? Wood, hay and straw which creates nothing of eternal value? Or, will it be gold silver and precious stones, as you strive for the rewards that are available to you in the future?

'What is the difference'? you ask. It is best to focus only on the actions that bring rewards.

Anything that encourages or raises the spirit of others, time given in prayer for others, kindness, generosity, compassion, love, all of these lead to eternal rewards.

There are opportunities for the miraculous all around you, every day. You have to be looking in order to recognize them and then take immediate action. Even the smallest act of kindness can completely transform the life of a single person and ultimately their entire family, or their town or city, even their nation.

You can never know in advance what the outcome will be, only I have that knowledge says God.

All you have to do is be willing to follow the instruction to *'seek first the kingdom'*.

Here is an important key. This *seeking* is carried out by your actions. The things that you say and do it in My Name are the things that bring the *Kingdom* into focus. The more that you walk in righteous obedience, the more clearly you will see it.

As it is written, some will not even *see* My Kingdom because their self-centered actions obscure their vision, especially actions carried out in the service of mammon. As it is written man cannot serve both of us.

Strive to do the right things for the right reasons. Be careful in your choices of thoughts and words as they can either build up or tear down. You have immense power at your disposal so be very careful how you use it. The tongue can be your biggest asset or your most powerful adversary. It has to be controlled, which can only be achieved through your thinking.

This explains why the battle for the minds of people is raging all around you every day. Marketing messages, television, social media, magazines and newspapers are all influencing the way that you think and even *what* it is that you think about. The majority of these things are not good for you. They will only lead to thoughts, words and actions that may take you further away from understanding the truth about My Kingdom. These things will seldom lead to any rewards, which is why I call you to focus on the desirable things instead. This is an extremely difficult thing to do, but you must understand that it is the only way to overcome the enemy" says God.

Romans 14:10
Colossians 3:2-4, 12
1 Peter 4:1
2 Corinthians 4:17
James 3:2-18
Philippians 1:29, 4:8
1 Corinthians 3:10-15
Matthew 12:36-37

271

125

THE KEY IS PRAYER

"Do not let complacency settle into your lives in any way says God. The victories you have seen are consequences of your obedience and your boldness in the spiritual realm with prayer. As I said before 'If prayer was your only weapon how much would you pray'?

When it comes to matters of the supernatural, prayer *is* your only weapon. Make sure that your thoughts are continually prayerful. That your words are powerful and prophetic. Do not waste time pondering on worldly frivolous things. See your activities as taking place on a spiritual battlefield, the enemy does!

Remember you are warring against principalities and powers that are seeking to gain control over your life. You can only defeat them by maintaining a spiritual mindset in everything you do. Remember that I said I will 'set a table for you in the midst of your enemies'? From this table we will plan and orchestrate your victories, from this table you will select the weapons that will wipe away the enemy.

The key to the positioning of this table is prayer. The key to the provision upon this table is prayer.

Keep sharpening your Sword of the Spirit. Speak out My Word with power and authority. Be on the offensive and not the defensive. No one wins a battle while retreating. An army loses when they start to believe they may lose.

You must be confident in your victory. You must stand on the Truth that 'Greater is He that is in you.' There have been setbacks, you have suffered some lost ground, but it does not mean that your victory is any less assured.

Keep pressing and pressing and do not let up. You cannot inflict a wound upon the enemy and then back off to see what happens. You must follow through. Seek to utterly destroy them and watch them flee from you".

Psalms 23:5
Ephesians 6:12
2 Corinthians 10:5
1 John 4:4

126

DEFEATING THE SPIRIT OF MAMMON

"Be aware of the spirit of mammon and continue to remove his *hooks* by ardently pursuing the things that will remove you from the world's monetary system. It is through that system of credit and debt that he gains control over so many. You can escape by following My financial principles and then you can teach others the way out. Be in great anticipation, for this will be a notable victory.

You have to create the life that is right for you, says God. That can only be based upon the plan that we have created together in pursuit of your purpose. Nothing that you do or decide can be based upon what other people want, do, or expect. This is the route that leads people astray. They embark on someone else's path and it leads them so far away from their own purpose, they end up getting lost.

You have to stop vacillating around your decisions. Once you have embarked upon a course of action, you cannot suddenly change direction, just because the 'next big thing' comes into view. Life is a constant procession of new things and new opportunities and it is impossible to maintain progress and focus if you allow yourself to be continuously distracted.

Focus! Yes, there are many excellent opportunities to which you can apply your gifts and talents, but rather be excellent at one than average at two or mediocre at more! You must have a plan and then seal yourself off from the distractions. If you know exactly what seeds you are planting every single time, you will know what harvest to expect.

There will be challenges so you need focused faith and to expect that the results will come.

Always be *allowing* and never *forcing*. Expect abundant and sudden breakthroughs. Remember that every miracle happens because someone asks for it and expects that it will happen.

The subject of taking oaths, making promises and signing written contracts or agreements is of considerable seriousness says God. If any such agreement puts you into the service of mammon, it must be avoided at all costs, for to serve mammon automatically removes you from My service and therefore from the fullness of My blessings. As it is written, 'Man cannot serve both God and mammon. My servants must make their contracts only with Me. Their agreements must only be in connection with their service to Me, otherwise they will no longer be serving Me because they have agreed to serve someone else.

If they are not serving Me, they have to be serving mammon by default. There are only two choices, to serve Me or to serve mammon".

Luke 16:13
Colossians 3:2
Proverbs 4:25-27
Romans 8:5-6

127

LAYING THE RIGHT FOUNDATION

"Any building will only be as stable as the foundation on which it stands. A person can look at any area of their lives and assess the strength of that area by asking the question: 'what foundation have I built this on?' If the answer does not line up with biblical principles, if you have built your own house instead of being a co-builder with Me, you have created a major problem for yourself.

The enemy delights in shaking buildings that are not on solid footings. Most often, he can cause at least some damage manifesting in problems in people's lives. Sometimes he can bring the whole house crashing down, causing major destruction. These principles apply to all aspects of life says God; personal relationships, business relationships, finances, physical well-being, spiritual well-being, marriages, everything.

A person should look at each of these areas and inspect very closely the foundation that it stands on. There is no point in ever trying to restore something that is built on a shaky foundation. The building will keep shifting and falling into disrepair, no matter how many times you fix it up.

In such situations, you have to reach back even further and enact a total reformation. This will require you to even remove the original foundation and start again from the dirt upwards, creating a new and correct foundation as you do it.

This time, you make sure that the foundation is built squarely on My principles, as that is the only way to build a house that can withstand any test. That is not to say that there will not be any tests, but when they do come, you will have the confidence to know that your house will stand.

Once you fully grasp this principle, you will easily understand why so many of My children are constantly suffering turmoil of one kind or another. Either their beliefs, their actions or their relationships are foundationally unstable. Of course, the only solid thing and sure thing in their lives, is their salvation because that is established in Christ, the unshakable foundation.

But here you see the answer to the question that is almost always on the lips of the unenlightened; 'How come you Christian believers have so many issues?'

It is purely because of this foundational instability. Re-examine your spiritual real estate. Look at every house you have and decide if it requires restoration or reformation.

Once you have made that assessment take appropriate action to get the work done. Remember, do not build alone! Any house constructed by men alone, is a house of cards and at some point, when it suits his purposes the enemy will blow it over and bring it crashing down.

Co-create your buildings with My Spirit, on solid foundations and they will be able to withstand anything, and you can inhabit them safely and be overcomers, says God.

It is important to have a *Foundational check-up* and make any necessary course corrections.

Spiritual: Foundation in Christ:

When you find that life has been self-centered, rather than God centered.

Correction Steps:

1) Sharpening the Sword of the Spirit. Reading, speaking and discussing the Word.

2) Continually invoking the presence of My Spirit and tapping into the power of the anointing surrounding you.

3) Continuous communication with Me. Dismissing all thoughts not consistent with My Word. Praise, worship and straight forward verbal communication. Understanding that prayer is an attitude of communication, not ceremony.

Physical:

Foundation has been to keep the body from getting sick. Your physical body is your vessel for dwelling on the Earth. The better you look after it, the better you can function in all other things.

Correction steps:

1) Keep increasing the knowledge of the body's systems and how to support them.

2) Some physical exercise should be a part of daily life.

3) Stick to the food or fuel principle. The more 'lifeless' food you put in the more unnecessary work has to be done to deal with it. Focus on life giving fuel which promotes energy and wellbeing.

Financial:

Foundation: Understanding the truth regarding the fact that 'man cannot serve Me and serve mammon.

Correction steps:

1) Learn to set and control budgets. Financial progress is impossible otherwise.

2) Have a planned giving project as part of the budget. Additional offerings should come from your personal resources.

3) Be committed that wherever possible, everything is purchased with funds you already have.

4) Keep studying financial principles and be disciplined to do accounting on a daily basis.

Integrity, accountability, purpose and passion, wrap these in your cloak of humility, hold it fast with the belt of truth and then wash it all in a bath of love. You will then start to glow with the *piercing light of righteousness*. This will cause you to be effective in everything you do and will lead you to the spiritual enlightenment that is attainable by those willing to walk the path. It requires total commitment, you must decide how committed you are".

1 Corinthians 3:10-11
Ephesians 2:19-22
Matthew 7:24-27
Luke 6:46-49

128

STAYING IN FOCUS

"Your future will not be determined by your past unless you allow it says God. There is no benefit to be gained from analyzing the things you failed to do previously as this will not contribute to your future. The only possible thing that can contribute to your future now is what you do today. What you did yesterday, last week or last year have all made their contribution, there is nothing now you can do to change those things.

Remember the importance of focusing your attention on the things that you *do* want so that you can attract more of the same. Going over and over old failures simply gives them energy and therefore it will attract more of the same. Only focus on what you do want in your life, focus on what you desire to attract.

You know better than anyone 'as a man thinks in his heart, so is he.' What are you thinking about? What are you giving energy to? These are the key questions for you to answer. Any kind of negative thinking, any kind of fear-based decision making is simply going to attract more of the same and that is not where you want to go.

I remind you about the formula* that I gave you, if you can develop it consistently into your life on the earth, then life on the earth will be transitioned into the joyful experience you desire. Living with the formula brings all the protection necessary to gain ascendancy in the spiritual battle. Without it you are simply dragged into the depths of the fight. That reflects why most believers find life to be a 'battle'.

It is just like business; there are simple specific things that have to be done on a consistent basis before success can be achieved and yet most people do not do them. Therefore, they do not get the result they hope for. It is the same with a formula, not using it means it cannot work for you, it is as simple as that.

Do not forget that time spent in an unproductive manner is time wasted and who has time to waste? What man knows the measure of his time to the extent that he can calculate how much of it should be wasted on meaningless pursuits? There are only so many breaths a man can take. If you knew precisely how many you had left how many would you want to waste?

Entertainment is a wonderful gift, I bless people with talent and ability to entertain. Like many things, the enemy can pervert it into something that consumes lives and prevents people from using their time effectively. Take control of that situation and bring your time back into its proper perspective. Building your legacy is far more significant than numbing the senses with meaningless garbage.

We went over and over the hours of watching television shows, it is the same old mountain. It is time to stop circling these mountains says God. They are wasting your time and limiting your effectiveness.

You have to be in control to be effective. With your understanding of spiritual matters, you know that if you are not in control of your life, someone else is and that someone else is only looking to destroy you.

My Spirit longs to guide your path, but you have to empower Him to do so by pushing the fleshly will out of the way. Take back control of your life, use the formula*, join with My Spirit and cleanse yourself and everything in your life from the stench of the enemy".

*See message #1

Proverbs 23:7
Psalms 90:12
James 4:14

129

RIGHTEOUSNESS AND FRUIT

"Blessed is the man who does not stand in the council of the wicked. In other words, do not take advice and guidance from those who walk in unrighteousness says God. A righteous person is one who walks according to My way.

An unrighteous person is by *default* a wicked person. There is no middle ground says God. You are either righteous or not. Wicked or not. Just as a man cannot serve both God and mammon, he cannot be both righteous and wicked.

The counsel of the wicked can never lead to righteousness. If you are a righteous person who *stands* in the council of the wicked, it does not turn you into a wicked person, it simply makes your righteousness ineffective. When your righteousness is ineffective, I cannot bless you, hence *'blessed is the man who does not stand in the council of the wicked'*. By the same token, blessed is *not* the man who stands in the council of the wicked.

Who are the wicked? How do you spot them? It is simple; they are the opposite of the righteous. By the very fact that they are not righteous, they have to be wicked. The easiest way to know if they are righteous is what? By their fruit of course.

It is a very simple discernment. The fruit being produced by people will immediately tell you if they are righteous or not.

You cannot make a judgment for it is not your place to judge, but you can observe based on your knowledge of the truth. The Word did not say 'do not be in the *presence* of the wicked'. You cannot be a light to the world by avoiding it. The key is not to mastermind with or take advice from unrighteous people. Your primary counsel is My Spirit says God.

Having said all this, you are entirely responsible for your own fruit. You cannot point fingers or blame others for the fruit in your own life. Whatever circumstances and conditions have blossomed in your life have been caused by the seeds that you have allowed to be planted.

You must take responsibility for that crop, just as the farmer who gets an unsatisfactory result. If there is fruit that you do not want to repeat, you must start over. Tear out that fruit and discard it. Eliminate the thoughts and behavior that produced it, prune that tree back to the roots. Now start adding food, which is My Word, to those roots, shine life giving light through My Spirit onto that tree, nurture it with righteousness and expect a bumper crop of fruit that is sweet to the taste, life giving and attractive to others. So much so that they will want to know how to get some for themselves. Then, the truth will spread and the number of those walking in righteousness will multiply.

I have provided a Formula* which you have never completely followed. As you know there is no condemnation from Me, just disappointment at the undeveloped potential.

The Formula is your guide. Like any other recipe, if you do not use it or you miss out certain ingredients, it does not work. Your body also works to a formula. Suppose it says today 'well I guess I won't bother with the breathing today' what would happen?

Every part of the Formula has to be applied to make it function and bear fruit. The hardest aspect for most is the issue of finances.

Many have struggled with this or have never been able to get control of their finances correctly because they have never successfully extracted themselves from the service of mammon.

This is where you should draw your line in the sand. In order to start serving Me, you have to stop serving mammon. Together we will eliminate all of your previous obligations and get you on track. My Formula will keep you on track. That way, you are standing in My council and not that of the wicked.

Concern yourself only with right thinking followed by right actions".

Psalms 1,
Psalms 17:15

*See message #1

130

ACT OF RESISTANCE

"As I have said before, many times, everything is spiritual. The spiritual battle is waged at a vibrational level. Your words and thoughts set up that vibration. So again, prayer is your only weapon in that realm, use it unceasingly. Pray without ceasing. It requires total focus and constant remembrance of its importance. Every inclination towards anger takes you away from your connection with My Spirit.

My Spirit will not function in an environment that is hostile. By allowing others to evoke bitterness or anger, you are cheating yourself from the power of your divine connection. When anger or similar feelings arise, recognize them immediately for what they are, the fleshly, worldly side of your nature attempting to gain control of your thoughts and actions causing you to behave in an unprofitable manner.

Apply the truth to the situation 'what does the Word of God say?' Once you have meditated on that, the way forward will be clearly defined. Everything you do must be done from a standpoint of love. The enemy cannot abide in an atmosphere of love. Acting in love is an 'act of resistance'. It is taking the very essence of evil and pushing it away with a force so powerful, it wins every time. I Am love. Take steps every day to demonstrate My love to others.

By focusing on the spiritual connection with Me, you can slow time down. Things do not rush by in the supernatural like they do in the natural. The goal is not to live a supernatural life hidden away from the world, but to live it in the midst of the chaos, providing a calming loving influence".

1 Thessalonians 5:16-18

131

INCREASE YOUR INTENSITY

"Your surroundings reflect the way that you think about yourself, about your life and your relationship with Me says God.

Chaos and disorder in any area will always reflect the same in some other aspect of your life. If there is no harmony and serenity in your surroundings, it will always make it more difficult for you to be effective in your spiritual life. Earthly mess will always signify a lack of excellence in your spiritual life.

If your earthly life is not planned, structured, effective, rewarding and enjoyable, it is because those things are not being addressed in your spiritual life first. It all starts in the spiritual realm. You have to address that first says God.

Trying to do it the other way around will just send you around and around the same mountain. You will keep wondering why things never change. Why, no matter how hard you try, you always seem to end up back at the same place. Make the changes first in the spiritual realm and watch them manifest in the natural realm.

I am calling you to operate at a new level of intensity. It should by now be obvious to you that the current situation is not acceptable and that there has to be significant and substantial change. It is not like we are having this conversation for the first time. Over and over, we have been through the steps that need to be taken and the things that need to be done differently. If you do not act on the decisions that we make consistently and with focus, then nothing can change.

If mammon is the focus, mammon will get the attention and will be the principle guidance system in your life. This renders you ineffective in pursuing our plans. As I have pointed out to you many times, there is no 'new' information required. You have all of the ingredients for righteous living. You have all of the ingredients for building towards the Kingdom; you just have to make the decision to apply them. You have to make the decision to step away from the world's system and into My system.

You have to be in constant contact with My Spirit to guide your every step. You have to realize that any steps taken in the flesh are not going to have the same impact. Any desire to do things yourself is nothing more than a carnal deception. My desire is always to do things together says God. You cannot do them on your own and then try to insert Me into the situation later to appease your own guilt. If you had not set off on your own course in the first place, you would never be feeling guilty. There is no condemnation in Christ.

Once you know that I have presented you with a door, you must press on through it. I *present* you with doors, but you must take the action to press upon it and walk through. You can even hold some of these doors open so that others can follow you through them. I have anointed many spiritual 'door openers' who have made the way easier for others. Learn to recognize these people. The doors they are holding open for those that are ready, lead to a wealth of wisdom and understanding. There are many others like them, but be careful, there are also those who appear to be doing the same work but will lead you astray. Test everything by the Spirit", says God.

Matthew 7:7
Romans 8:1
1 Thessalonians 5:21
1 Corinthians 14:33

288

132

YOU ARE NOT OF THIS WORLD

"Your success can never lie in the things of this world, because you are not of this world says God. If you can truly understand this, it will make things so much easier for you. For those that focus their thoughts around the earthly, the temporal, their achievements and rewards will be taking place in the here and now, in the earthly realm, and as such will be temporary in nature.

Maybe they will bring brief moments of joy and attention, leaving the flesh feeling satisfied, but to what end?

As you know, if those pursuits have added nothing to the platform established in 1 Corinthians 3 what is the point? This is all foolishness.

Look at what Solomon said about all of his wealth, all of his possessions, all of his achievements. Where is all that today? What has it profited him for even one second since he left the earthly realm? Yet the spiritual wisdom he acquired lives on. That door is still held wide open for those with the good sense to walk through it.

Think only from an eternal perspective says God. If you have grasped the truth in the fact that everything is Spiritual, everything is already taking place at an eternal level, you will realize that to think on any other level is a complete waste of time and a deception. It is the hardest thing for the human mind to embrace, that the world in which they live on the earth is merely a manifestation of the collective consciousness of all the people on the planet.

If chaos rule in their minds, what do you think would be most in evidence in their surroundings? If greed, money, power and self-promotion are the main focus of most of the 'leaders' in the so-called civilized world, what circumstances do you think that is going to create for the people that they are able to influence?

Do not forget that they will also be holding doors open, but woe to those that are pouring through those doors for they lead only to greater deception and for many, to total oblivion.

Be warned and spread the warning. There are many of My sheep that have gone astray and are lost beyond these doors says God. They are obviously still of the fold because My brand is upon them, but they have been made ineffective by the deception that is upon them. They need to shear off that tainted wool that is covering their spiritual eyes and return to the fold.

We are working on matters of eternal importance. There is no more time for experiments. To be set apart and separate, you have to be different from the world. I did not say to be 'disguised' in the world so that there is no discernible difference between you and the world.

I call you to leave behind the plans of men and the ways of the world and to follow My ways says God. Press forward and keep your eyes firmly focused on My truths and you will become blind to the lies of the world".

1 Corinthians 3:10-11, 5:9-12
John 15:19, 17:14-16
James 4:4
1 John 2:15-17, 4:5, 5:19
Philippians 3:20
Matthew 16:24

133

NO-ONE KNOWS THE HOUR

"I have said many times before, if My children knew for certain the hour of My return their whole lives would change says God.

Just like when you were small, you know your mom and dad will be coming back at about 9pm in the evening. Therefore, whatever 'undesirable' thing you were doing while they were out, was no doubt wrapped up and all of the evidence removed by about 8.30pm, so that by the time they arrived, everything looked 'normal' and as though you had been behaving exactly the way they have asked you to before they went out.

Can you remember such a situation? How about the time when as a young child, you were in the middle of doing something that you should not be doing and you heard the slamming of car doors, the feet on the pathway outside the house? They had come back unexpectedly! They were about to come in the house and you were not ready! Now, you scurry around, anxiously trying to hide the evidence of your misdemeanor, desperately trying to make it appear that you have been behaving as expected.

Remember the panic? Maybe even the dread that your actions were going to be discovered and that you were going to get into trouble. Maybe you were even going to be punished?

Remember how that felt? That fear, that dread, that anxiety? It was completely self-inflicted. For if you had behaved exactly as expected of you, there would never have been any need for you to suffer such trauma.

This is a *type,* an *example* of things to come.

Now imagine if you take those feelings and multiply them a million times. You will not be even close to one percent of the feeling that some of My children are going to experience on the Day of judgement. When they realize that I have returned at an unexpected hour that they are not prepared for and are not ready.

Oh yes, says God, this is the time when many will realize why they had those experiences years before, and the fact that the consequences of being unprepared and disobedient are the same today as they have always been.

Were you ever rewarded for being deceitful to your father? Did you see improvements in your relationship when you deliberately did the opposite of what you knew he wanted you to do? When you failed to live up to the responsibility he trusted you with, did he then grant you more responsibility? I know the answers are obvious; however, they are not so obvious that people realize the spiritual significance and apply it to their lives. If it were so, My return could be even sooner.

No, people still see their spiritual life and their physical lives as two separate things, two different worlds. This is just comprehensive ignorance.

People need a different perspective. How comfortable would the teenager using drugs or the husband watching the 'adult movie' be if they thought that they were actually going to get caught? Think about those feelings; think about what excuse they would be making up to justify their actions.

This grieves me so much says God, because I see all of these things all of the time and then I feel the pain of the lies and the excuses. These are sins upon the sins and are more painful.

How about you? Are you grieving My Spirit with your behavior? Are you ready? Or are you acting in a way that shows how glad you would be if it turns out that today is the Day? How about now? Are you ready now?

Or are you waiting for 'something' before you get ready? Are you going to change things for the better once you know for sure that 'He is on His way' Are you thinking 'surely it would be more obvious? After all, God wouldn't do that would He? He is not going to just show up taking everyone by surprise. I mean, He is not going to come back yet if only a few people are ready? Is He?

No, we have plenty of time'

Never forget, after millions of people took part in the Exodus from Egypt after they saw with their own eyes miracle after miracle; after they spent 40 years going around and around in circles in the desert 'getting ready', how many of them were actually ready to step over into what I had prepared for them?

How many of that generation were allowed to take their families with them and 'go in'? The number was two! Out of all those millions, two made it through and yes you have perceived correctly says God, that was another shadow of the things to come.

I stick to what I say; if you do not do the things that you know that you need to do, there are consequences.

Just like with your earthly parents, you did not stop being their child when they came home early and found you at fault, but there are invariably some consequences that are physically and emotionally discomforting to you and so it is going to be for many on that Day that I choose.

Make no mistake, no one knows the hour, but everyone should behave as though they think it is soon. Everyone should behave as though it could be tomorrow, or today or in a moment, because it really could.

Do not spend time trying to figure out the day or time. What use would it be if just as you realized that *now is the hour*, it actually *is* the hour!

What would have been added to your account other than being wise in your own eyes? Remember how you feel when someone phones and says that they are going to make an unexpected visit and they will be there in 1 hour? Can you see yourself rushing around, picking things up, trying to get yourself 'looking right' to receive your visitor? You know how that feels?

How about an even worse situation? There you are, not dressed properly, hair untidy, last night's dinner dishes still in the sink, a pile of washing you are 'going to get to' in the bathroom. Then the doorbell rings and it is the person that you met at the church a couple of weeks ago; the one who said they would 'give you a call sometime'. Well they did not call, and they are here right now, and you know that they just saw you through the kitchen window.

Can you get a sense of how that would make you feel? The point is made. No one is ready, My people are not watching, you are not ready, it is time to change, indeed.

As a believer, in the midst of this wicked world you have to take immediate, massive and drastic action to change your status. You have to move from a situation of chaotic unpreparedness to a situation of total readiness, heightened expectation and yet calm assuredness.

It will be an outward manifestation of 'the peace that defies human understanding' and it can only be attained through Spiritual perception".

Ephesians 5:15-17
2 Peter 3:10-12
Luke 12:37-40
Matthew 24:37-44, 25:1-13
Romans 13:11
Revelation 3:2, 16:15
Mark 13:33
Numbers 32:11-12
1 Thessalonians 5:6

134

THE REJECTION OF SELF

"These are the days of the completion of the equipping says God. I am revealing the final pieces of the puzzle. It has only been a puzzle to those that were truly seeking the Truth. There are many that for a long time have been confident in their own picture. Where there were missing pieces, they simply created their own, but their picture is both incomplete and spoiled.

To be alive to the Spirit, in the *fullness* of its potential, you have to be dead to the world. To be dead to the world, you have to be dead to yourself. Self seeks only after the world and the adoration of man.

Self rejects everything of the Spirit, it is cursed.

The only path to righteousness it through My Word. Self cannot perceive the truth in the Word and will seek to reject it.

The moment of Salvation starts a conflict within every believer.

A conflict without end, that has to continue until the separation of the spirit and the flesh. The battle for the salvation of the soul is waged between the flesh that seeks to keep you in control of the actions of your body and My Spirit who desires to carry out My plans through you.

This will only transpire through separation from the world.

You cannot walk in unrighteousness and serve Me, says God
You cannot lie and serve Me.
You cannot be double minded and serve Me.
You cannot pursue mammon and serve Me.
You must press through with the things I have shown you and walk in faith.
You must lose your life to Me now in this world, in order to gain it back with glory in eternity says God.

If you take the glory now, your reward is complete.

If you give Me the glory now, I will return it to you multiplied at the appointed time".

1 Corinthians 4:5

1 Peter 1:9

John 12:25-26

Romans 8:7

Ephesians 3:19

Proverbs 2:1-11

2 Peter 1:5-11

Matthew 16:25

135

RICHNESS

"Pray for everyone you meet. Pray with everyone you can. Bless everyone you can with kind words and with hope. Encourage everyone you can. Find something good in everyone you meet and let them know.

Life can be simple and elegant. Life can have richness without needing riches. Riches can promote marriage with mammon. *Richness* promotes My Spirit.

People never see Me through riches; they always see My grace through *richness*.

Today is the day for change says God. Even a little leaven spoils the whole lump. You cannot entertain any unrighteous thoughts or carry out any unrighteous actions or speak any unrighteous word. To do so, is to introduce a little leaven and the outcome is obvious.

Stand up in your righteousness; let your *yes* be *yes* and your *no* be *no*. Do not behave as the world does.

Be full of faith in the face of your accusers. If you have erred, I will restore you says God, but I cannot do so while you continue to wallow in your iniquity.

Using one shortcoming to protect yourself from another is a fool's plan. Free yourself from all strife and connection to mammon and look only to Me to lift you out of the situation.

Hold your heads high, you are My chosen children and are not to be subject to the abuses of this world. Free yourselves from the shackles of mammon and follow Me only".

Ephesians 4:29-30
Matthew 5:37

136

FLOWING IN THE SPIRITUAL MINDSET

"You live at a time where the cultural expectation is 'instant' everything. The contrast is, when focused from an eternal perspective, life does not only produce outcomes and results here and now, it can also produce harmonic flow that extends for eternity.

If your thoughts and actions are to be effective from an eternal perspective they have to make a positive contribution to the flow.

If your every thought and action is centered upon an immediate temporal worldly need, it is impossible to start the momentum that will cause the flow to occur.

You cannot live in the spiritual realm with a worldly mindset says God.

Declaring yourself as *separate* from the world is one thing, living in a manner that is consistent with the declaration is entirely different. Look how short the time is since you understood the necessity for the change. In less than one week you have been blown in every possible direction to the point where you are already at the door of doubt and unbelief. Do you imagine that this level of focus or belief is going to carry you when any difficulties arise?

It should be clear enough, that if you are going to attempt to walk this path in your own strength, you will not be able to do it. As My Word declares: 'Greater is He that is in me, than he that is in the world' and 'Not by might nor by power, but by My Spirit'.

These are examples of what to feed on in order to provide the necessary strength.

'Let the weak say I am strong' can only work when you are prepared to recognize your own weakness. To harbor secret delusions about how strong and resilient you are is foolish. That kind of strength only leads to destruction.

All these truths are in My Word says God. There is nothing new required. Just to be *doers* and not just *hearers*, it has always been just that".

1 John 4:1-6
Zechariah 4:6
Isaiah 40: 29-31

137

STRIVE FOR THE PRIZE

"The only way that you can be confident that you are constantly on the right path, the straight narrow path, is to measure your activity. The surest way to attain the prize of the high calling is to teach others how to find the same path. You cannot teach them how to walk in the path. That is a matter between them and My Spirit says God.

This is a task of enormous difficulty with never ending challenges for it requires you to 'live in the world' without being 'of the world'. That is easy to say but proves impossible for most and will remain impossible unless you are prepared to completely surrender the flesh and your earthly consciousness and turn them over to the control of My Spirit says God.

Yes, there is a general assembly that will contain billions; there is a great cloud of witnesses, impossible to number in the human perspective, but those that attain the prize, that earned the right to be called and then chosen out of the resurrection to be co-heirs with My beloved Son, these will be a tiny percentage.

To be among this number requires total dedication and the readiness to suffer loss in your time on the present earth in order to gain that prize in the coming Kingdom. Most cannot consider such a proposition, because their faith in the reality of the Kingdom to come is not fully developed.

Yes, they understand that My Son will soon return; they have a vague concept of what His bride will look like and the taking place of the marriage supper. Some have a picture of the millennial reign, but it is incomplete.

The greatest error is that most are trying to find a way to understand and embrace these truths that does not place any burden on the level of comfort they have created for themselves in this world. I have no regard for the things of this world that are being controlled and developed by the one who has disappointed Me the most and for whom I have already reserved eternal damnation.

The current age is purely a preparation for the return of My Son to prepare for the Eternal Age. Through these times I am able to set apart those that will work side by side with Me through the millennial reign to make ready for the eternal reign.

At that time the cycle will be complete, and My vision will be fully in view as it was always destined to be. The outcome was never uncertain in any way, only the will of man with which I blessed him had to be revealed. Without it, I would have had no need or desire to involve man in the process at all.

The best teachers are the *examples*. The best way to learn something is to teach it. Be aware though, the mantle brings with it an extra burden of responsibility. There is nothing more disappointing than a double minded teacher.

Be a sign, not a stick, lead but do not push. You cannot lead if you are not sure where you are going. My Word is your map and a lamp to your feet. Without these you will stumble and if you take your eyes from either, you will lead people on a long journey around the mountain.

Only when they see the 'promised land' for themselves can they 'cross the Jordan'. You cannot carry them; you cannot make boats or bridges for them. You can only demonstrate how to find the map and the lamp for themselves. My Spirit alone can work the perfection of their understanding and remove the scales from their eyes. This is a true revelation of what it means to pick up your cross on a daily basis.

The knowledge alone of this work is a burden. The willingness to carry out this commission is a heavy burden. It is the cross that race runners have to bear. If you do not carry it, you can run at the pace of the world with seemingly no effort. The burden of destruction always feels light and easy. The easier it seems for people, the further they are from My perfect will for their lives says God.

A race runner must not even contemplate such relief, for to find it will mean that he has lost his way. As I have stated before; if your life looks the same as the lives of those that do not have this knowledge, it is the same as those people and therefore you have left the only true path. Being a Jew to the Jews and a Greek to the Greeks does not mean to live as they do, it means to speak to them from their perspective so as to gain their attention. You do not become a light to the drunk by becoming drunk or to the adulterer by doing it yourself!

Wisdom will guide you, the wisdom that is only available through My Spirit led application of My Word. Walk in it, breath it, live it. I will make the way for you if you will make the way for Me" says God.

Hebrews 12:1
Matthew 7:14, 7:21, 8:11
Philippians 3:10-15
Galatians 5:7, 5:17, 6:9
Hebrews 3
Hebrews 4
2 Timothy 2:12, 4:2
Romans 8:17
1 Corinthians 9:24-27, 10:1-13
John 5:22, 6:63
Revelation 15:4

304

138

THE TRUTH WILL MAKE YOU FREE

"Anyone who studies the Word and lets My Spirit minister to them as they do so, will naturally discover the truth in it says God. This is not something that can be taught by man because it is a condition of the spirit, not a blind following of man's rules.

My Word says that 'the truth will make you free'. These truths are only apparent to those that are ready to set aside their will and to subject their soul to the instructions of My Spirit. Followers at such a level exhibit such total commitment and belief in what they have discovered that it serves as unction to others to want to discover the same truths for themselves.

All truth is contained in My Word says God. It is a recipe not a menu. Leaving out any ingredient will spoil the end result and make it less than it should be. This is also the case with teaching the truths regarding the coming Kingdom. It is impossible for anyone to aspire to being counted among those in the out-resurrection if they do not walk according to the Word, if they are not examples of My Spirit directing their every thought, word and action!

Avoid telling people 'here is what you should do'. Rather let them witness what you are doing. Be *doers* of My Word, not just *hearers*.

Doers are the examples that urge the hearts of others to do the same. Hearers simply tell others what they should do without necessarily walking in the same truth that they talk about. Hypocrites! These are double minded empty clouds! Let your actions confirm the truth that you speak or be prepared to miss the mark. Of those to whom much is given much will be required".

John 14:26
Philippians 3:11
Luke 12:48
Psalm 73:25-26

139

ATTRACT SUPERNATURAL INFLUENCE

"The worldly human condition always operates at a different pace and with a different expectation to the spiritual. If you continue to approach every situation using the faculties of your worldly mind, you will only achieve results at that level.

In order to attract supernatural influence and enter the flow, you must be able to step back and wait on Me says God.

Remember that when you have done *all* it is time for you to stand. Be sure then that you have in fact *done all.*

If you make a dam in your stream, the flow stops and it becomes more and more difficult to remove all the debris to get it going again. The more consistently you add to the flow, the easier it will become. Right now, imagine your stream and in the middle is an ugly pile of sticks, leaves and pieces of wood, it has almost completely blocked the flow of the water. The water has backed up and is brown and murky due to its inability to proceed forward.

As you walk in obedience a few sticks are removed. As you put out more light into the world, a few more and each one releasing a little more of that life-giving water to continue its journey. An encounter with doubt, unbelief, fear that you do not immediately overcome through the power of My Word, will add a handful of mud or a few more sticks says God.

Be very aware of this, because you can undo the progress of an entire day by letting these old enemies gain traction against you.

That is why I tell you to make records of everything. That way when the lies come, you can immediately overcome the adversary and declare 'Look what God has done'.

Just like the river on a bright sunny day, once you are in proper *flow*, My glory from that flowing living water will be reflected in your face and shine from your eyes. To the natural mind this whole perspective sounds like nonsense. The spectacular heights of the resulting flow sounds like a children's tale. Remember these are the same minds that label My life-giving Word as a collection of fables says God.

The level of faith required to enter into this realm may appear impossible to attain and it is not to seek to elevate yourself above others 'for the first shall be last'; It is to enter into the *fullness* of what is available to all that run the race. As the pieces come together more and more will see. The more the world is removed from the picture the easier it is to see this glorious truth says God.

Here are some observations; the spiritual ambience in your house has dropped, where is the Spirit filled music? My Word says 'when two or more agree' are you not two? If there is power in two or more do you see no merit in employing that? If you cannot walk in humility with each other, how will you do so when much is entrusted to you? Excellence is a state of being, not a state of mind. You cannot 'think' excellence. It is something that you have to do. Love, help and encourage each other into the flow. Building each other up in this way also removes twigs and leaves. Each day of progress will produce an immediate change in the color of the water and you will start to feel the change in the flow. Therein lies the joy of a purpose filled life flowing in the Spirit and reflecting My glory" says God.

2 Corinthians 3:18
Ephesians 3:19
Psalms 27:14
Isaiah 30:18, 40:31
Matthew 20:1
1 Corinthians 9:24-27
Hebrews 1:3

140

MAINTAINING THE COVERING OF THE ANOINTING

"To maintain the anointing, you must pray without ceasing.

Ask Me about every decision and work to maintain the constant presence of My Spirit to override the influence of the world. Look for the Kingdom perspective in everything. If there is none, then the decision makes itself.

Consider everything from a standpoint of love. If something will not allow you to demonstrate love to others it is pointless and therefore has no place in your future.

In order to maintain momentum, all things pertaining to your spiritual life have to be continued regardless of circumstances. This creates the flow and will keep it flowing. This removes debris from your river and will eliminate dams.

Maintain single-minded confidence. When you 'know that you know' let that be it. Do not regress the next day to 'I thought I knew'. Sinking into doubt and unbelief is not acceptable. Be strong and of good courage says God.

Be courteous, kind and humble but not a respecter of men.

Look only to Me for approval says God. Men may nod and approve which may show you as right in their eyes. It is all meaningless unless you are operating in My will and be sure to be 'about your Father's business' and no one else's.

Learn to speak out My will and watch the miraculous unfold. In order to do so, you must first discern only My will. This comes through obedience.

Do not give time to laying up treasures for yourself in the earthly realm. It is of no value to you. Learn to look at every situation, person and opportunity through spiritual eyes. Worldly eyes will focus only on the world's perception which is always the wrong view.

People create what they perceive to be success for themselves. Often, they then declare Me as the author of their success.

My desire is that as many as possible should be saved. Rich, poor or in between is of no interest to Me says God. I am concerned with hearts and souls, not material success.

There are few that can have material success without losing their focus on Me. That is a strength of My Word. It causes man to stay focused on Me as their source and not the world. It is impossible to live according to the Word and be dedicated to the world.

That is why the world hates My Word. Anyone grafted into the Olive tree without understanding this is still of the world. Protected by the blood and assured of salvation but unable to attain to the promise of the rewards of the Kingdom.

The narrow path, the straight narrow gate that few will pass through, is My Word says God, My unfailing plan for righteous living. In the absence of My Spirit, it is empty law keeping, only serving to highlight man's weaknesses and disobedience. In harmony with the anointing of My Spirit it is an unstoppable force of righteous power. It creates the platform for the power of My Spirit to break through into everything you do. 'Not by *your* might, nor by *your* power, but by My Spirit" says God.

Romans 11:17-24
Ephesians 3:6
2 Corinthians 1:21-22
1 Thessalonians 5:16
Philippians 4:6
Matthew 6:19-21, 7:13-14

141

RUNNING THE RACE, STRIVING FOR REWARDS

"Look at how a runner is required to race at the worldly pinnacle of all races, the Olympic Games. Each runner is allocated a lane, once the start is made; he has one small lane, not much wider than himself, in which to run. He must stay within these lines, if he strays outside of the lines for even a second, he may be disqualified and must stop and wait for another chance on another day. The lane restriction is so tight, that even placing 1 foot on one of the lines for one second can cause disqualification.

Why would attaining rewards in My Kingdom be expected to be any easier says God? It is the greatest prize ever offered to man in the history of the universe. Can people really expect it to be easy? My people perish through lack of knowledge. Indeed! Says God.

To know My Word is to know that these rewards present the greatest challenge that a man can pursue and their attainment is for those that endure to the end. Even Paul was unsure. Only by suffering through the uncertainty can the necessary perfection of your soul take place. You have to remove self. To become *self-less* is essential because self will always seek to serve self and if self is being served, I am being neglected says God.

Serve Me by serving others and the focus on self is eliminated. When you put your focus on others, I come quickly into view. Self-centeredness makes it impossible to see My grace and hear My wisdom. Walk according to My ways and you will know My ways. Walk according to the ways of this world and you will know the ways of this world and enjoy your rewards in this world. You can have your treasures now, or you can defer your enjoyment for a more perfect eternal treasure.

Staying within those lines, on that straight and narrow path, requires extreme focus. Only by keeping your eyes on My Son can you hope to keep on track. His atoning blood saves you from death and allows you to start over each time you fail. There is of course a reward for those that run with hope and especially those who cross the finish line.

There are so many who although the blood has saved them, they have not even started to run. They do not even realize that there is a race to participate in, let alone the significance. The veil of religion is blurring their vision of the truth and their ignorance will not add to their foundation says God.

A believer filled with the hope of attaining to the prize of the higher calling, hastily preparing their wedding garment to attend the banquet as part of the bride, is a delight to Me. The sense of purpose that is ignited by these truths is uplifting and inspiring. People are hungry for it. They have grown weary of the empty promises of man's plans and schemes.

To whom will you look for approval when you are walking in My ways? Prepare yourself, be set apart and under My anointing at all times, ready to impart at all times. Stand up in your righteousness, I am calling upon those that have ears to hear. Those that will refuse to hear have their own agenda.

I will pull on the hearts of the right ones. Push on the doors to see where they are. I will draw them. You have to be visible in the spiritual realm as well as the worldly realm. Your level of spiritual *tuning* must be elevated to the highest level ever. This is a deeper blessing of the Word, it brings the physical discipline which is required to release the spiritual flow. The subjugation of the flesh must be complete for the flow of

314

the Spirit to be at its peak, this is only possible through consumption of the life-giving Word.

The more you *release* the more flow will come to you. I will send you a raging torrent of spiritual sustenance says God. Continue to remove the debris with which you have blocked the river of your anointing. You have released a trickle but the strong current that will thrust your vessel into full sail still has not broken through. Keep pressing forward with urgency as you do not want to be forced to wait for another tide. Your appointed time is for this hour so be committed to the voyage and obtain direction and provision for yourselves from the stores in My word.

Avoid the temptation to jump into someone else's boat. You have done that many times and it has been to no avail as that is not what I have called you to be. Make your tents, let down your nets as required but once you set sail, do not leave your vessel, this is a lifelong voyage which will take you into the millennium and beyond. So be sure that your commitment is one hundred percent because many vessels have come to grief on the rocks of iniquity. They have many names but all lead to loss. Your voyage will be joyous and filled with wonders and delights and the exhilaration of feeling the closeness of My direction at all times. It is the greatest and most vibrant blessing available in the earthly realm, to be navigated and blessed by My Spirit. Beware to never let others steer the course of your vessel lest they sink you on the rocks leaving you to have to dry dock and carry out repairs. Fly your flag of hope and set your course for Me" says God.

1 Corinthians 9:24-27
Philippians 3:10-14, 2:16-17
Hebrews 3:1, 11:26
Matthew 5:12-20, 16:27
2 Timothy 4:8

142

PRAYER AND DISCIPLINE

"My Word instructs you to 'pray without ceasing' says God. The essence of this instruction is that you keep your earthly mind focused on spiritual matters so that the evils of the world cannot get a foothold in your life. Prayer is not a ritual. It is a communication channel. If every decision is made in consultation with Me you will not go astray.

The war between thoughts raging in your mind can only be won by divine influence. The peace that defies human understanding only comes through disciplined communication. Remove anything from your life that promotes stress or anxiety for these are not My design says God. Outline your intentions for each day and consider them prayerfully for guidance.

Without discipline you are like a long grass in a strong wind, bending first this way and then that, showing no strength. Let My strength be within you so that you may stand firm like a tall oak. The confidence of My wisdom will be your backbone and your discipline to listen for My voice in all you do. This will bring the calmness and increase of wisdom that will enable you to stay focused.

Be blessed and encouraged because recognizing the need for an increase in discipline and wisdom is the most important step in attaining it".

2 Timothy 1:7

Revelation 3:19

Philippians 4:7

143

THE SPIRIT IS YOUR 'GPS'

"Fill your days with steps that take you in the right direction says God. The steps that lead you closer to Me all face the same way. If you go off on a tangent or focus on things that are not of Me or part of My purpose for your life, you will be led astray. You may end up standing still and making no progress. Worse still, you could end up losing ground and going completely in the wrong direction if you are making decisions in your own strength. That is exactly what will happen. Every time, guaranteed.

The biggest problem is that the enemy can shroud these misdirected steps in temporary glory or success which will only take you further away from your path. That is why constant consultation with My Spirit is your 'GPS'.

Like any 'GPS', it is only effective if you ask it the right questions. It will not direct you where to go otherwise and you will be left trying to find your own way. Let My Spirit be your spiritual 'GPS' so that you can stay on track and make corrections when necessary.

All decisions should first be prayed over and then discussed with Me to be confirmed with My Spirit, and then acted upon. This will eliminate mistakes.

Remove any behavior or thought pattern from your life that would grieve My Spirit because these things block your communication or can cut it off altogether. My Spirit will not abide in a situation where it is willfully brought into an unholy atmosphere by the selfish actions of a selfish and self-willed child. Do not cover yourself in darkness through your own thoughts and actions and desires.

Bathe yourself in the calming light of glory that fills you with joy and abundant energy. This can only be achieved in accordance with My will for your life. Stay on track, stay in constant communication and always be ready for action. The enemy never rests in his desire to destroy you. Likewise, you must never rest in your pursuit of the perfection of your calling.

Step forward into the things that I have called you to do and I will make the way for you. I will open the floodgates to an abundant flow of resources which will allow you to move at a rapid pace and make up for lost time. I will restore to you the things that you should have already received but did not because of your disobedience. I will restore them to you because My love for you is absolute and unwavering. The only reason the flow stops is when you block it through your actions. I have already purposed it, I am never double minded, but if you are it invalidates My decisions and creates a barrier between us.

You can erect a barrier between us by your words and actions. I never remove such barriers unless I am asked to do so says God, because they represent free choice. Having such choices is what makes the possibilities for mankind so rich and exciting. Choose wisely".

John 14:6
Jeremiah 6:16
Psalms 16:11, 19:14, 25:4, 119:35, 139:23-24
Isaiah 2:3
1 Corinthians 2:5

144

THINKING BEFORE SPEAKING

"Thinking before speaking is a most powerful skill. The ability to do so is a gift that I bestow upon everyone says God, but it is the least used of all gifts. Exercise this gift and you will become a Spiritual power house. You will become so effective in the Spirit realm that the enemy will run from your presence.

Every thought, every word or action that follows the thought will have one of two outcomes. It will take you towards the fullness of My power operating through you, My glory being reflected by you and My love radiating from you, or it will diminish these things and lead you towards darkness.

Understanding this will clearly show you how much of the time people are standing still in a spiritual sense or moving forward so slowly that it hardly makes a difference. Some are moving rapidly backwards towards the darkness.

This is why you see some people that I am using seemingly fail or fall short. I will work through them when they are flowing in My assignments but if the choices they are making elsewhere drag them back towards the darkness, they have to reverse that themselves by changing their choices.

Look at any place you travel to, any event that you attend or any work you do, as a mission to find those dormant seeds and germinate them. Where there are no seeds, plant some. Where there is a shoot, fertilize it with words of wisdom. Where there is a fruit bearing tree, encourage it to increase its yield and to move to a higher level.

You must know that there is no higher level of understanding in this matter. Once you know that *everything is spiritual* there is no further enlightenment necessary. The key now is to walk out that knowledge on a consistent basis and resist returning to the state where only some things are spiritual which renders you ineffective in the spiritual realm".

James 3:2
Psalms 19:14
2 Corinthians 1:12

145

I AM

"I am the God of Abraham, Isaac and Jacob. I am the creator
of the entire universe perceived and unperceived, discovered and
undiscovered and everything in it. I am enormous and powerful
beyond comprehension. I am able to create or destroy anything I
choose.

I have chosen to love you.

To envelop you in a love so all-encompassing that humans do not have
the mental faculty to find an emotion to describe it. You just have to
be it, be *in* it and be *of* it. You can breathe it, you can taste it, you can
feel it in every cell of your being, but you cannot create it, touch it or
describe it.

I am the power that makes everything work, good or bad. I am the
absolute judge and decision maker. I *provide* the choices, you *make* the
choices. My judgments are based on your choices, it is that simple.

When you work in My power there is no striving. When you make your
decisions with My discernment, there is no uncertainty. When you
speak out My wisdom, there is always clarity and understanding.

This is so simple, it is the simplest thing. It is just one principal. Put Me
first says God.

If you put Me first, I can reward you beyond your comprehension,
because that is where I find My delight."

Hebrews 1:2-3
Isaiah 45:7
Psalms 36;5-9
2 Chronicles 20:6
Job 26:7-14
Psalms 147:4-5
Jeremiah 10:12-13
Romans 1:20

146

SPEND TIME WITH ME FIRST

"It is good to rise early and spend time with My Spirit says God. Before the noise of the world has the opportunity to disrupt your thinking.

I have told you to spend time in My Word before you sleep.

Make sure that My truth resonates with your cells as you regenerate.

Rise early and reap the benefits from that superfood. You can achieve more in this time than at any other time of the day, because the purity of what you produce will be the highest".

Psalms 5:3

147

FEED ON DIVINE TRUTH

"If you are not feeding the cells of your body with My divine truth, what are you feeding them with? Your physical body is an outward manifestation of your spiritual body. If there is something wrong in your life spiritually, it will invariably show up somewhere in the physical realm.

There are many reasons for sickness and disease in the world and one of the principle reasons is the lack of attention that people pay to their spiritual lives. While it is true that I might sometimes use a physical infirmity in a person as an instrument to bless others, physical problems are often self-inflicted through spiritual ignorance. Understanding the truth in My Word will help to improve this situation.

Regardless of how bad things are, they will always look better under the Lamp of the Truth. You have to take a stand and be able to see your future in order to walk into it. This vision of your future picture needs to be brought into focus. Once you have that picture, you must put *action* to your faith.

The time is short and there is an urgency in the current days. You have to prepare and choose if you are going to embrace the truth or continue in ignorance" says God.

Hebrews 11:10, 12:2
John 9:1-12
Proverbs 4:23
Exodus 15:26

148

THE WORD IS LIKE A MIRROR

"My Word is like a mirror says God. It is not only used to educate and to edify, to encourage and to correct, but also to reveal. When you look into the mirror of the Word you will often see things in your own life that will bring you joy. You will also see things that should cause you to reconsider certain thoughts and actions. If the Word is a mirror, what does 'you will know them by their fruit' say about you?

Looking at yourself from My side of the glass, what fruit do you have on display from the various aspects of your life?

These are hard questions says God. You are always happy to look at the fruit produced by others, but how much consideration have you given to your own? How much work do you need to do to improve the quality and quantity of your harvest? Is there even going to be a harvest this year? Have you been paying attention to that which is growing? Have you planted any new seeds?

Remember there can be no fruit without seeds and even seeds are of no value unless they are planted. Once planted they should be nurtured and given attention. Then they will produce even more seeds and a new cycle of blessings will begin. If you need more fruit in your life, just ask Me and I will show you how to get the seeds and where to plant them. I will work with you to nurture them and produce the harvest.

Be warned though this is not something that you can do by yourself. It has to be a joint venture between you and Me. This is the way that you get to serve Me and Me alone.

Striving under your own strength, producing fruit for material gain and personal glory is also possible. For many it works very well and they are revered and admired by the world. They are celebrated and honored for what they achieve and they have their reward.

That route does not serve My intentions. That route puts you directly into the service of mammon and as you know, there is no way to serve both of us. You have to make a choice and focus on the path of your intention"

2 Corinthians 9:10
John 15:4-5
Matthew 3:10, 7:15-20, 12:33-37
Psalms 17:14

149

THE CHOICES OF LIFE

"Life is a series of choices. Every choice has an impact, in fact a double impact. Every choice affects your life here on earth and it also has eternal consequences because it builds upon your platform.

What are you building with? You must be dedicated to the preservation of the physical vessel. Choose life in your application of exercise and diet. The more life there is in your diet, the more *life* there will be in your physical body.

Choose life in your financial resources. Money as a spiritual object is dead until you start using it. If its first use is for your own ends, it stays dead and it sucks you into the service of mammon and remains dead and promotes death. It becomes an instrument of death. I requested your first fruit says God. It is for your benefit not Mine. When you give the first 10th of your harvest for your first fruit, you spiritually activate the rest of the crop. You effectively breathe life into it by honoring My Word.

Now you have *live* resources at your disposal with which you can develop more life and more abundance.

You cannot afford to miss any of these ingredients so that you do not end up being encircled by your circumstances. It is important to pursue only your own purpose. Circumstances are often designed by the enemy to take your focus away from where you should be going says God.

You can spend hours absorbing garbage into your spirit through the television screen and that needs to be avoided. Likewise, you can absorb even more through the internet. Remember that the idea is to reduce the amount of time spent staring at a screen so that you can spend more time with things that will add value to your life. You should not look to reduce television time so that you can spend more time in front of the computer.

There is a time for that, but it predominantly needs to be productive time. There are so many distractions online and it is important that you do not get sucked in and end up following the herd.

There is no point in 'extending your days' if they are not going to be days that are *effective* and with *purpose*. You want to see the things that you do having a positive effect on the lives of other people and if you truly are My servant, you will be effective in that role.

The only way to physical wealth is by choosing life in your food and life in your body. The only way to spiritual wealth is by choosing life in constant interaction with the living Word and through prayer, praise and meditation. The only way to financial wealth is by activating the life in your resources by passing the germ of life, the first fruits, as instructed.

The only way to true emotional wealth as a human is by choosing life in every area. If you do that, it is impossible not to live at a level of emotional exhilaration that is unattainable any other way. Once you have created this balance, you will easily discern the full spiritual implication from an eternal perspective of every choice you make and action you take".

Psalms 90:12, 91:14-16
Proverbs 3:1-2, 9:11, 18:21
1 Kings 3:14
Romans 8:28

150

THE WORLD GIVES NO SECURITY

"The world can never offer security says God. There is no security in possessions or things or assets. The only security comes through My Son, the *eternal security* that exceeds the value of every material possession on the earth all added together.

Houses are just possessions and they do not hold the key to security. They can disappear in the blink of an eye as can every other thing that is made by man.

On the day that the trumpet sounds, many will find that every last thing that they had considered to be their security will be gone in a moment. The only thing remaining will be the *offering* represented by what they have produced as fruit from the seed created through the *working out* of their salvation.

Once you understand the source of your true security, everything else falls into place very easily. Finding a dwelling place is then based on how it will further what you will add to your foundation. It will not become an idol to you or a stumbling block to others.

You are sojourners on the earth; you are on a journey leading to your permanent residence in the millennial kingdom. Avoid thinking 'we have arrived' until I confirm that to be the case. Take your joy in My presence being in the place where you abide and not in the place itself.

To create attachment to a place is to detach yourself from the fullness of our relationship. You ought to dwell in Me and I in you.

I am your home, your house, your land, your refuge, your source of food, your living running pure water. I am your comfort and your comforter, your castle and fortress, your shelter from the enemy.

I am your inspiration, your mentor, your guide and teacher.

I am your Everlasting Location.

Abide *in* Me and *with* Me and wherever you are you will always be at home".

Philippians 2:12

Colossians 3:14

Revelation 11:15

1 Thessalonians 4:14-16

John 14:2-3, 14:6

1 Peter 1:9

1 John 5:12

151

WHAT IS LEFT BEHIND IS ALL THAT MATTERS

"Demonstrate to others that they can be 'all they can be' without having to sell their soul to the devil. Every good thing and every desire of their heart is available to them through Me says God.

Achieving success with humility is not only possible, but the only path to a true sense of achievement and a contented heart. Riches gained through a competitive spirit will always bring a bitter aftertaste at some point. However, richness gained through love, wisdom and unselfish effort brings not only prosperity in the here and now, but also it builds more prosperity from an eternal perspective.

There is nothing wrong with goals and the measuring of achievement as long as the purpose behind them amounts to more than just material gain. 'He bought a lot of stuff' should not be the epitaph of choice.

It is plain that when a soul leaves this planet he does not get to take his 'stuff' along. The only thing that gets acknowledged, the only thing that I ever get to see, is what is left behind in the hearts and minds of those you affected while carrying out your purpose.

What are you sowing into other people? Take a close look because that is where your eternal rewards are going to come from.

Long after the memory of the cars and the houses and the clothes and all the other stuff has faded, the only thing remaining will be how you were 'being' to those around you. To those whose reality you had an opportunity to impact.

Keep your purpose in the forefront of your mind as you interact with people. Measure every decision you make, every goal you set, every thought you make and every action you take against its potential to take you further towards your purpose or not.

Anything that is not in harmony with that purpose, that is not vibrating at the same frequency as that purpose, is obviously of no value to you and should be immediately cut off.

Remember that every moment spent pursuing something that is not in harmony with your purpose is a moment that is wasted. How many hours, weeks, days and months, even years will all of this wasted time add up to"?

James 1:17
Philippians 2:3-11

152

FLOWING WITH GOD

"I never changed the flow of the days or the seasons or the times says God. It is man that changed it to suit his own ends and his own agenda. The majority of the world lives on a timeline that is contrary to My design. They are shackled to the schedule of the enemy, out of the natural flow of creation and in the flow of manipulation.

Through this counterfeit flow comes competition and striving, sickness and disease, unrighteousness abounds, because to serve the enemy's timeline is to serve the enemy. These are difficult truths says God, because they make it necessary to change everything so that you are moving completely against the flow of what appears to be normal and correct. The fact is, the appearance of it being normal and correct is a deception and the deception keeps many from the fullness of My blessings.

Understanding the natural flow of time is essential to those seeking the Kingdom. It is difficult to stay on the straight and narrow path when marching to the beat of the time clock of the adversary. You cannot demonstrate this to others unless you are first overcomers and press into the cycle of life as I designed it, for it contains unimaginable blessings.

Whose timeline do you imagine we will be using in the Millennial Kingdom? Only in My timeline of flow will you will find the natural restoration of the physical body. Empowering, inspirational dreams and visions and the energy and strength to carry out all of your daily activities.

Leave the creatures of the night to commune with each other. Let those who hunger after the service of mammon seek their ideas and inspiration from the councils of evil. You are to be separate and set apart so that My Spirit can instruct you towards the things of life.

To commune with the Essence of Life brings understanding, wisdom and faith. To do the opposite, brings the opposite. To each his choice says God. I do not inflict choices on people. I make them available and then watch and observe. Half measures do not produce half results. They always produce *no results of eternal value*. Only dedicated, fully focused, obedient children can aspire to the adoption. The requirements are plainly set forward.

There is no negotiation or flexibility. The path is clearly defined for those that have eyes to read the map. This map has only one true path. There is no other way, no detour, no alternative route. Just the *straight narrow* way for the Kingdom seekers. To know that you are on this path should bring unspeakable joy. Reverent fear serves only to keep you on it. Be blessed and enjoy the journey".

Galatians 4:4
Romans 8:14-17
1 Thessalonians 5:7
2 Timothy 4:7
Hebrews 12:1
James 1:12
Matthew 24:13
Psalms 177:18-21, 19:1-16
Ephesians 1:3-10

153

THE WORD IS THE ONLY TRUTH

"It is easy to validate any claim that a written word has originated through the prompting and guidance of My spirit and everything is to be tested against My living Word says God. If there is a contradiction in evidence the writings are not of My Spirit. Am I to be double minded? No! I am the same yesterday, today and tomorrow for eternity.

There is no point in time in which I will decide to start contradicting Myself. Anything in My living Word that has been suggested to be a contradiction, is simply man's inability to properly understand and interpret that which is written.

My Word is the standard against which everything can be measured. Every thought, idea, word, action. It can all be weighed against the truth of the living Word. If it contradicts the instructions that I have placed with you since the beginning, you will know that it is a human variation of the truth. Variations are of no benefit from an eternal perspective for they add nothing of substance to your foundation and in many cases can be destructive.

I have been *selective* since the separation of the sons of Adam. This is an established pattern that has never varied to this day and is always associated with choice. Cain made his choice, the sons of Noah theirs. Esau made his choice, the sons of Israel theirs. On it goes, throughout history until today. Choices that everyone must make on their own and then live or die by the fruit of those choices. Will it be to bring themselves comfort and joy in the here and now with no regard for others? Will it be to embrace the deeper joy found only in My living Word? 'Each to his own' say the people of the world. And so it is each to his own choice.

There are many in this day that are saying 'Thus says The Lord' or some version that suggests the same thing. How will the truth be revealed? Only by returning to the root of all truth can you move past the requirements of 'itching ears'. Everything was written in the beginning. Everything since is a validation of what was stated in the beginning and a repeat of the same cycles.

'There is nothing new under the sun': There is a deep truth in this statement for everything that *is* just keeps repeating itself, striving towards perfection, but falling short because there is only One that is perfect. There are My words, there are My people. When My Words and My people become one, My light illuminates the clear path to eternal separation from the world. It has always been there, it is just not visible through the eyes of the world, only through the eyes of My spirit dwelling within man. That Spirit is fed through the fountain of light, life and truth in My Word.

Everything must point back to those Words says God. It must confirm and harmonize with those Words and it must compel to feed more voraciously on those Words. If it does not, or if it offers contradiction, it is a lie from the purveyors of evil and will bring death to those sheep that embrace it as truth. There is only One Truth".

John 14:6, 16:14
1 Thessalonians 5:21
1 John 4:1
Hebrews 13:8
James 1:17
1 Corinthians 3:10

154

OIL & WATER

"Righteousness and the flesh are like oil and water says God. They do not mix! If one is in ascendancy, the other is suppressed, there is no other possibility. To walk righteously requires the constant suppression of the flesh which is only achieved through My Spirit says God. For the measure of My Spirit to grow within you, it has to be fed and nurtured.

There is only one food for My spirit and that is My living Word, the sustenance of all life. Without the truth of My Word, everything righteous would die.

The Word contains everything pertaining to life and righteousness and also reveals the plan of the enemy. It is impossible to walk in the supernatural realm without the protection of My Spirit.

To know the absolute power of that protection requires faith and 'faith comes by hearing and hearing by the Word'. The more you absorb the truth, the stronger and more confident you will become.

The Word brings authority, discernment, wisdom and righteousness. When these are all in perfect balance, they will cause a spirit of love to emanate from you that will bless everyone that you come into contact with. People will seek to share this love and every life that is touched will bring glory to My Name.

In order for this to come to pass, you must continue to devour My Word. Let it permeate every fiber of your being, every cell should be alive with the truth of My vibrant living Word. Be aware, this is no small task; this is not about *knowing* at an intellectual level.

This is about *being*.

Every thought, every action, every decision, every idea, every conclusion, anything that you write, the words that you speak, must all come from the same perspective.

They must all be illuminated by the glow of righteousness which can only be provided by My Spirit," says God.

Ephesians 3:19, 4:13
Galatians 5:16-17
2 Peter 1:3
Romans 10:17
John 1:9, 14:26, 16:13-16
Ephesians 1:18-25, 4:19-20
Hebrews 4:12-13
Proverbs 16:9

155

REGRETS

"The biggest regret that people express at the end of their lives is not 'I wish I had more money, I wish I had more cars, more houses' no, it is 'I wish I had more time'.

Knowing this, you can see how vital it is that the time that you do have is *never wasted.*

People would love to get back all of the hours they wasted on frivolous nonsense that made no positive difference to their lives whatsoever. They cannot get it back. They have no control over anything that happened even 1 second ago, only now is yours to act upon and decide how it will unfold and what you would do with it. Choose wisely, because every choice has eternal consequences.

What is your purpose? Only I can create your purpose and place that within you. The logic for this is simple. I am the Creator of everything. The enemy does not create anything, he simply perverts that which I created by deceiving the vulnerable about certain details so that they often think they are pursuing My plan for their lives, but they are not.

How do you know if the purpose you are pursuing is from Me? Does it benefit only you? Or does it bring benefit to others? Does it put you on a pedestal or does it illuminate My power working through you? Does pursuing it require you to do anything that you know would grieve My Spirit?

The big danger for people that start to get significant levels of success in their lives, is when they believe that they are solely responsible for it and they do not acknowledge the fact that it is only by My grace that they are where they are. Many times, you will hear people state that 'I am so grateful'. Well *who* exactly is it that they are *grateful* to?

That distinction needs to be included in your gratitude. Sure, I know your heart, but your mouth will speak out what is in your heart. Understand the importance of knowing your *source*, of knowing *who* you are and *whose* you are".

Psalms 39: 4-8
Psalms 103: 15-18
Psalms 90:10-12,
Psalms 27:13-14

156

THE QUESTION OF AUTHENTICITY

"How authentic are you in your spirituality asks God? There are many that declare My name in the presence of others, who quote My Words and yet their actions are not consistently in line with what they profess to believe. Knowing the truth is one thing, living the truth in thought, words and deeds is a completely different thing.

Knowing the truth is the same as being a 'hearer' of the Word. 'Faith comes by hearing' as it is also written 'faith without works is dead'.

The ways of the world are a contradiction, they will always represent the lie that runs closely to the truth but will be the way to destruction and never to happiness. True happiness is the surety of basking in My Presence for eternity. The joy of knowing that My hand is upon you and that it delights My heart to count you among the number of My chosen ones.

There is nothing within the world that can lead you to these riches says God. The world's paths will only lead you to deception, particularly for those that do not hear the admonition 'do not store up for yourselves treasures on earth'.

It is impossible to be authentic without walking in righteousness because authenticity is a fruit of righteousness. Once people see the truth in you, illuminated by your righteous actions, your authenticity is confirmed and this will give you the ear of kings, leaders, moguls and many others who would usually not even listen.

Authenticity opens doors that would usually be closed and it produces favor beyond measure. Even the world craves the purity of its fragrance. Once something is revealed as a *fake* it is mostly impossible to restore people's confidence in the thing or the person. As such, it becomes an article of derision. For this reason, you must be vigilant in your pursuit of righteousness and it is imperative that the evidence of your authenticity is always freely available and be blatantly obvious to anyone who seeks validation.

Do not be burdened by this says God. To fall short is part of being authentic; otherwise there would have been no requirement for Grace. Living the righteousness required by My Word will maintain your authenticity. Your inability to do everything in it perfectly without flaw, illuminates My Grace, glorifies My Mercy and validates your weakness when you are not being led by My spirit.

The more you are led by My spirit, the more authentic you will be. A servant walking in My spirit carrying out tasks under the guidance of My spirit can never miss the mark. Once the flesh is allowed any input the picture immediately changes because the flesh always seeks to do the opposite. It has no option because that is its nature.

Walk upright in your authenticity. Seek righteousness by living out the truth in My Word which I have written on your heart. Increase your wisdom and understanding by giving it away to others that are seeking the authentic in an ocean of counterfeits and liars and I am not speaking of the world" says God.

Proverbs 3
Psalms 103:13-14
2 Corinthians 12:9
Romans 3:24
John 1:14

157

DECEPTION

"In ancient days past, My people would consistently turn away from Me and give their attention to other things. They would make gods for themselves and lust after the things of this world. They felt that things could be better and easier for them if they *blended in* more easily with their surroundings.

This is a deception and one that is even more prevalent today than it was before. Men continue to manufacture their own distractions in the name of progress and convenience, they continue to produce item after item that will supposedly 'make life easier'. Nothing under the sun makes life easier says God, except to walk righteously with Me. To follow My commands and keep counsel with My Spirit. This makes life easier, because with it comes purpose, eternal significance and even rewards.

The inventions of man can be of benefit if used in connection with your divine purpose. Be warned though, if all you use them for is to satisfy the lusts of the flesh more readily, you become the author of your own misfortune. Excess in any regard is a fruit of satisfying the lusts of the flesh and will keep you from the blessings.

The most powerful tool available for those pursuing good health is My Word says God. The most powerful tool for those seeking wisdom and peace in relationships is My Word. For those seeking success in business, My Word.

I gave you My Words as the living life-source, the answer to every conceivable question, the ultimate infallible instruction manual, the final authority. You can only rightly understand it through the revelation illuminated by My Spirit. To read the Word in the absence of the Spirit is like putting a spoon into an empty bowl and attempting to feed yourself.

All who know Me have access to My Spirit says God, but We will only work with those that ask and who are prepared to subdue the flesh through prayer. Subdued flesh produces humility and humility provokes the flow of the Spirit and makes the way for the soul to hear the truth in My Word. Creating worldly success of no eternal significance is a question of doing more work. Righteous success bearing fruit for eternity is a question of doing more Word".

Galatians 5:24
Romans 13:14

158

THE MASTER KEY HOLDER

"What value are all the academic honors to those who do not know My truth? says God. An educated fool remains a fool and all his learning will profit him nothing in the Day that counts. All eternal wisdom is in My Word. Only those who build their bodies with that food can present themselves before Me as acceptable.

Only in the light of the truth in My Word is the true glory of the promises revealed. I am the Master key holder of every key says God. The academics of this world hold keys, the politicians hold keys, the leaders of religious organizations hold keys, Hollywood has its own keys as does the music industry. The leaders of nations have keys also, but all of their keys open doors that lead only to loss. Their keys do not even fit into the lock of the doorway that leads to My Kingdom.

That key is only available to those that seek earnestly after it. Even those that discover it and they are few, will find it difficult to hold on to. You cannot hold it at the same time as any other key. In order to keep it you must be prepared to sacrifice and give up your other keys. This is a conflict for the flesh which will seek only after the things of the flesh. Deep calls to deep from the path of the truth says God, but you will never hear its call if your keys have taken you through the wrong door.

Study to show yourself approved and feed on My living Word and My Spirit will present you with your key. Hold it as the most valuable treasure you will ever receive in the natural realm. Guard it carefully and keep it oiled and polished by walking the righteous path.

In this lies the blessed hope that the key you hold will open the door to the inner sanctum of the bridal chamber on the Day of the wedding celebration. Some keys will lead only as far as the gathering room but will not open the closet that contains the wedding garment.

Some keys that have not been oiled or polished will break off in the lock.

There will be weeping and gnashing of teeth.

What key are you holding says God? The best-looking key in the wrong door is like an empty cloud, nothing will come from it and then it will just fade away and be forgotten".

Psalms 42:7, 112:10
1 Corinthians 2:14
Matthew 22:13
1 Timothy 6:7
Revelation 19:8, 21:1-27
Matthew 25:30
Matthew 16:19
Revelation 1:18

159

LOVE AND PRAYER

"The love between you and your wife is a key ingredient to spiritual harmony says God. You must never abuse it with contentions and strife. There can be no cross words, profanities, no accusations, no manipulations, no coarse joking. Nothing that can disrupt the natural order of things as I have declared them to be.

All of these things are grievous to My Spirit and gain much ground for the enemy. This is not the time for giving ground, we must gain ground every day and walk upright in righteousness and victory. You are precious in My sight and should resolve to be set apart from the world so that My love, My glory and My Spirit can shine through you in everything that we do together.

'Husbands love your wives just as My Son loved the Church' and 'Wives submit yourselves to your own husbands as you do to the Lord'. As simple as it sounds, the lack of understanding and the lack of application of so simple an instruction has brought the world to where it is today. It was the failing that caused the fall and that continues the work of the enemy to this day.

You must understand that nothing you do in the midst of contention can bear any approved fruit. The enemy will continue to try and blind you from the joy and the power of prayer. You have to break through this last barrier says God.

I will not do this for you because it is an act of the will. 'My will be done' can only happen if your will is deliberately put to one side. Walk in this victory and you will find praying together as natural as eating together. After all, it is a more valuable sustenance and more necessary. As I have said previously 'if prayer was your only weapon how much would you pray'?

Again, I point out, the only way you can fight this enemy is on a supernatural level in the realm of the spirit. In the spiritual realm prayer is your only weapon! Any barrier, or resistance that you can feel is the enemy's last bastion of defense. If you understand that you are powerless in the absence of prayer, that you can achieve nothing except by My Spirit, it should be obvious to you that the more the enemy can keep you from praying the less effective you are.

You have to pray about everything at every opportunity. The disciples did not need to do this as they could walk with My Son and just His presence empowered them. Today is different says God. My Spirit empowers you through prayer.

In the 'religious world', prayer has been instilled as the means through which people can ask Me for what they want. It is so much more says God. It is the only line of communication between us through which we can implement the plan outlined in My Word. It is another missing piece, a misinterpreted piece. You cannot walk out the Word or strive for the prize without prayer. No one will gain a full revelation of the truth about the Kingdom without prayer.

As you have learned 'the end is in the beginning' so just as prayer is the beginning of salvation it is also the end of salvation and the 'end' of salvation. You must today embrace the power of this truth and nothing will be the same again.

1 Thessalonians 5:17
Romans 8:26, 12:2-12

Psalms 17:6, 141:2, 145:18
Ephesians 1:18, 5:22-33, 6:18
Luke 6:12, 18:1
Philippians 4:6-7
1 John 5:14
Colossians 3:18-21

160

WOULD YOU WEAR THE COAT?

"If being one of My chosen children meant that you were required you to wear a bright yellow coat every day, would you wear it, or would you be too self-conscious?

If people get uncomfortable in the presence of the words; Jesus, God, LORD, Yahuwah, Yahuwshua, Holy Spirit, what does it say about those people? What is going on inside them that causes an adverse reaction to these life filled words?

They will happily receive words like abundance, prosperity, success, attraction and there is nothing wrong with any of these things. They are all things that I want for My children says God, but I want them to happen in the context of a deep personal relationship between you and Me. That way they will be eternal and come to you without regret.

To have any of these things in the absence of this relationship will bring only stress, strife and eventually destruction.

The reason for this is that the only way these things can be achieved without this relationship, without pursuing My purpose for your life, is if you are in the servitude, knowingly or unknowingly, of the god of mammon.

This is the evil one made manifest and he is fully in tune with his plan, which is to separate us. He wants to drive a wedge between you and Me and to keep you from the fullness of the joy you will find in My love for you.

You find many supposedly successful people that will reveal to you that deep down, they are still not happy or content, that there is still something missing in their lives.

These are perfect examples of what happens to those that end up in the service of mammon. What is worse is that they keep themselves from a deep relationship with Me through their choices which means that one Day, I will have to deny them in the same way that they have denied Me. I will have to say, 'I never knew you'. How sad will that be?

You can change it though. Any person can make a new choice. Acknowledge Me and I will acknowledge you. Invite Me into your life and I will jump in with both feet and love you and protect you. Then together we can create for you the most abundant prosperous, enlightened life you could ever imagine.

We will create success and attract joy at such a level because you can achieve anything through Me because I am your Strength, your Source and your Provider"

Zechariah 4:6

1 Timothy 6:6-19

2 Timothy 2:12

Titus 1:16

Matthew 7:23, 26:70

Proverbs 3:6

161

IS YOUR SILENCE GREAT?

"How many times has someone questioned your position on the Torah, says God? If your answer is a small number, your silence is great. How often are you standing up to defend the position and authority of My Son? If your answer is a small number, your silence is great.

The grace of salvation, the power and joy in My Word, the hope of the Kingdom, these are the building blocks of righteousness declares God. A stable house must contain all of them. The grace of salvation is the foundation and the cornerstone is Christ.

Studying My Word to correctly understand the Torah builds the walls strong straight and true. The hope of the Kingdom puts in the windows and the doors which bring in the natural light which is necessary to fully appreciate the beauty in the truth of My eternal plan for you. My Spirit anoints you to build and provides guidance and strength through revelation.

Those building other houses are building castles of sand in which there is no truth, and no eternal stability. They may adorn them with riches and they may have an appearance of significance but only those built with the anointed ingredients will stand.

If people are not questioning the way you are building, you are building in secret and for whose benefit is that? To be all things to all people is to end up as nothing to any of them. You have to be one thing to any and all people that you come into contact with. You have to be truth manifested in flesh and bone. Think the truth, speak the truth, walk out your daily lives in the truth.

A little compromise, an adjustment to accommodate a sin, is still a lie. A little leaven spoils the whole lump. In other words, any leaven spoils the whole.

This walk is so at odds with the way of the world. It is impossible to appear as they do and still stay on the path. If there is no friction in your life, you cannot get polished. If there is no controversy in your life, you are too much in agreement with what is around you and that will seek to absorb you and make you ineffective.

It is very necessary to stand up in your leadership you cannot lead from the middle or the rear. Proclaim the truth to all who have ears to hear and eyes to see. Where there is no resistance there can be no real progress. Do not seek to blend in. To look the same as the world is to be like the world. You cannot be of the mind to build your own house first and build Mine later.

Build only My house and I will take care of yours. Why would you waste time on a temporal building when My eternal project has already started? If your actions are not building for Me, where is their merit? What is their point?

Can a man reclaim the day and use it again?

There are so many ways for provision they cannot even be counted. You cannot make the way of provision your focus says God. They are My issue not yours. If you make them your issue, they become an outlet for your own strength and will cause you to lean on your own understanding".

Proverbs 3:5-6
Ephesians 1:17-23
Matthew 6:33
Jeremiah 29:11

162

SIGNIFICANCE OF RIGHTEOUSNESS

"Man's understanding only leads to man's rewards says God.

You may have to receive such rewards in the course of being in the world but use them only to reflect My glory working through you.

In order not to fall into the deception *of* being of the world, be sure that anything that you attract is a byproduct of your diligence in promoting My agenda and not your own. The enemy drapes so many in the appearance of approval but how quickly it dissolves away leaving only misery despair and bewilderment.Then they pick themselves up and head off back around the same mountain.

'Seek first the Kingdom' has more substance than anyone can imagine says God. There is no time to let things 'fall into place'. You have to pick them up and put them into place.

An ounce of action will outweigh a 100 pounds of thoughts, plans and ideas every time. A plan of action that is not adhered to and acted upon is like a huge table of food that remains uneaten. It holds all the promise of provision but is only spoiled. Trying to eat it the next day is pointless.

Be relentless in your determination to establish My system, My timetable, My plans. This is where you consistently see the resistance because this step will put you fully in the flow which you know is desirable. The enemy also knows the power of this flow and strives

354

to keep you from it. 'No weapon formed against you shall prosper', applies to those walking in the fullness of My protection says God.

A man walking naked into the battlefield will surely perish.

Those cloaked in the armor of righteousness will surely deflect all the fiery darts of the enemy with the shield of Faith. These are not new ideas to your ears. A man knows that if he stops breathing oxygen he will die. He breathes it every day without fail without reminder. He does not need Me to urge him or encourage him to do more of it or to keep it as a priority. How much more then should you seek to breathe the oxygen of My purpose, for that is breathing life into your eternal being which is not of this world. It is important to understand the significance of your righteousness. If you are not righteous, you are blended in with the rest of the leaven and can bear no fruit. If others misperceive your confidence in the truth as arrogance or self-righteousness, then let them wrestle with their own imperfections. Walking in the truth will shine a light to their feet.

Your calling is clear, now you must walk in it daily and take only the steps confirmed by My Spirit. Yes, it is a long and winding road but there is a joy to be found in the suffering that the human mind cannot be appreciative of. The radiant glow produced through your willingness to walk this path brings a joy to the Spirit.

The suffering is for the flesh and the soul that wrestles against the direction of the Spirit. When your spirit unites with Mine and follows the path of truth you can enter into the realm of unspeakable joy that will one day be the very atmosphere in My coming Kingdom.

Breathe deeply says God, fill yourselves with the power of My Spirit and walk".

Isaiah 54:17
2 Corinthians 4:17-18
Isaiah 55:8-9
Proverbs 3:5-6
1 Colossians 1:24

163

DO NOT GAMBLE WITH TIME

"Address everything in your life that needs addressing says God. Do not teach about finances as a person troubled by debt. Do not teach about food and eat garbage.

Do not teach wisdom and walk in foolishness. Do not preach the goal of the Kingdom and then not strive for it. Do not talk about love and not give it. Do not extol the merits of praise and worship and not engage in it and do not ask for healing without expecting it to be so. Do not ask how to ascend if you are not prepared to come up. Do not ask to be separated and then live the same as before. Do not ask for more anointing, use what you have and that will produce more.

Do not ask Me for messenger angels to assist you and then do not do the work that they can help with. Do not ask to hear My voice and then not act upon My advice. Do not compromise your confidence in Me to appease the lack of understanding of others. Do not waste your time pursuing the things of this world.

Set your heart upon the things of My Kingdom to come and call upon My name and hear the counsel of My Spirit. Let the miraculous flow through your hands as you operate under the Spirit filled power of My anointing.

Shout your message from the rooftops. Let your passion for the truth demand the attention and the audience. I will cause the doors to fly open for you as you stride boldly towards them.

Proclaim My name to the world says God.

Proclaim the safety of My House.

Proclaim the awesome beauty of My coming Millennium Restoration.

Herald the arrival of the Harvester, because the great harvest is soon coming".

Galatians 6:9

Revelation 14:15

Matthew 9:38

164

164 VIBRATION AND FREQUENCY

"Do not let the 'new age fools' of the world monopolize for themselves words like *vibration and frequency*. Let the light of the truth of My Spirit shine on this and you will see how to understand this in Spirit and in Truth.

Your level of effectiveness will be significantly enhanced when you take time to enter into the *fullness* of My Presence says God. The advanced instruction, equipping, teaching and training takes place in the heavenly realm, not the earthly.

The more proficient you become at reaching the desired frequency, the easier it becomes, but you have to press through and be consistent.

The frequencies of the world distort the portals and hinder many sheep from the equipping. When you vibrate only with the frequency of the earthly realm you are confined to the earthly realm. You must tune your own spirit to the frequency that permits access to the heavens by setting up an internal vibration that resonates with the frequency of My Spirit.

To enter into this realm, means to leave behind the realm of the world. This will require the abandonment of the frequencies of the world and that of the flesh, which constantly seeks to subvert your plans by directing your attention back to the unceasing demands of the worlds system. Subdue the flesh and tune in to the Heavenly frequency.

It is time to step boldly forward. There can only be so much preparation as only action begets fruit.

Cultivate an expectation of the miraculous. I will send to those that are ready a new anointing of Spiritual confidence and boldness. You need have no fear of the esteem or knowledge of others. When you are about My business, My supreme confidence goes before you. We will deal with all matters in the supernatural first so that the natural has no option but to fall into line.

Remove any obvious links to world. You cannot operate as holy and set apart if you are part of the worlds agenda.

Everything must be Kingdom focused. To have a different effect, you have to be different. You have to be set apart and permanently conscious of your purpose".

John 1:41
Ephesians 3:19, 4:12-15
1 Corinthians 2:10-16
Romans 14-17
Matthew 16:19

165

HEALING AND FREQUENCY

"Vibrational frequency is so important because without the correct resonance, even when you hear what you know is wisdom, your system will only retain it and take positive action upon it if your receptors were vibrating at a frequency that will cause the knowledge to be absorbed. It is possible to 'hear' but without absorption.

The parable of the sown seed speaks about frequency: The ground into which you sow has to be prepared with the correct level of vibration to promote maximum fertility.

That is why the frequency of the sower is so important.

The same is true with healing. The body manifests a realignment of cells immediately it is instructed to do so. If the cells are allowed later to lapse back into the same disorder, the challenge will reappear.

The seeds of wisdom and healing must be sowed into fertile ground.

Prepare the ground first before sowing and teach the possessor of that ground how to set up and maintain the correct vibration for the seeds to bear fruit.

Prayer in its purest form is the exchange of vibrational frequency from Me to you through the Spirit, the tuning fork of life.

Anything other than the divine vibrational frequency will ultimately result in death and destruction. Righteous resonance promotes restoration and pursues eternal purpose.

This resonance promotes abundant provision says God. Provision of purpose for My people, provision of resources and opportunity in preparation for positioning in My Millennial Kingdom. It is time to emerge from the world's matrix and move to a vibration of supernatural resonance which will allow the equipping, training, sustenance and protection of those called to My assignments.

They are revealed by their frequency says God. If the trumpets of Jericho had sounded the wrong notes, the walls would still be standing today. There is no need to hold auditions, 'deep calls to deep says God.

Vibrational discord is the disqualifier so that there is no requirement for analysis or judgment. Speak only peace in all situations, it is the revealer of frequency.

Do not strive to curse or condemn, that is a perception of warfare from the enemy which causes My people to destroy themselves. Use the warfare of wisdom, building up a vibrational atmosphere of righteousness creates the resonance that will tear down every stronghold, bind every strong man, vanquish powers and principalities for nothing can withstand the power of My Spirit.

Death begets death, but life overcomes all.

Vibrate with Life, speak Life, resonate with the frequency of Life and My glory will explode all around you in an abundance of light".

Matthew 13:1-23
Psalms 42

166

GRAFTED INTO ISRAEL

"The sands of time are running out for My people that are hard of hearing says God. The writing is once again on the wall. My chosen children must return to the land while they can. There will be times of much persecution and of difficulty for My children abiding in the lands of the enemy.

Gentile believers are missing the 'frame around the picture'. Israel is that frame and without it, the picture is both distorted and incomplete. They will never understand the Kingdom without the frame. My chosen ones need the frame to understand the true perspective of Israel. How can a nation prosper if they do not understand themselves? The natural tree requires the grafted in wild branches to produce the choicest fruit. The two components have a cellular dependency on each other says God.

The integration of the two frequencies produces a divine resonance of supernatural power which destroys principalities and powers and combined with My Spirit is an unstoppable force preparing the ground for the return of Messiah.

The picture and the frame have to be complete and everything you do has to have that perspective, or it is a meaningless work of the flesh".

Revelation 21:1-27
Romans 11:11-26

167

RECIPE FOR EMPOWERED LIVING

"Are you taking all of the steps you are supposed to take and following the formula* and the system? Do you make a list of your tasks and then complete them? Does your time have ordered structure or is it chaotic? Is your environment neat and does everything you do ring with excellence?

Are you following a budget and is your record keeping kept up to date on a daily basis? Are you keeping your refreshing times and is there praise and worship taking place every day in your home and work environment? Is diet and exercise a priority for you and are you giving your first fruits?

If the answer to any of these questions is no, you are not keeping a disciplined lifestyle says God. Structure, order, record keeping, and accountability are all Kingdom attributes. The better organized you are the more you will achieve, and you will flow more powerfully in the spiritual realm. The enemy thrives on chaos and indiscipline. If he can cause you to lapse into disarray he can make you vulnerable and his demons will be able to attack you and hinder you.

It is necessary for you to walk in victory all of the time. This requires the diligent focus of a warrior. There is no time for further preparation says God.

This battle has already started, the lines are drawn, and the weapons are being deployed and used. You must maintain an attitude of alertness, of vigilance and walk with the confidence of the anointed but be sure that the cloak of humility is in place as those walking in arrogance will suffer loss.

Anything that deviates you from your purpose must be rejected. Be firm in your focus, be dedicated and committed to your purpose because those of the world lead only to destruction."

*See message #1

Philippians 2:3-4
1 Peter 5:6-7
James 4:6-10
2 Chronicles 7:14
Micah 6:8
Proverbs 11:2

168

LED BY THE SPIRIT

"Everything that you do must be conceived of the Spirit and carried out by the Spirit. If not, it is a work of the flesh and where is the profit in that? Only works of the Spirit produce fruit says God. Faith without works may be dead, but faith with works of the flesh, even more so as they produce fruit that contains strange and dangerous seeds. When these seeds are planted they bring forth division and destruction among the sheep.

Once a plan has been conceived and approved of by My Spirit, be sure to bring the work to completion under that same protection. Any attempt to inject self into the situation will cause the project to fall short of its objective. Stir up and feed My Spirit that is in you. Present to Him a pleasing abode, a clean and functional vessel with which to operate. Multiply His strength, building it up with the sustenance of My Word and your praises and thanksgiving. Take each step with the bold expectation of success worthy of an anointed warrior but remember that the glory is not for you to wear and that humility looks like a precious stone on your foundation.

Do not proclaim an intention without first seeking the discernment of the Spirit within you and remember that 'If God wills' should always be your primary consideration.

The man that does My will is protected by My divine anointing and powered by My Spirit. The man doing his own will is vulnerable and within the grasp of the enemy.

My Spirit is like a protective force field that encapsulates the wearer. The inertia of non-activity causes its effectiveness to diminish. Just like faith without works, these works of the flesh remove the protection altogether. Much worse, the words coming forth from your mouth, words spoken in the flesh will instantly grieve Him and cause the protection to be withdrawn. Many more could have been destroyed if not for My grace.

Prayer before decisions, building up of the Spirit through My Word and taking actions directed by My Spirit, these are the keys to fast and effective progress says God.

There is much to do and much is required of those that know how. Let this be a burden of joy for those with eyes to see and ears to hear".

Ephesians 4:29-30
James 4:13-17
Mark 3:35
Ephesians 4:13-16
2 Corinthians 6:17-18

169

DO NOT CONFUSE PROVISION WITH REWARD

"I can bless you in any way I choose says God. There is no limit to the ways I can bless those that I choose to bless. Be strong and of good courage, seek My face and seek first the Kingdom for which you must prepare.

Your vision must be from the eternal perspective otherwise you will continue to assess things from a temporal worldly viewpoint in which there is no righteousness.

A single righteous task pursued to completion is of far greater value than 100 grand plans of man that promise great wealth and deliver only distraction.

You are entering a season which will only look different to the previous years if you walk a different path.

What now? Will you return to the same thought process where every intention is judged purely by its potential financial profit? What progress did that produce in the past? Are you not pretty much back where you started?

What now? Will you set yourself on exactly the same route that you took before, or will you choose a different path?

To renew your mind, to make changes, to experience the creation of something new you have to be prepared to let go of the old. Stop clinging to the old ideas, the old relationships which bore no fruit.

Move on to new things, to new thinking, to new habits, new ideas.

Let the lovers of money pursue money for the sake of mammon, but you should not be counted among their number unless you want to reap their reward.

My rewards cannot be measured in man's esteem. *Do not confuse provision with reward.* I tell you that no one will see My reward before the judgment, but My provision is in abundance and it is only limited by your assignment and your faithfulness.

When I said 'I will supply your needs' and am 'able to do immeasurably more than all you can ask or imagine' it was to allow you to be confident in My desire that you should be well provided for says God.

The enemy keeps people in poverty by controlling their thinking. You must strive to control your own thinking because it takes work and effort because of the war with the flesh which is striving against you. Make your business My business".

Galatians 6:3-10
Romans 8:6-8
Ephesians 3:20
Philippians 4:19
2 Corinthians 11:1-3

170

THE BIG PICTURE

"I am bringing My kingdom to the earth for 1000 years and then the eternal Kingdom. These are My plans, this is My 'big picture' and it is set in stone. No amount of money, no level of success, no amount of pleasure or deviant behavior, no wars, no peace treaties, no religions, governments, groups or ideas of man will change it in any way.

Man can either embrace it and prepare for it or reject it and suffer the consequences. Only those that believe in My name and then call upon it have the choice anyway. The rest are lost from the beginning.

Many strive to save themselves in their own foolishness with their money, their material success and their soothing words of esoteric nobility, their courses and programs, breakthroughs and discoveries of secrets, but at the end of the day they have nothing says God.

They are a vapor, empty clouds bearing no fruit. When their blink of an eye on the earth is done, they are gone and in the Day to come I will not know them. I will deny them as they have denied Me now. I made My position clear, those who deny Me will be denied by Me.

I will bless those that bless My land and those that do otherwise will be cursed. Heed these words lest you be cursed by the Almighty, these will be mighty and terrible curses."

Revelation 20:1-15
Revelation 21

2 Timothy 2:12
Genesis 12:1-3
Isaiah 62:1-7
Numbers 24:9

171

TREASURE IN HEAVEN

"There are no new answers say God. All you require is obedience to
carry out what you already know. You can never be obedient in the
flesh, it is physically impossible. It follows then by default; you will only
be obedient when carrying things out in the Spirit.

My Spirit is fed and activated by prayer.

There is no alternative scenario. You have to stop considering prayer
from the religious perspective. Prayer is simply *communication*. It is like
your own 'personal instant messenger' that you can use to get your
instructions from the heavenly realm as opposed to the worldly realm.

Any instructions that come from the world can only have one
outcome. This is extremely simple, yet you have still not embraced the
simplicity. If you are not acting on My behalf under the direction of
My Spirit, who are you acting for?

There is no reward in selfishness. There is only loss involved for those
following the ways and whims of the world.

Pursue excellence. Half measures bring half results, but there are
no half rewards. It is not your own rewards that should ever be in
focus anyway. There are so many that do not yet know that they *could*
qualify. There are so many that do not know that they *could* suffer loss.
The truth of the *fruit and rewards* message is powerful, poignant and
necessary for you to hear.

Start putting one foot in front of the other and I will order your steps says God. I will cause you to walk briskly and then to break into a long-sustained run.

Your natural mind wants to bog you down with the worries of this world. That is why you have to work on building new *thought trees*.

I know your heart, but let Me tell you, there are many hearts filled with great honorable intentions that will remain unfulfilled, because they either tried to carry them out in their own strength or just decided that such things were not for them to do after all.

Not by might, nor by power, but by My Spirit, says God.

It keeps coming up because it truly is *the* only way that you can keep living in the natural realm and at the same time make accomplishments in the supernatural realm.

Remember that those accomplishments are *the only ones* of any eternal significance. Nothing that you accomplish on this earth can be transferred into the supernatural.

When you gaze upon your foundation at the judgment, you will see only the treasures that you laid up for yourselves in heaven if indeed you have done so.

Everything of any material value on the earth, will have remained on the earth and will not add one iota to what you lay out before Me as the sum total of your effort in My name.

Anything done by any other name, even your own, will prove to have been futile.

Why would you worry about being accountable to the things of the world before you can be accountable to me? Surely if you follow My instructions I will bless you and attend to your needs."

373

1 Corinthians 3:12-15
Matthew 6:19-21
Romans 8:6-8
Acts 4:12
Philippians 2:5-13

172

THE RIGHT COMPONENTS

"There never seems to be enough time, because you are still operating on your time schedule and not Mine. It is *not* about following rules and laws. It is about understanding the components of a harmonious relationship that bring peace to your soul and cause every day to be fruitful.

There are things that you can do in any relationship which will put a strain on it or cause you to lose it. There are many sheep that have fallen out of relationship with Me as they are so busy building relationships with the world. They are trapped in the service of mammon, trying to get 'just a bit more money' or 'a bit more established' and then they are going to come back to Me.

Fools! For no one knows the Day or the hour, especially those that are not even looking. Even now, with so many signs so perfectly presented, they will reason it away as just the way things are today.

Be a part of the awakening. Do not get caught up with those in slumber. Many of them will not get the chance to wake up before it is too late says God.

Be anxious for nothing for I will never leave you nor forsake you. You have to ask people, 'God is faithful but are you faithful'?

Are they carrying out My will for their lives or their own?

Whose purpose are they on? Theirs or Mine? This is so important for those following church programs and other objectives conceived by man. It will all come to nothing if not ordered by My Spirit says God.

You create your own anxiety and stifle your own potential. With everything that has been revealed to you, with every tool and all the knowledge you have at your disposal, you still lose focus on *who* your source is. You also lose focus on *what* your objectives are, the reason *why* there is only one way to live, *where* you are making the mistakes and *how* you can easily get back on track.

More importantly, you have everything you need to stay on the right track.

It is better that you do not keep coming back saying 'why, why?' or 'please help' and 'how do I? or 'why me'? when you already have all of the answers but will just not subject the flesh enough to give those answers the power to operate in your life.

Do what you know needs to be done and everything else will follow."

Deuteronomy 31:6
Ephesians 6:18
Hebrews 13:5
Mark 13:35-36
Romans 13:11-12
Revelation 3:2
Matthew 26:41
1 Thessalonians 5:6-8
Matthew 25:6-13

173

WHERE IS THE TIME GOING?

"For some people, their weekly use of time looks similar to this;

Total Hours in the week = 168 hours
Time spent sleeping 56 hours
Time spent in church per week- 2 hours
Time spent in prayer per week – 1 hour.
Time spent reading the word per week- I hour
Time spent serving others per week- 1 hours
Total time spend on My business per week- 5 hours

By contrast:
Time spent watching TV per week- 14 hours
Time spent working- 40 hours
Time spent on sports and hobbies- 7 hours
Time spent on socializing/entertainment- 4 hours
Time spent in the car- 6 hours
Total time spent on the world's business 71 hours

Total hours used = 132
Remainder = 36 hours

The things to which people give their time and attention will determine
My choices to bless them says God. I am always willing, but I will
not contradict My own principles. Even in this crude example, the
complacency of many sheep is perfectly illustrated. It would still leave
any person a full 36 hours per week with which to make a difference.

Even if they spend 2 hours per day eating, they would still have 22 hours per week available. Imagine if everyone claiming to walk My path, suddenly devoted 20+ hours per week to doing just that! Imagine the increase in prayer volume! Imagine the level of activity in the spiritual realm. It would create an instant spiritual revival.

Many more would call upon My name. Many would grow up in their faith and mature and start preparing for My Kingdom. Many sick would be healed. Many lost would be saved, just through the increase in supernatural energy. The world would change very rapidly!

The reason this is not happening is very easy to understand says God. My people have become complacent.

They are distracted by the issues of this world. Failing to realize that the issues of this world can only be addressed successfully through an understanding and application of the truth".

Matthew 6:21

174

COMPLACENT SHEEP

"The issues of this world are causing it to stay on track with its destiny which was set and sealed before the beginning. There is no alternative ending to this script.

The two sequels, the 1000-year millennium reign and the eternal Kingdom have already been written.

All that remains is the final casting and allocation of roles.

The sheep are blinded says God. How I long for them to remove the blindness that they themselves have caused to cover their own eyes. Many have so blinded themselves with the glitz and brightness of the world that they do not even see My Word if they pick up the Book.

Will they stand before Me on the Day declaring 'I never had the time, we thought you would let us know'? The signs are here for all to see. They just have to remove their eyes from the world and all of its deceptions for long enough to focus on what is actually happening rather than what appears to be happening.

If these matters referred to the lost, I would have said so says God. I speak of the complacent sheep, those who will still be trying to put a 'new roof on the building' when the time suddenly comes upon them. The reality is soon to be revealed and preparation crushes complacency.

Proclaim the need for thorough preparation now. Everything must be ready. Five of the 10 virgins were found to be short of oil and in the hour to come, it will be too late to get more and no one else can share theirs with you.

This is oil that must be produced in you and through you. After all, you do not hold your lamp in your hand, you are that lamp. The *crushing of self* on a continuous basis will produce in you a continual flow of that precious oil which will keep your flame burning brightly and light your way to the Kingdom and the marriage supper.

Only those with full lamps will find their way to the door in time. Those in the darkness of their complacency will stumble and wander and arriving at the door will find it closed. The reason I describe them as 'foolish' should now be obvious says God. If your eyes fall upon these words, see it as a wake up to shake you out of your complacency.

Look at where your time is going and make the changes you need to make, lest you also become one of the fools", says God.

Revelation 20:4-6
Revelation 19:7
Luke 19:11-26
Luke 12:35-38, 21:36
Romans 13:11
1 Thessalonians 5:6
1 Peter 4:7, 4:18
2 Corinthians 1:8-9

175

PERFECT TIMING

"Press through in your understanding of times and flow says God. It is far easier to stay on My agenda when you are in harmony with My timing. Set your physical clock to work in congruence with My Spiritual clock and not the distorted version of the world.

If your body is conditioned to walk with My Spirit, it will work when it needs to work and sleep when it needs to sleep. These needs cannot be determined by the world's thinking which will always be contrary to My plans.

Use the knowledge that you have been given to infuse life into your bodies and let My Spirit magnify that life.

The enemy gleefully uses poor health often caused by poor nutrition, to reduce the effectiveness of many people. Pharmaceutical medication disrupts the frequencies surrounding many, making it more difficult or even impossible for them to hear My voice.

This is the season for making provision for what is soon to come. You should have an increased sense of urgency in all you do and be ever watchful for the signs. Beware though, do not spend so much time analyzing the deeper meanings in the signs that you neglect to prepare. Be looking for My glory and the clues that lead to righteous expectations.

The signs of evil are in abundance but be sure to let people know the error of spending time in the analysis of evil. Whichever way you hold it up to the light, its nature remains unchanged and must be dealt with in the spiritual realm and not the natural.

There are many sheep who know every detail of every evil thing or conspiracy they discover but who still lack understanding in the truth of My Word.

'Seek first the kingdom' is the instruction. The keys to My kingdom are found in the knowledge and actions of the Truth.

Detailed knowledge of the components of evil may well help to some degree to avoid them, but it builds nothing upon your foundation. Be sure that what you learn to avoid from the enemy camp will lead you to righteous actions with eternal perspective.

The purpose of knowledge should be simply to build faith, leading to action. For Faith without works is dead. Knowledge that does not pertain to your faith is pointless.

There are no rewards at My judgment seat for what you know says God. Only for what you *do* with what you know. Doing nothing with your knowledge also leads to loss.

This further clarifies the necessity of being on My timeline and not that of the world.

Once you overcome the ties to the timing of the world, you will find that you always have more than enough time to do what I require and abundant time for rest, recreation and restoration. My timing is always perfect".

Ephesians 1:17, 4:12

Colossians 1:9-10

176

THE NUMBERS

"Declare the love I have for Israel and extend to her people the olive branch of shalom, be crusaders for truth. Burn off the dross of the lies that blind the eyes of even My sheep who are deceived by the tricks of the age-old enemy.

The battle continues to rage in the spiritual realm and is reflected in the natural realm. Declare to the saints that they have to fight now! Picking up your weapons when the battle is over is of no use declares God. We all know the ultimate outcome, but to the victors go the spoils. You cannot be a victor as a spectator.

You can be part of a cloud of witnesses *or* be one of the victors that has been the object of their witness. It is a powerful and fearful choice, but each must choose.

You shrink from accountability and record keeping for fear that it may reveal the reality of your progress. The sand still runs through the hourglass and stands still for no-one. I will not extend a man's days without purpose says God. Fill the days with purpose and passion to pursue it and enjoy the fruit of the Psalm that declares the satisfaction of long life.

Whenever you have been employed by the world and have been asked to give an accounting of your actions so that your results could be analyzed, you have complied.

How much more should your complicity be assured of with regard to carrying out My tasks? I am the God of order and structure and precision. Everything is about the numbers because I created the numbers. All truth and all creation is contained in My living Word which includes the names and the positioning and the meaning of the numbers.

The numbers never lie. They always reveal the exactness of the situation. A man without accountability is a wild man with no direction. To whom will you choose to be accountable? To the world who offer nothing other than lies leading to ultimate destruction?

Look at the magnificence in the precision, accuracy and infallible life-giving truth in My Word. I worked all these matters through righteous ones who were accountable to Me. Those who remained set apart were blessed throughout their days. Those who chose to be accountable to others, turning themselves from Me were required to pay the price for their disloyalty.

Bring your results before Me each day and let us together consider the fruit of the day and order your steps for the next.

Make no mistake there will be those at the Appointed time who protest ignorance as their defense. 'I did not realize that I could spend time everyday under your wing, under your guidance, asking your direction and your advice. Do not now judge the work that I did in my own strength because I never knew any better'.

Lies, all lies declares God. Ignorance is no defense and the judgment will be sure and fair for everyone. To whom is given much, much is expected.

Consider this; if everything you do is carried out under My anointing, with the guidance of My Spirit and the assistance of My Angels who are My messengers, how much wood, hay or straw would be added to your foundation? Yes, the answer is very obvious.

The fallen nature which abides in all men will rebel at the concept of dedicated and complete service. After all, it can only use you to pursue his plans when you are not serving Me says God. The battle for control of your temple wages incessantly. It does not stop and will never stop until it is ultimately redeemed.

Vigilance is therefore imperative and your records will bring your attention to potential holes in your hedge before they ever appear. Your numbers will help you to maintain your flow. They will cause a buildup of your faith that will increase your confidence in your divine calling.

You will walk more fully in the power of the anointing that is upon you, thus making provision for greater and greater measures of it. It will compel you to keep your armor in peak pristine condition at all times and the edge of your sword will be sharpened to a supernatural level that can cut through anything in the natural or the supernatural.

You will be more easily able to ascend and descend to and from the heavenly realm with the tools and keys that you acquire when you walk in the confidence of your positioning.

Whether by compass or the stars, a man needs to know his numbers to be sure of his positioning. Be only on My timetable, My dates and times. My seasons and appointed times are the only things that have any connection to reality. Everything else is a lie and a deception. Just as you have to know precisely what you do with every unit of money that flows through your possession, you need to have the same diligent accounting of the use of the heavenly currency, your time.

Every moment of time is precious. It is the only resource that there cannot be more of so cherish it accordingly. Know where and how you are spending it.

As you know there will come a Day of reckoning when the fruit of how you spent it will be inspected. Why take the risk of a surprise?

Daily reckoning will allow you to keep a full awareness of your positioning at all times, it will equip you to adjust and to pursue your hope of election with more confidence than ever.

Why would I make rewards available if I would not encourage you to strive to attain them? You cannot enter into the Rest before the appointed time of the rest. On the 8th day comes the eternal rest from everything, until then keep account and work.

I declared to 'bless the work of your hands', not the 'rest' of your hands. I told you to 'work out' your salvation, not to 'rest' it out. I said that 'faith without works is dead' not 'faith without rest'. Yes you should rest from working in your *own strength* which is both fruitless and pointless and leads only to destruction. *No work of the flesh ever produced righteousness*. A seed can only produce after its kind.

Rather present yourselves as willing vessels ready to work under the guidance of My Spirit, to bear fruit that you can offer up as a pleasing fragrance and add to your foundation with gold, silver and precious stones.

Resting inappropriately before the appointed time is like the 'folding of the hands'. It adds wood, hay and straw to your foundation because 'so much as you *did not* do to these the least of Mine, you *did not* do unto Me'.

Wrong action and no action look exactly the same and produces the same fruit.

You have to push through and perfect this so that you can teach it. The tools are all available, just come up and get them, then put them into immediate action".

2 Peter 1:10
Revelation 14:13
1 Peter 5:8
Philippians 2: 12-13
Matthew 25:26-30
2 Corinthians 5:10
1 Corinthians 3:11-23
Hebrews 4:12
Psalms 91:16
Matthew 25:46
Proverbs 24:33

177

A SENSE OF URGENCY

"If you knew that My return was in precisely 1 year, how many of the next 365 days would you want to spend pursuing the lusts of the flesh and the desires of this world? How much time would you want to invest in talking about how to make money for the sake of 'increasing your net worth?

How many houses would you like to acquire? Cars, boats, and other vehicles? How many would you need to own? How much gold and silver would you need to stockpile?

If your day is measured by how much money you made that day or how many people you talked to about making money that day or how much you sold of this or that, what a sad empty day that is.

Let your days rather be measured by the miracles you see, the time spent in My Presence. By the power of My Spirit working through you. By breakthroughs in the Heavenly realm and by making provision for those engaged in My service. By the blessings for the poor, the widow and the children in need.

My nature is to turn all things to good says God. I can bless the smallest seed sown in humble expectation of the miraculous and create from it a mighty tree of blessings and restoration to help those in need and there are many.

Use every resource and talent you have available and I will also send more. Everything is possible through My Spirit".

1 Corinthians 2:5

178

ACTING ON KNOWLEDGE

"Knowledge that is not acted upon is like rain falling upon ground in which nothing has been planted says God. No plan, no purpose, no grand declaration of intent is of any value while it remains only on the paper or in one's mind.

Noah did not start work on the ark the day before the rain came.

If you plant a *thought tree* and then do not 'water it', the tree dies. Remember that the old tree only dies when the new tree's root system takes over and strangles the root of the old one.

You cannot walk in righteous humility if you say one thing and do another. Let your 'yes be yes', is the admonition. Not let your 'yes be maybe' or 'when you get around to it'.

There will always be distractions.

The key is whether or not you allow yourself to be distracted by them. Remember that the worlds systems teach: 'get done everything that pertains to the world; to business, to making money, to sports and hobbies and to have fun. Then, if there is any time left, you can use that for 'doing good', going to church and spending time with spiritual matters.

Then what happens tomorrow? When their lives are suddenly ended, and the Day comes for reckoning?

You cannot set an example unless you are *being* an example says God.

Talk is cheap, it is easy to write things down when you have a gift for writing things down, but *you have to act* on what you write and what you say.

Exercising obedience is never easy because it always conflicts with the flesh. It still has to be done though, there is no alternative. Diligent obedience is the call. Not occasional or sporadic, but diligent. Only through the consistent application of food to the root systems of the new *thought trees* can they thrive, grow, and finally kill off the old.

No number of different versions of accountability sheets and other record keeping systems are of any value unless they are utilized on a daily basis. The actions upon them will never become habits unless you force your own will into subjection.

You must be able to become a co-ruler with Me in your own domain before you can become a co-ruler in My domain.

You will not see people ruling and reigning in the Millennial Kingdom that were ruled by their own wills in their time on earth. All will have to fight this battle says God, but esteem and reward is reserved for those that are victorious and who overcome".

Luke 19:17-19
Acts 1:3
Matthew 5:37
Hebrews 11:16
1 Peter 5:9
Revelation 3:12, 3:21, 22:12-14
1 Peter 1:17-21
2 Corinthians 1:12-22

179

THE EXPECTED OUTCOME

"Back then to diligence, focus, obedience, all the things that the flesh wants to be opposite to. Unless of course whatever you are doing causes you to be diligently focused and obedient to the things of the flesh. Then watch how easily it all falls into line.

The key is the expected outcome of the effort, says God. Is it fruit bearing of millennial and eternal consequence, or material, fleshly and temporal? Efforts towards the latter are futile says God, they create nothing but straw and his companions.

It appears that you are once again seeking the 'magic bullet'; the one ingredient that I have kept back from you until this time. There is no such ingredient. You have been in possession of all the tools for quite some time. Tools are of no use to the idle craftsman. A good tool that is used inappropriately will never produce the desired result. The tools also have to be used in the correct sequence. You cannot place the screw first and then drill the hole.

Everything has its proper time, place and application and you must stick to the approved sequences.

Keep being aware of the battle. It is unceasing because you are living in the land of the enemy. If the battle ceases, you have either surrendered or My Son has returned and taken victory.

This is not what the human mind wants to hear. They are mostly waiting for 'heaven on earth'. That is not an option, so do not waste time or effort in anticipation of it. Keep moving forward in faith.

Maintain an attitude of *obedient excellence in all things* I have shown you. Subdue the flesh and build up and encourage the Spirit.

You must push through the natural resistance to being righteous, that is always uncomfortable in appearance. However, if you are set apart for long enough, even the things of the world start to feel unnatural and that is your goal.

Pray about every decision before you make the decision says God. Most people fall short in this regard. They make the decision first and then they pray about it and ask Me to bless what they have already decided to do. Of course, if a child asks Me for bread, I do not hand him a rock. My provision is far superior, My plans far more effective than anything that man can conceive".

Ephesians 4:13-16
Isaiah 55:8-9

180

THE TRUTH IS THE TRUTH

"Faith without works is dead says God. I will bless the work of your hands not the work of your minds. I provide you with the talents, the seeds, the ideas, you must be good stewards with them and take the action. Just take the steps and I will meet you in the field.

Pick up the phone, I will give you the words. Raise the pen and I will guide you what to write. Press upon the doors, I will cause the right ones to open. Every action you take will be fueled by My Spirit while you keep your focus on My beloved Son. He is the author of your faith, hold tightly to Him in all things.

Start casting your fishing lures into the stream, I will cause the right ones to bite. The fish feed best when the stream is flowing. Prayer creates that flow and sustains it. If your lives reflect truth, that is all you require for any project.

My Word says that 'the truth will make you free' and you will see that Word in its purest form, as resting in the truth will make you free from the need for any form of manipulation or exaggeration in order to attain success.

The Truth is the Truth.

There are many that need to be helped today and My love has the answer for them. Show boldness in your expectation of gaining support from others, walk in the divine authority I have provided for you. When your focus is purely on bringing benefit to others and glory to My name, I will remove barriers and soften hearts. Where you tread, I will bless", says God.

Hebrews 12:2
1 Corinthians 13:12-13

181

CONSIDER EVERY THOUGHT

What then should be the focus of the renewing of your mind? Pray without ceasing was the exhortation. Only through divine connection can you build the thought trees that will produce fruit of eternal significance. To produce new thought trees with the part of your mind that is tainted by the flesh will just bring more thorns and more poison.

Consider each thought and its relevance to My purpose for your life. If the thought would lead to a word or an action that is outside of My revealed purpose, you must take that thought captive and turn it over to Me says God.

This will be your strength in staying on track and on purpose. This is why your days have to be ordered and planned in accordance with My Spirit. You have to give your mind the track to run on and then carefully select only the thoughts that will keep it on the track.

A mind allowed to enter the day with no track, will run here and there, out of control, often with severe consequences. If you have a job to go to every day, you usually have the track laid out for you by the company. You have to rise at a certain time and take your pre-planned route to get to the place of employment by a set time.

Then you have to spend your day carrying out the tasks that you have been allocated. You know what you will be doing. You are not permitted to give energy or focus to things that would not benefit your employer during the time specified for work.

Next, you take your preplanned route back home again. This is an example of where your thinking is being controlled or heavily influenced by others, but at the same time, it demonstrates that man *can override his own will and control what he thinks about if the incentive or reward is considered worthy enough.*

Consider the value of the rewards to come and think and act accordingly. There is no time to wait and see or 'I will just do *this* first and then change'. You do not know the *day or the hour* says God. There will be many who will be found in the process of *getting ready* to make things different. Just completing this task or that before setting their own will to one side. The message to them is simple: too late is too late. Time waits for no man and neither will judgment".

2 Corinthians 5:10-11
Romans 14:9-12
2 Corinthians 10:5
Revelation 14:13
Daniel 12:2-3
Revelation 20:1-15, 21

182

TREASURE YOUR WIFE

"This is a simple situation to address. If you follow My ways and My commands everything that you ask for is easily attained.

The way a man behaves toward his wife is very important to Me says God.

It is a measure of his willingness to follow My Word and My calling. If a man will not revere his wife above all earthly things, how will he ever revere his King above even his wife? It is My joy that every wife should be loved completely. She should feel so blessed by the attention of her husband that the enormity of the love is almost overwhelming in the physical realm. How much more powerful is the knowledge that My love for her is even greater?

My love produces a light so powerful that it completely surpasses the glitter of the trinkets and baubles of the world. It is brighter than any diamond, more elaborately woven than any earthly garment. This Love reflects the beautiful tapestry of My robes, My anointing and the light of My spirit. It offers to all that have eyes to see something that the world can never provide.

It is all part of a spiritually aligned marriage. A diamond cannot polish itself. Your responsibility is for the polishing and safekeeping. If a man cannot properly care for this, the most precious earthly gift he can ever receive, how would he qualify to be trusted with anything in the

Kingdom to come? Make no mistake, there will be many that have a high expectation of the rewards they have earned, that will suffer loss due to their neglect of their wives.

'As Christ loved the church' is a hard command, but a command it remains. Can your right leg take a walk without the company of its partner on the left? Can your brain receive a message that your heart doesn't hear? Can the eye see something that the soul doesn't picture? A husband doing anything independently of his bride is equally unprofitable.

A team has to be a team. Two horses going in opposite directions will go nowhere. Point them both on the right path and they cover much ground swiftly. The princess instinctively knows what is required of her in the presence of her prince. It is triggered automatically without pressure or prompting.

Only when her delicate nature is damaged by neglect will she adopt the abrasive contrary nature of the women of the world. The wise man knows the spiritual significance of these principles. Those that are unprepared for the reverential love required for an anointed, Spirit filled wife, should rather not marry in the first place for there will be judgment for those that neglect 'so great a gift' says God.

There is nothing worthier than a called servant walking in humility with the might and power of My Spirit welling up within him".

1 Corinthians 13

183

THE COMFORT ZONE

"Whenever you try to make progress, there will always be more things trying to keep you either where you are or back to where you were before. Therefore, moving forward in life will always feel more challenging than just staying where you are or going back to where you were, says God.

If you are not feeling any resistance, you are in the 'comfort zone' and that is a dangerous place to be. The comfort zone is the easiest place to suffer loss and reversal, because it causes you to let down your guard. You are in a far better condition when you can feel the resistance to your progress. Knowing that it is there will cause you to be vigilant and make sure at all times that you are watching for those people and things that would prevent you from achieving your goals.

Look at the people that you spend your time with and interact with the most. Do they contribute positively to your life? Do they add value? Do they encourage? If any of these responses are negative, make sure that you either cut that association or at least reduce the amount of time that you spend with them.

You have to continually feed your mind with the right information and being surrounded by negative contrary people does not benefit you in any way. Sometimes, due to family situations you have no option, but even then you can consciously avoid conversations that give people license to sow negativity".

Revelation 3:1-2, 14-20,
Zephaniah 1:12
Proverbs 1:32

184

FOCUSED ACTION

"Intentions without actions are like empty clouds says God. They look great, they puff themselves up and present the promise of so much. Then they fritter away, having produced absolutely nothing. This occurs because the heart of the cloud is empty, it was an intention without substance. The substances required to make an intention valid are faith and action. By adding these to your intentions, miracles can happen. It is important that both elements are present.

Acting on your intentions without the faith to believe that you will achieve your objective is a waste of time. Where doubts exist, failure becomes a possibility and therefore in itself an intention.

Having the faith and not putting it to work through correct actions is just as unproductive. As it is written, 'faith without works is dead'.

There are so many people with great intentions that are useless to them because they will either take no action or they doubt the outcome, nullifying any effort they make.

Combining faith and actions together produces focus.

Once you achieve focus you will always have the strength to follow through on your intentions. The equation is therefore simple: Identify the intentions that line up with the pursuit of your purpose. Discard any that do not. Apply focus to these intentions and then through faith and action combined you will witness sudden and immediate results.

You cannot fail to move forward towards your purpose because failure as a possibility cannot exist in the absence of doubt.

Focus eliminates doubt and it is important to focus on just one intention at a time until the intention is completed.

You need to get clear on the intention and seek the support of My Spirit to cleanse your mind of any distraction.

Pray for supernatural focus and wisdom to apply to your intention and take action".

James 1:5-8
Colossians 3:2

185

THE MOST IMPORTANT MEASUREMENT

"Quit worrying about 'over-spiritualizing' things says God. *What* or *who* are you worrying about? Are you afraid that your obvious love for Me will scare people away? Are you worried that people may think that spirituality and business should not mix? Do not fall into that trap says God. This is a huge deception.

You know full well that you are in a battle that cannot end until the Judgment seat. Every choice and action you take based on that choice will have an impact on your outcome. If you want your outcome to be incredible you have to constantly remind yourself of the fact that all matters are Spiritual matters. As such, you are either following Me or you are in deception and are following the enemy.

Being 'on purpose' at all times means having the belief to boldly declare that purpose and following it. Give no heed to the opinions or criticisms of mere men. After all they will not be there when you meet with Me to discuss the rewards.

The measurement of 'what did I place upon my platform today?' is far more important than any other measurement. This should be obvious to you as it is the only measurement that has any eternal consequence. Are you living for the present moment or for the eternal picture?

This is a distinction that many people have no perception of. The mere knowledge of it can cause the lost to believe! It can cause those that believe to be overcomers as they realign their intentions with a purpose that has an eternal perspective."

Psalms 118:6
Matthew 10:28
1 Corinthians 3:12-13
2 Corinthians 5:10
Revelation 3:21-2

186

I WILL ORDER YOUR STEPS

"Structure is a good thing says God. It keeps the mind organized and focused and minimizes distractions. An unstructured life is very easily swayed all over the place and will lack focus.

Consult with Me daily and let Me order your steps.

Do not go into each new day blindly hoping that it will just unfold. This will cause you to waste much of the day figuring out what you want to do next.

Let My Spirit guide your every move and decision and do not lean on your own understanding. Be careful what you allow into your spiritual realm. Remember that the eyes and ears are gateways to your inner man. Fill your soul with the things that are good. Cut out the noise of this world. Get yourself into a frequency of supercharged spirituality. Hear My voice and see My hand in all that you do.

If you start a project, be committed to finish it. Be in the habit of asking for guidance before everything that you do.

Do everything 'So as to Me' otherwise, why would you want to do it anyway?

We are talking about a new lifestyle. You are either a person who prays or you are not. You are either a person who keeps records or you are not. You are either a person who by nature saves money or not.

They are all choices, says God.

The choices you make are made manifest by your actions and the results that they bring. If you do not like the results, you have to change your actions. In order to do this, you must make different choices. In the Kingdom to come, there will be tasks to be carried out on a daily basis, things to be organized and followed through with. These 'habits' therefore, will not suddenly change at the resurrection.

It is something to be perfected where you are right now. It is the only way to master the separation from the world. You have to be in control of your time and your resources, otherwise you end up serving unrighteous mammon. All the teachings I have provided make it possible to be *in* the world and not *of* it. You just have to do the things the way that I told you to do them and not let the flesh get in control".

Colossians 3:24-26
Proverbs 3:5-6

187

CHOOSE YOUR THOUGHTS WISELY

"Focusing the mind on things of goodness and purity is the key to clear thoughts says God. A mind encumbered by the lusts of this world is unable to think clearly. This renders it incapable of clear accurate communication with My Spirit which will cause the thinker to be ineffective or even to be deceived.

That is why I tell you to incline yourself towards the things that are beautiful, decent, loving and righteous.

Protection of the *thinking part* of your body is equally as important as protection of the physical parts of your body.

It can 'poison' your system just as surely as eating the wrong food, drinking the wrong drinks or speaking the wrong words.

While they are still thoughts, words can be taken captive and rendered null and void before being released.

Filling your spirit with wonderful powerful anointed thoughts will empower your physical body in a way that you have never experienced.

It is however a challenging task because the enemy also seeks dominion over your thinking, so you must be vigilant and consistent.

Remember that this is a choice, so you should choose your thoughts wisely".

Philippians 4:8
2 Corinthians 10:5

188

WALKING IN RIGHTEOUSNESS AND TRUTH

"There is a *completeness* in being a true believer says God.

It requires an elevated level of both discipline and obedience. This is not a burden, as it is so grounded in love, that the yoke is light. Only by removing the veils formed by the corruption of religion and the evil self-centered desires of man, will the full brightness of My light be revealed.

The Spirit within you naturally embraces truth so these are not hard lessons to learn, just different in the details. The message never changes; it becomes more powerful and more accessible through the application of pure Truth.

There is a new awakening coming and a restoration taking place and only those with eyes to see and ears to hear can participate. Never has 'study to show yourself approved' been more significant. There are many eloquent educated scholars with vast memories and instant recall who can recount every detail of anything they have read. However, salvation of the spirit was always only about being open to receive My gift. Salvation of the soul on the other hand, is not about what you know; it is about what you do with what you know.

I do not want you to waste time proving to others why they are wrong. Just one glance around the world which surrounds you is more than enough evidence of that. Demonstrate what is right by *walking* in righteousness and truth. Follow My ways on My agenda on My timeline, keeping My commands and carrying out My will. This will provide the overwhelming evidence that will change hearts", says God.

James 4:17
Ephesians 2:8-9
1 Peter 1:7-9

189

RENEW YOUR MIND

"How much more joy is there in the presence of God than in the presence of the imagination and foolish pursuits and plans of men?

If you are spending more time with the whims and fantasies of men than you are with Me, what does that say about where your passions lie?

The ship's captain has to set the course; he has to know his destination before he sets off. Then he has to continually chart that course and check his position relative to his objective. If he fails to maintain his vigilance, if he is inconsistent in checking his charts and recording his progress he will invariably lose his way.

If you find that you are going through the same situations over and over, you can surely see that nothing is ever going to change in this regard unless you do. This is the way that I want things done so it is you that has to change says God. You have to change through the renewing of your mind.

If you truly think differently, the words you use will be different. The actions you take will be different. Your goals will be different. They will all lead you inexorably on the path to fulfilling your eternal destiny. Why waste time with the temporal?

It was you who perceived and understood that; 'If eternity is real, you are already in it'. Once that level of revelation is attained, to then continue with the temporal is fruitless. Temporal focus is only for those lacking revelation regarding their eternal positioning. You must now use your 'new thinking' to pursue your eternal purposes.

To bring hope where there is none, to be an advocate for the disadvantaged and the discarded, to help others to connect with their divine purpose as the purposes of this world are of no consequence.

Make your decisions based only on their eternal impact.

This can never be measured based on a perceived inconvenience or interruption in your own equilibrium. If your life looks 'well balanced' in accordance with the world's perspective you have obviously slipped back into the box of conformity. There is no glory to My name through those conformed to the ways of this world.

Use this new thinking consistently in your life. Change is as simple as changing your thoughts. Changing your thoughts is not a question of adding new thoughts and expecting them to coexist with the old thoughts. No, the new thoughts have to *replace* the old thoughts, permanently.

The old thoughts have to be abandoned and completely eliminated. Every time the old thoughts try to resurface [and they will] they have to be captured, stopped in their tracks before they can result in an action. Then they are replaced by the new thought and acted upon immediately which will strengthen the root system of that new thought.

This process will ultimately cause the complete demise of the old thought system. This may not be news to you but be careful that you have not simply increased the size of your forest of thought trees. If you have planted your new trees alongside the old ones and have not tended the new ones consistently enough to strengthen their roots, the old ones will keep sprouting new leaves and even dropping new seed, says God.

The level of thinking required to prevent this takes focused effort and *separateness* from conventional thinking.

Every meal you eat should be a celebration of life. It should be a time of thanksgiving and joy and never be taken for granted. When were you last truly grateful for the blessing of a meal? There are so many that would love to share in your favor and yet you seldom give them a thought.

How aware are you of My plans, My calendar, My festivals, My cycles? All of these things should be of more focus to you, otherwise I would not be revealing them to you.

Eliminate any thinking that portrays you in a worldly perspective. Walk in the confidence that you are hand-picked ambassadors in My service. You are to truly be a light to the world. Not a flicker or a glimmer, but a light. The light that I provide to the earth never diminishes.

I cause the earth to move to promote rest and growth, but the light is always present as should yours be. This is only possible through Spirit based thinking. Earthly, temporal thinking always has the root of darkness as the fallen nature of man is at its core. You must rise above the fallen nature and center your focus on Me and let the Spirit guide your thoughts. This has to be a voluntary surrender of your flesh as We will not take control by force, that is the way of the deceiver.

Chart your course, set sail with supreme confidence and consistently monitor your positioning. Life will look very differently to you very quickly because you will be regarding it from an eternal perspective.

In every believer, I have created a plenteous tree of magnificent potential. Now tend it properly, watch the succulent fruit burst forth. Eat, share, and distribute seeds to others who are ready to plant and develop their own trees. I speak of these things to you today, in the knowledge that once you read these words, you will understand that you are ready to embark on this journey.

There have been many false starts and foundering, but these have just equipped you better. Any recent intensity of enemy activity is their final attempt to dissuade you from the truth. Step forward in boldness, maintain constant contact with the Spirit.

The only way to build up the spirit within you is through interaction with My Spirit that I set apart for your instruction.

Self-instruction leads only to self-destruction. This is a law and must never be overlooked.

Personal development can be a valuable thing but only when combined with the truth of My Spirit will it lead to glory.

You have nothing to fear from the scoffers says God. Be a beacon, shine brightly and never permit the darkness suffered by others to negatively impact your purpose. If they try, you can always increase the brightness of your light!

Darkness is darkness and all the same. None of it can stand in the presence of true Light. The world cries out for true wisdom. They keep searching but in vain, for they do not really know *what* it is they are searching for.

Only the actions of right thinking, holy and set apart children will lead them on the right path. Those actions are the physical manifestation of the truth of My Word walked out in loving humility, which is the only *true power* available to an earthly person in a physical body.

All other illusions of power are corrupt.

My thoughts, words and wisdom are both divisive and decisive. They cut to the heart of the truth and separate those called from the deceptions of the world. Share them in spirit and in truth, with the humble self-assuredness of those that 'know that they know'. Be prepared to witness a massive outpouring of power and grace and glory and the time for divine positioning is upon you.

The plans of men are being set aside and those counted among My true servants, few though they may be, are entering into a time of unprecedented ascendancy that will confound the so-called wisdom of this world".

Matthew 5:14-16
Hebrews 4:12
1 Corinthians 2:2-16

190

PRAY PLAN EXECUTE

"If you marry yourselves to the world, you will end up behaving as the world does says God. You need to utilize situations that permit you to maintain your separation from their ways.

In other words, do not settle for doing business in the way of the world. Approach your business with a supernatural spiritual mentality. Expect to produce supernatural results that are not possible using the world's systems.

If you measure everything against their metrics how can you expect to be any different?

Pray, plan and execute. That is the step-by-step system that will work says God. Without the prayer first, you are planning in your own strength which is a waste of time and will not bear fruit.

All of the prayers and plans are pointless if you do not discipline the flesh to carry them out to completion.

Good intentions produce no fruit; neither do they gather rewards.

Your mind is capable of producing an output of wisdom and productive activity that will astonish you, but only when it is being controlled by My Spirit. That is why you have to become disciplined like an athlete.

Your ascendancy over your own flesh has to be total and complete as it will constantly seek to subvert your intentions. It is important to win this struggle for those that control the flesh walk in victory".

1 Corinthians 9:24-27

191

ACT WITH MILLENNIAL INTENTION

"The most specifically detailed plans are of no consequence if they are not acted upon says God. What is the point of a 90-day plan, or five years, or seven years? A plan with true Kingdom intention will be a plan that extends into My Millennial Kingdom soon to come. Any plan that is designed to get you to the 'next level' is based on man's fallibility and lack of faith.

You take the steps with 'Millennial intention' and I will take you to the levels that you need to be at.

There is a joy to be found in discipline and obedience, in maintaining ascendancy over the flesh and walking by the guidance of the Spirit dwelling within you.

Always be focused on consistency, constantly applying My principles and the power of My word to everything that you do. It is time to live the true set apart life of a believer, where you are operating in the world without being of the world. This requires diligent application of all the things you have been learning.

You all have your schedules, your talents, your projects. Now you need sustained focused action. Only My Spirit can put it all together through you using your Millennial mindset. If the worldly mindset of greed, gain and self-gratification is given a foothold, you will remove yourself from the blessings. Beware of even a little leaven.

I delight in excellence, but it must be measured against My standards, not those of the world. Excellence is demonstrated by example.

Speaking of it and writing about it is one thing, but *being* it is an altogether different thing and the only one that has any power.

I call upon you to be excellent in everything you do. Have excellence in marriage, be excellent stewards of your resources, demonstrate excellence in your business pursuits, speak with excellence. This kind of excellence brings peace, harmony and healing to all situations and it can never be questioned or criticized. It shines My light into even the darkest situations.

Many of My people are returning to understanding and they are seeing for the first time the true depth of the deceptions of the world. They are finding a hunger for the truth. There is only one source of that Truth, My life giving Word lived out by example in the lives of My children. Transcending barriers of race and religion, restoring My family values, rediscovering the importance of community and family life. People need to witness the example of excellence in this lifestyle.

Pursue good health and prosperity through feeding the body with life-giving nutrients and feeding the mind and the soul with the life-giving sustenance of My word.

Apply My standards to everything that you do and I will bless the work of your hands abundantly beyond your perception. You just need to be sure not to construct barriers that block the flow of the blessings. These are created when you decide to impose your will or ideas on any situation.

My blessings cannot flow through man's will. Not by might, nor by power, but by My Spirit", says God.

Revelation 20:4-5
Ephesians 4:26-27
1 Peter 2:11-12
Zechariah 4:6

419

192

SEPARATE

"To declare yourself as *separate* from the world and then continuing to live exactly as the world does is pointless says God. There is no separation for those who choose to remain as the world is.

As I have said to you before, if everything about your life looks the same as that of the people in the world, there is no difference. You are being a worldly person.

To be set apart from the world means to give up interest in the things of the world and to be interested only in matters of eternal importance. It means to cease to be interested in self-gratification and self-obtained 'security' and to be interested in serving and helping others to the extent that your actions bring glory to My name."

1 John 2:15
Matthew 5:16, 6:1
1 Timothy 6:11
2 Timothy 2:22

193

TIME FOR BOLDNESS

"If Prayer Was Your Only Weapon, How Much Would You Pray?

I ask you that question as an important sign says God. Communication leads to righteous action, and to blessings and even rewards. It all begins with the communication. Set aside the will, allow the Spirit to be the guide and the mentor.

You cannot see what I do in the natural realm, only the spiritual. You cannot see into the spiritual realm through the eyes of the world, only through the Spirit that is placed within you.

Just as you have learned about water, that it has to be balanced and energized to flow and bring life. It is the same with the Spirit within you. The more you are removed from the impurities and toxins of the world, the more life there is in your spirit. This is the level you have to be at to be effectively led by My Spirit.

The less there is of you, the larger and more powerful I will become through you. Now is the time for boldness. While boldness in your own strength leads to destruction, boldness in My name leads to victory.

Why do people spend endless hours focused on the temporal meaningless things of the world and yet they spend zero hours in trying to help or be a blessing to others? The more of your time that is dedicated to producing fruit that will fill the souls of your brothers and sisters, the more joy you will find in your own lives".

Philippians 2:3

421

194

THE DECEITFULNESS OF RICHES

"The worries of the world and the deceitfulness of riches have become your own flag says God. You constantly worry about paying this, and taking care of that, structuring a deal here and a deal there, locking things in, putting things on a secure footing.

These are all terminologies connected to the worries.

Only those embracing the worries will seek comfort in these agreements with men. Are they truly any source of comfort? Has there ever been an agreement in the past that produced any comfort for you? They are only as true as the words on the paper and if they are not My words, then where is the truth?

Doing what you are supposed to do is all that is necessary to produce resources to handle any situation that arises. I have never varied My position. I remain the same, every day all the time. Most of you however are twisting this way and that, trying to get yourselves into the right 'shape' to 'fit' into the situations that you are busy creating to solve your problem.

The only problem you have is disobedience. There is nothing missing that would keep you from walking in the fullness of your calling, you have it all at your fingertips.

It will never be a question of you needing to be 'at a certain place' from a worldly perspective before you can be effective in the Spirit.

You can only be effective in the Spirit when you are prepared to leave behind the things of the world.

Entering into the Spirit is just like the eye of the needle. All the worldly perceptions of success and material gain cannot go through.

You have to see that they can play no part in the process. The concept of 'when I have money I can be a blessing to others', is just a lie from the enemy. It is a deception because it contradicts My word.

The essence of it sounds like 'once I have served mammon, then I can serve God'. What nonsense is that? Serve Me first and I will cause mammon to be your servant.

Focus on Me and you will see mammon under your feet. Focus on mammon and all you will see is more mammon and you will surround yourself with his evil cohorts, which will blind you to the truth and keep you from walking in the fullness of your purpose. Thus, the 'deceitfulness of riches'. See how the 'worries of the world' cause you to focus on mammon and so the cycle continues.

The only way to break that cycle is to obediently pursue the things that I have placed in your hands.

'Seek first the kingdom' says God. There is nothing that needs to be added. Then your hearts will be filled with the joy that you seek.

Knowing that you are in harmony with My plans and purpose is what brings the hope and the expectation of fulfillment".

Mark 4:19
Hebrews 13:8

195

THE FOOD OF LIFE

"My anointing can produce a divine calm confidence says God.

A confidence that permeates into your spirit, fueled by the love of My Spirit. This *inner peace* is fueled by My Living Word and by the continued communication between us when you pray without ceasing.

In the space created through this peace, you have the ability to see things clearly for what they really are. Through My Spirit, you will walk with discernment at a supernatural level that will provide you with a unique advantage in negotiations and decision making. This peace permits you to immediately see the correct course of action in any situation.

Be sure to eliminate any participation of the flesh, for it will only cause you to believe a lie and your path will then become obscured and distorted.

Your body becomes whatever you put into it most. If you put into it high quality nurturing nutrients with live ingredients containing life, it will flourish. If you put it to work through exercise, it will flourish, if you do the opposite you will produce the opposite results.

The same can be said of your spirit and soul. If you feed them on a worldly diet of bad news, conspiracies, fantasy, unholy images, the vain imaginations of men, lusts of the flesh, the deceitfulness of riches and the worries of this world, it will produce stress and fear. A mentality of lack and scarcity then prevails. This in turn causes *reactions*, rather than *responses*. Then infirmities appear in the physical realm causing more focus on that, than on the solution which is the Life in My Word says God.

My Word is the food by which all things can be sustained, healed and nurtured. My Word is life itself.

Those that feed on it will thrive abundantly, for to feed on it is to digest it and act upon its truths and instructions with unwavering faith. The more the Word is consumed, the bigger and stronger your faith will become.

Look at how the world assaults My people, physically and spiritually. It is all designed to allow the evil one to gain control over them and to keep them from the truth.

You are called to shine light upon the truth".

Romans 8:5-9, 13:14
Galatians 5:17

196

WHAT DOES IT PROFIT A MAN?

"How does it profit someone who claims to know Me, to know My Name and to understand My standards for love and righteousness and yet he lives just the same as the world lives?

A person that is called to be holy must be 'set-apart'. If this is not the case, he is not living such a life and his choices will always be tainted by the world.

Choices should be made based on the Word, not the world.

Take every decision and weigh it against the wisdom of My Word says God; if there is a contradiction, the decision is made for you then by wisdom.

True wisdom comes through making decisions out of the Spirit and not out of the will. It is impossible to be both faithful and willful at the same time because they are the antithesis of each other.

Only those prepared to set aside their own will, can aspire to wisdom. Otherwise, from the willful man you will receive only 'opinion'.

Wisdom and opinion look similar at first glance, but opinion usually glorifies the man, whereas wisdom glorifies the Spirit and My name.

A man that is wise in his own eyes is an opinionated fool. Any man who sets himself up as 'wise', is not, else he would not have elevated himself.

Wisdom and humility are married to each other and one cannot exist without the other.

This holds a great truth; a 'wise' arrogant man is a deceiver; a humble fool is but a fool; *you will know them by their fruit* is an unfailing test. It is also powerful for self-analysis says God.

Keep your eyes on your own fruit as this is the easiest measure of your own progress.

Remember, temporal fruit is of no eternal significance. View everything through your Millennial mindset as this gives the subject true perspective. If the outcome of a particular course of action does not carry over into the Kingdom, what is the point in pursuing it?

Time is precious and should be treated as such. You have discovered the significance of balance and harmony at the spiritual and cellular level. The more aware of this you remain and the more you pursue its knowledge and perfection, the better equipped you will be to tap into the vast well of supernatural strength that exists within the Spirit within you.

It requires an understanding of and a pursuit of holistic excellence; this is the only path that offers the hope of being set-apart and supernatural power.

It is not the power that is the key, it is My Spirit wielding the power through you that transcends your perception of human potential. Power wielded by men only ever brings destruction and sorrow.

Power wielded by My Spirit brings love, joy and hope and the peace that all men long for in their hearts.

The more you become set apart, the more you become more Word-full and less will-full, the closer I will draw to you.

Then I can use your light to shatter the lies of darkness and deception".

2 Corinthians 1:12
1 Peter 1:15-16
Proverbs 4:5-9, 8:12-21
Galatians 5:22-23

197

SHABBAT EXPLAINED

"Shabbat is a celebration of being 'set-apart' and a rest from all labors. A time for reflection, restoration and renewal. If it contains elements of the other days, it is no longer set apart.

You cannot experience this restoration unless you are prepared to fully set the day apart on My terms and not yours says God.

It must be special and unique and not resemble the other days. How can you show someone a set apart day if that day looks the same as the others? It is no longer set apart, it is just the same. Set-apart means to be different to, to appear different, not to appear the same.

It is the same thing with those that are called to be set-apart from the world.

You have to be different to the people of the world, you have to appear different and not be the same as the people of the world. Otherwise you are one of the people of the world.

My Son walked on the earth and was *in* the world, but He was set-apart, nothing in Him was *of* the world. This is how you need to be also, to be set-apart. Every decision has to be made with the counsel of My Spirit and the mind of Christ, otherwise it is a decision of the flesh which keeps you tied to the world.

You still perceive financial prosperity and abundance from a worldly fleshly perspective. What is this perspective adding to your foundation? I can release the flow of abundance beyond your imagination, but it is pointless unless it is part of the eternal picture and contributes towards the building of the coming Kingdom.

The worldly concept of 'once I succeed on the world terms, I will be able to contribute significantly to the Kingdom' is a fool's errand says God. In being set apart, your plans and aspirations have to be Kingdom centered at the outset.

That is why divisions between what you see as *ministry*, things relating to Me and *business,* things relating to provision, are not acceptable. You have to be of one mind and one focus because, as My Word says; a *house divided against itself cannot stand.*

The Sabbath day is a 'fast' from the things of the world. To rest and cleanse your mind from the way the world wants you to think. It is to nurture and fertilize the 'thought trees' you have established that grow contrary to the world's ideals and that feed only from the roots of truth in My Word. If you allow it to be infected by the world, you will introduce toxic food to those roots which must be avoided at all costs.

You must jealously guard the set-apart nature of this special time. By the same token, your refreshing times should be seen as mini Sabbaths sprinkled throughout the days. If you do not take them, you will allow your day to lapse away into the worldly way of thinking.

You must operate like 'spies' as you are living and working in the land of the enemy. Your mission is to be a light to other members of your family who are suffering from 'Stockholm syndrome' and who have temporarily forgotten who they belong to and what their own mission is. There is no business worth pursuing except My business and when your business and My business are one and the same your success is divinely assured", says God.

2 Corinthians 6:17
2 Corinthians 7:1
Matthew 12:25
1 John 2:15-17

198

WEDDING GARMENT

"There is only One you should serve, One you should follow and One on whom you should depend exclusively, and this is no mystery to you.

If your business plans are centered around your own survival, that is all they will ever produce, your own survival. They have to be realigned purely with Kingdom principles in order for the blockages to be removed. Weave the thread of the Kingdom truth into everything that you do and say.

My people are hoping to find truth. As misdirected as so many are, they will turn their heads more easily than you think if the spirit within them hears even the faintest whisper of a reminder of the righteousness that bought their freedom.

Shout out your message of truth in everything you do and stand up boldly in Me and I will stand up for you in ways that you cannot yet even perceive.

Does your conversation sound like someone who is part of the world? Then expect the rewards of this world and the empty pointless successes they deliver. Start sounding like a you are on a 'Kingdom mission' showing that you are striving for Kingdom positioning and you can chase the rewards of the Kingdom.

There are millions upon millions of people hoping for and longing for an understanding of these truths. They know in their hearts that there must be more, that they do not have the complete picture, but they do not know where to look or they would already be looking there.

Giving Me the glory after succeeding on the world's terms is easy, yet pointless. 'Do not lay-up treasures for yourself on the earth' was more than just a good idea. It is an absolute prerequisite for the acquisition of a wedding garment. Such garments can only be purchased with Heavenly currency says God. As I have said many times, you will bring nothing with you to the Judgment. All that you have produced pertaining to eternity will be waiting there for you.

The wedding garments required for entrance into the marriage supper of the Lamb will be given *only* to those that have already earned them by laying up for themselves treasures in the heavens out of their diligent obedience during their time on earth.

You cannot whip out your checkbook or credit card and declare 'I'll just buy one now please'. You cannot roll over your retirement account for a wedding garment or exchange your stock portfolio. No! Only those who have *pre ordered* and *pre-paid* for their garment will receive that reward. That is what it is, a reward for service not a gift of grace like salvation".

Romans 8:18
Luke 21:34-36
Revelation 19:6-10
Matthew 6:19-21
Matthew 22:9-11
1 Peter 1:17
Jeremiah 31:16

199

THE WORD IS YOUR PROTECTOR

Your protection comes from the Word and the trust that you have in the power of that Word says God.

It was with that Word that I spoke all things into being, with that Word the heavens were aligned and earth was given form and everything in and on it was created.

This Word has formed history for all time. Despite all this and the knowledge of it, you need Me to remind you of it.

The Word holds the key to every answer you would desire to hear.

My love for you was complete before and it remains complete today. I am the same yesterday today and tomorrow. My Word declares it and it is so.

'Hedge building' is not a difficult task, but maintaining it is a constant consideration. The enemy will continue to attempt to make holes in your protective hedge and never forget this, it only takes a small imperfection in that hedge to begin the formation of a stumbling block.

Many have tripped over these blocks and fallen. That is not the heart of the issue, the most important thing is that there is no merit in repairing the hedge but leaving the stumbling block in place. You will just end up falling over it again.

These blocks are actually the iniquities that are not properly dealt with. They will literally 'block' you from making further progress because you cannot help but to repeatedly fall over them. Just casting them out is not the answer, because the enemy will simply wait for another hole in your hedge and craftily slide them back into place.

At times this is so subtle you would not even notice that it is happening. In some cases, they are built one on top of the other until there is a complete wall between My Spirit and yours. This is not necessarily the case now, but it would become the case without attention. As you have seen, the body needs certain nutrients to create the adequate defenses of the immune system, the most powerful and complete mechanism for human physical healing. It is the same thing with the spirit and the soul.

You simply have to feed it the correct 'nutrients' to create your own hedge, your 'spiritual immune system'. In the same manner, this is the most powerful and complete mechanism for human spiritual healing. It is a literal supernatural growth hormone and healing elixir. Where do you find this amazing tonic? In the life of My word. I Am that living Word and in it lives every comfort and treasure you seek.

The hedge of protection – My Word
The full armor – My Word
My unceasing unwavering love – My Word
My plan for your lives – My Word

Continue to quiet the noise of the world and you will hear Me better says God. Look around with your spiritual eyes and you will see Me everywhere.

As with David who was greatly deceived by his own iniquities, My forgiveness is always absolute. He was still a man after My own heart. This is so because these iniquities are not a part of who you are. They are a temporal attachment, either acquired or inherited through spiritual disobedience, either way they can be removed and permanently eliminated through prayer and effective spiritual warfare.

The enemy will never cease to look for opportunities to reattach them, but if you maintain your protection you are safe. My Word declares it. No weapon formed against you shall prosper. No means exactly what it says. Iniquities are like enemy 'sleeper cells'. Just like in the world they can be identified, broken up, utterly destroyed and steps can be taken to prevent their return.

I still have many wonders available to you says God. We must all walk in the same direction. Of course, there is the fear of 'friction' because our path is so opposite to the world.

This is only a reminder that you are going in the right direction. Once you start moving, the anointing oil of My spirit will start to make it easier to slide through the resistance. You have to make the effort to get this oil flowing. That is where many fall short, the first moment they encounter the pain of resistance they turn back to the easier direction and go with the flow.

This is a joyous day in this realm says God. I knew this moment would come I just had to wait for you to realize the source of your pain. Do not ever forget though I do not build hedges for people, I simply supply the materials and the instructions. You have to be willing to take the necessary actions. The fatted calf is indeed ready"

Psalms 5:11-12, 40:11, 138:2, 139
John 1:1-5
Hebrews 13:8
Isaiah 54:17
Revelation 22:13

200

WALK IN OBEDIENCE

"Once we have discussed something and I have provided you with
a path or a solution, make sure that you are obedient in taking My
counsel. The main thing that holds people back from the results they
deserve is their lack of obedience says God. It seems that they are
waiting for something easier, or a solution that they like better.

Understand that this will not happen. Just like the Israelites who went
around and around the mountain for 40 years, you have the right to
make the same choices. My position never changed, and it took them
40 years to get in line with My will for their lives. How much longer do
you want to take?

Feed on the Word first. Then everything else will taste better.

The Word is your living spiritual sustenance. What would happen to
your physical body if you stop putting fuel into it for say 3 days? How
about 3 weeks, 3 months?

Of course it will grow weak, become increasingly ineffective and
eventually it will shut down and die. For optimum health the physical
body needs to be cared for carefully, well fed with the correct nutrition
and properly exercised to keep everything working. Your spiritual body
works in exactly the same way. Its sustenance comes from My living
Word and its exercise comes from you using the Word and doing what
it says to do in your life on a consistent basis".

1 Samuel 15:22
James 1:22
John 14:23

201

THERE CAN BE VALUE IN DISAPPOINTMENT

"Disappointments are often blessings in disguise says God. There is a season for everything and everything has a season. When following a dream, make sure it is yours, following the dreams of another person could lead to a rude awakening.

Fiscally responsible prosperity will always glorify Me, so I do not prohibit it. Acquiring the wealth is never the issue, becoming a psalm 52 man is the problem. Stay in harmony with My plan for your life and with My Spirit power and ensure that this fate does not befall you.

Escape the hooks of the world to a greater degree, the decision is yours to make. If you want to be blessed, be in the habit of doing things that provoke My attention.

Do you really think I am interested in who is winning the game or the latest episode of some television show? I am interested in the spirits and souls of the people I created. Nothing else matters to Me.

They have been the sole focus of My attention since I created them. All the other things are man's creations, which serve in some way to dilute the relationship.

My concern is for the eternal not the temporal. One will soon replace the other and then, where will you be? What will you be doing? In those answers you will find the purpose that you are seeking.

If you truly grasp the significance and the uncertainty of time, you will appreciate the folly of 'options'.

'What does it profit a man if he gains the whole world but loses his soul?'.

Ensure that every project, every action is propelled by a soul saving motivation.

Do not miss the fact that the greatest assurance for the salvation of your own soul is found in the saving of others through your example".

Psalms 52:7
1 Peter 1:9
Philippians 2:1-4, 12-13
Matthew 8:36

202

BREAKTHROUGH

"Taking a trip should not require you to 'step out' of My anointing. In fact, it is more important than ever when you expose yourself to new situations that you abide with the fullness My Spirit.

Your ability to be a light to others will be diminished if you do not maintain your close interaction with Me at all times.

Your discernment from teachings will be so much more precise from an anointed perspective. It should be 'business as usual' from the spiritual point of view, regardless of where you go and how long you go for.

Drink from the well every day without fail.

The success of your plans will reflect your diligence and your ability to stick to what we have discussed and planned. Let go and let My Spirit take control.

Being 'reasonably good' at being obedient, you will get 'reasonable' results.

Press forward now and provide Me with 'breakthrough' obedience and I will return it to you with *breakthrough* results," says God.

Ephesians 3:19
Colossians 1:19
Ephesians 4:13

203

KEEP YOUR SPIRITUAL EYES WIDE OPEN

"Sometimes in the natural realm it becomes necessary to take a step
backwards before any progress can be made says God.
There is little point in embarking on or continuing on a journey with
a hole in your water bottle. If you do this, you would end up stranded
in the wilderness where you would die without water. This is the most
painful death because you actually *had* the water, you had enough for
the journey, but lost it through the unnoticed hole and by the time it
was discovered it was too late.

I have made it known to you that repairs were necessary and now it is
up to you to make them. The water I speak of is My Living Word. It
is necessary to cleanse, purify and repair your vessel to be prepared to
receive the abundant flow I am about to release for you.

I will flood every aspect of your being with the power of My rivers
of Living Water, but you have to be ready to receive, retain and renew
your cleansed vessels to a level that you have never previously known.

Remove all the hooks of the enemy as I reveal them to you, repair
any holes because that is where they come from. Many people remove
the hooks from their lives but fail to realize that every removed hook
leaves a hole, which can act as a doorway for spirits seven times worse
than those that were removed, to gain entry.

When basking in the joy of restoration which I desire for you, it is
easy to underestimate the importance of continuing to prepare for the
journey ahead.

Cleansing and washing in the Living Waters will remove all of this pain and will soothe both spirit and soul.

The truth and power in My living Word will bring strength and healing to your physical bodies. You have to be willing to pick up once again, the keys that I had handed to you and unlock further wonders of My treasures so that you might share them with those with ears to hear.

You are already seeing irrefutable evidence of My guidance and presence, so you need have no reason to doubt the direction to move in.

Keep your spiritual eyes wide open at all times, never fall into the pit of complacency again says God.

You have been plucked from its jaws and set once again in a favored position on the mountain, but you must continue to climb.

The higher levels provide a greater view and cleaner and more fragrant atmosphere. Remember though, the higher you are the further there is to fall.

Those that start imagining that they achieved such heights through their own power, effort or understanding start to 'glow' in their own self-glorification.

This glow causes them to be easily identified as targets by the enemy causing many to fall or to be literally 'shot down' from the mountain by the arrows of hatred.

You *cannot* immerse yourself in worldly things and then expect the sweet heavenly fragrance of the anointing to be the result.
You must swim in the Living Waters, drink them in and let them perform the miracles that only they are capable of.

Cleanse, repair, refresh and renew. These are daily requirements for those that are developing in the world for a season says God. When this is consistently applied you will be astounded by the power of the results.

There are no new revelations. Just reminders of things that those with the world in their eyes can no longer see."

Matthew 9:14-17, 12:43-45
Mark 2:18-22
1 Peter 2:1-3, 13-16

204

RICHNESS

"If good health is your goal do only the things that you know will promote good health. Eat correctly, exercise regularly, sleep properly, get sunlight, breathe deeply, nourish the body and the mind. Use kind words and be calm. Energy spent trying to be someone other than the person you were called to be is energy wasted. Be authentic and passionate but be those things under the guidance of the Spirit and not the driving of the ego.

If financial success is your goal, follow My principles says God. Rather pursue *richness* for that is a holistic manifestation of spiritually balanced success rather than 'riches' which would be success measured by the world's standards. Never deny the Source of your success because that source, which is the truth in all the things I have shared with you, is the energy that allows you to effortlessly maintain your status of richness.

The moment you lose connection to Me, your Source, the ego will insert itself and claim glory for the success. The material gains will indeed be 'riches' in the eyes of the world, but they are temporal. The *richness* I speak of is an eternal condition that sets us apart from the world.

It is this power that allows you to be *in* the world and not *of* the world and yet still have a major impact *on* the world.

You should exude *richness* every day. It is not measured in dollars and cents, in age or physical strength, it is not measured in intellectual knowledge or material achievement. It is measured in outcomes and the impact that you have on the lives of every person that you get the opportunity to help.

Follow My Word, follow My formula*, do what you know to be right and you will feel the 'Cloak of Richness' on your back. Wear this cloak with humility and blessings will be in abundance.

Where *richness* abounds joy and rewards, both present and eternal, are always close by."

*See message #1

Psalms 23:5

Matthew 5:6

Ephesians 3:19

John 15:19

Matthew 5:3

205

HUMILITY

"Focused passion promotes action says God. This is why it is so important to know exactly what you should be doing. So many are rendered inactive and certainly ineffective, because they made the wrong choice regarding where to focus their efforts. Many are striving in their own strength rather than yielding to My Spirit.

This produces surface level results that have no eternal relevance.

Maintaining constant contact and surrendering to the greater wisdom of My Spirit takes *discipline* and *effort*. It is so easy to go the way of the world and revel in any success as though it was your own personal triumph. Humility is a golden key. It unlocks a door in the spiritual realm that leads to many wonderful blessings.

Calmness, peace and quiet confidence; these are all traits of the humble. In humility a leader can achieve success beyond the comprehension of those who measure only by material gain and position. Humility transcends worldly achievements because its rewards also have an eternal element that the ego driven achiever will never see or understand. The acronym for ego (E.G.O.) 'edging God out' is very valid.

Anyone driven by their ego is always going to be self-absorbed and driven by greed rather than gratitude.

Wisdom and understanding are both fruit of humility, making it even more important to pursue the path of a humble leader.

Always look to give credit rather than take credit.

Praise the efforts of others rather than seek praise. Even though it may seem counter intuitive, humility builds character and boldness because the person who does not need accolades can walk with the confidence that My Spirit goes before him and that together we can achieve anything. This is a great contrast to the ego driven leader who feels the need to constantly assert himself less his followers see him as 'weak'.

The position of a servant leader is certainly desirable, it brings a largely unique approach in the material driven world, but all great leaders have always been those with a servant heart which of course could only be attained by one who walks with humility. There are many successes coming, but I want you to be ready to except them with a humble heart so that we can build upon them to great levels and be sure that they are adding the right materials to your foundation."

1 Corinthians 3:10-11

Colossians 3:23-24

Philippians 2:3-4

Hebrews 12:11

Proverbs 6:23, 15:33

Psalms 25:9

James 4:6

Matthew 5:3

Luke 14:11

1 Peter 5:6-8

Micah 6:8

206

FOCUS

"A man cannot reap without sowing and he cannot plant in one field and harvest from another says God. Giving yourselves too many fields at once that need planting is foolish. You will scatter seed haphazardly and in insufficient quantity because you are rushing. Then you will not have enough time to tend the field properly and you will end up with a less than wholesome crop.

The key at this stage is focus. You have to drill down to that core desire, that purpose which you will be happy to work on diligently for the remainder of your time on earth. The one thing that will bring excitement and passion into your life. The thing through which you will feel the greatest sense of connection to your eternal calling.

You have to work on that until it becomes an abundant self-sustaining testament to your commitment to excellence. When that crop is deeply rooted in the nutrient dense soil of Faith, it will be bountiful and will produce its own supply of seeds. These seeds will be encoded with the same energy of power and abundance that can then be shared with others who also wish to plant."

2 Timothy 2:3-6

207

YOU HAVE TO BE ACCOUNTABLE

"Lack of accountability usually results in no action. If you are not held to a standard how can a standard exist? How do you know if you are making any progress if you have no intention behind your thoughts, words or deeds? People that move blindly always bump into many obstacles and even stumbling blocks. You have to *see* the end at the beginning, because a journey started without a clear picture of the intended destination will either take too long or could even result in getting completely lost and stranded in the wilderness. Take good account of the Israelites, their disobedience and lack of wisdom and understanding cost them 40 years in the wilderness.

Order your steps and hold yourself accountable. Sounds simple enough, but the flesh will constantly rebel, especially in the absence of Spirit led decisions and actions. It is easy for the flesh to resist if you do not bring it under control through prayer and meditation in My Word.

The daily application of Truth is what is required. Why else would I say, 'pray without ceasing.'? The desire of the flesh to gain control never ceases, so it has to be constantly controlled in order to accelerate progress. Plan a step, act and then make that step. You have to complete every task and stop leaving things half done. After all you cannot eat something half cooked, you would not want to read half of a book. You cannot be half healthy or half committed it has to be 100% then it is much simpler. You cannot pursue more than one objective at the same time unless one leads to the other on the same trajectory. This again is so important in connection to your daily actions, your daily reporting and accountability. Work on this and it will become a source of much joy. This will cause you to experience the enhanced power of the threefold cord says God. The synergy it creates is somuch more than the combined power of two. Continue to push through and be disciplined. Take care to work with joy and delight in what you do.

This again is why the vision has to be constantly worked on and kept in clear focus. Once you lose sight of it, even for a moment, it is easy to start doing things that will shift your direction. You do not have to move much off course to eventually miss the target completely, so take great care with this.

There are many that are on paths that will lead them straight past their rewards and they are completely oblivious to the danger, because they have not constantly checked their map against the truth.

They have not kept the level of accountability that would have shown them their error. It does not matter what anyone else is doing, it does not matter what the latest thinking is. What does matter is that you do the things you are called to do and be consistently obedient and only then will you make the right progress.

The Spirit I have placed in you knows when you are on the right track, as do the ministering angels assigned to your protection and assistance. Use these great gifts and outcomes will indeed be incredible.

I do not give you all these gifts, tools and talents so you can just set them aside. I make them available to you so that you have a real opportunity to attain the desires of your heart. You have to be willing to use them effectively to bring the things that you have asked for to fruition.

Many ask for outcomes but are not prepared to provide the input that I require. This is the simplest part of wisdom and understanding. You have to do the works, to fuel the Faith. *Be, do* and *have* make so much more sense in this context.

You have to *be* a spirit filled obedient servant, this will cause you to *do* the necessary things to create the outcomes you seek. Then you will *have* all of the consequences of those diligently focused actions. It really is that simple.

Return to *being* and then the *doing* and *having* become attainable. You cannot just *have* as that route will always end up with a *being* that is controlled by the success of the outcome and not the other way around. That path leads only to death and misery. Take immediate action to do what you know needs to be done and then be accountable to keep yourself on track".

1 Corinthians 10:1-13
Romans 8:9
Proverbs 25:28
Galatians 5:16
Philippians 4:8-9
Matthew 26:41

208

TRUTH TRIGGERS

"You still have to spend more time with the truth that is in My Word says God. You must ingrain the truth into the depths of your soul. Imparting man's wisdom serves only man. Everything you teach has to be rooted in My truth.

The true 'truth triggers' are found in My Wisdom; all others are just 'ego' triggers.

Only My truth will cause a man to dig deeply enough to find what really empowers him.

Can you see the importance now of Wisdom and Understanding? Without these, man is a fool moving from one worldly success or failure to the next but never experiencing the joy of a deep connection with his divinely inspired purpose.

Success for the sake of the flesh will bring material gain and surface level satisfaction, but the glow of inspired accomplishment, that can only come through a connection with My purpose for your life, is a feeling that cannot be matched by material gain. This is the genesis of true joy.

Study the Word, eat the Word, speak the Word of Truth and the connection will come through at the deepest level.

The truth in My Word builds faith, and with it the strength and courage to act. These are the actions that build for the future and that lead to eternal rewards, the only rewards that matter".

Hebrews 11:6
Proverbs 2:2-11
Revelation 22:12

209

SPEAK THE TRUTH

"I can only provide you with the blueprint and the tools necessary says God. It is required of you to override the flesh and read the blueprint and pick up the tools. There have been many that were well equipped with the tools and talents to create wonderful outcomes but produced little or nothing because they let the fleshly thoughts take precedence.

This is why My Word is so important, it orders the mind and suppresses the carnal mind's desire to only pursue worldly objectives. In the absence of the Word, the carnal mind is left to its own desires. Keep My Word on your lips, speak only the truth, do not compromise on this.

One lie will lead to more and that is the way of the evil one. Eventually you get so entangled in the web of lies it becomes very difficult to get out. This has become the fate of so many of My sheep says God.

Being caught in this web, they are rendered useless and are incapable of building any rewards upon their foundation of salvation.

Remember that you have to control the 'food' that is presented to your spirit.

A diet of peace, love and good things, time spent praying and sharing your love of the Truth, these are the building blocks of strength. These are the *proteins* for the Spirit of Truth placed in you. Endless hours of television dulls the spirit, reduces production and saps the life energy from your soul. This is the way of destruction as it wastes the one thing that should be of most importance to anyone pursuing their purpose; it *wastes their time.*

If your purpose is the driving force behind your life and your actions, then wasted time is time where you are 'off purpose' and that time can *never* be regained.

You cannot keep looking for new answers, you already have them all"

Romans 8:6-11
1 Corinthians 3:10-14

210

SLAY THE GIANTS

"Magnifying My Spirit within you activates spiritual discernment which will always be superior to carnal discernment. Fleshly decisions usually bring rewards to the flesh but do not feed the Spirit. You have to become your own David says God. Regardless of how big the giants in your life appear to be, you cannot dwell in fear.

Pick up your stones and move towards the enemy. You will be shocked at how quickly they diminish once you assume the victory.

The easiest way to defeat most giants is to let them see that My Spirit within you makes you bigger and more powerful than they are! This will send most of them running.

For the others, My Words are the most powerful stones you can ever pick up. Those words delivered between the eyes of the enemy are unstoppable. That is how the truth will make you free. Base everything on the power of that truth.

Faith *without* religion is still faith. In fact, it is very powerful because it is the one thing that can truly ignite the spirit within every person, because it is pure and unadulterated by the plans and schemes of manipulative men", says God.

1 Corinthians 2:14

Philippians 1:9-10

Hebrews 4:12

211

ENCOURAGEMENT

"Why do people resist accountability? Because it shows up areas of disobedience says God.

If your progress in any area is not measured, how is it possible to know if any progress is being made? This is a vitally important area.

You need to be keeping records and then using the data to adjust your strategy and direction. Remember that a spacecraft is off course almost all of the time, however there are continuous, tiny adjustments being made. Likewise, it should be the same with your spiritual walk. There should be little adjustments made all of the time.

You will only truly know where you are at any given time when you have absolute clarity on where you are going.

In the same way, you have to keep accurate records of your daily progress, so that you can correct any deviation from the true path, before you end up completely off track.

Fuel your thoughts with My Word and let it nurture your spirit and inspire your actions. You are realizing increasingly the necessity to remove all obstructions to the flow of My Spirit power to work in your life. This is the only route to the desires of your heart. If your heart's desires were of the worldly carnal type, you would be able to achieve them through worldly carnal means.

This will not work for you, so stay in the flow of the supernatural and that which you desire will flow to you. No situation is irretrievable and any challenges you currently face can easily be overcome through obedience. They are miniscule in the scale of what is about to unfold. Therefore, do not waste time fueling them with energy or attention. Rather spend that time on taking the action steps required.

Be bold in your expectation to function at the highest level in everything that you do and make sure that you are resolved to *not tolerate mediocrity*. To do so, is like burying your talent.

Encouragement comes through making progress says God and making progress comes through encouragement.

Be consistent in your encouragement of each other, and your uplifting of each other as well as other people. Always strive to help other people feel encouraged by any interaction they have with you. Leave them with a sense of increase. A sense that you have deposited something beneficial within them as far better results will come by offering encouragement rather than criticism".

Philippians 3:13
2 Peter 1:9

212

EYES TO SEE

"An idea here and there does not make a plan says God.

They may be *part* of a plan, but the plan itself has more substance.

A clear picture of your purpose and how you will pursue it is the blueprint. It is a perfect vision which you can focus on and take steps towards every day. I will cause many things to come into your lives that will take you towards this vision and help you to live out this purpose.

You have to have eyes to see to make sure that you do not miss opportunities or get deceived by the enemy.

Be aware that division brings dilution and will make you and your wife ineffective. It is the threefold cord that holds the greatest power so always strive to use that. Check the attitude of your spirit before anything that you do. This attitude is determined by the amount of self-influence you allow in any situation. Being willing to relinquish control and allowing My Spirit to lead is most difficult, because the flesh constantly resists and wants to direct the spirit, which only leads to frustration.

My Spirit is to be the leader not the follower. *My Word and your prayers are the fuel that provides the strength and power necessary for the Spirit to always rise above the attempts by the flesh to regain control.*

Keep looking for opportunities to bless the lives of others with your gifts. They are everywhere around you.

The battle in the spiritual realm wages relentlessly. The enemy will not withdraw.

Keep pushing through with courage and confidence as these two confound his plans. I am your strength says God. Start operating purely with this strength at your core and rapid transformations will occur."

1 Peter 2:11, 5:6-11
I Chronicles 28:20
Deuteronomy 31:6
Ephesians 6:10
Psalms 27:1
Isaiah 41:10-13
1 Corinthians 16:13
Provers 3:5-6

213

THE POWER OF THE SPIRIT OF GOD

"Be aware that you should not ignore the supernatural realm says God. It is the higher plane where the Spirit within you can achieve great things that will then manifest in the natural realm.

Ignoring the supernatural or the importance of the strength of the Spiritual does not mean that it is not there, it just makes you less effective. As you know, every victory must first be achieved in the Spiritual realm if it is to have any eternal impact. Without that, it is just an earthly waste of time, a vain imagination.

Feel the presence of My Spirit in every endeavor.

I will give you the words to speak out and the confident attitude, measured with humility, that you need to walk as a warrior amongst the wickedness of the world.

This is the most splendid and powerful force that will help you to achieve much in compressed time.

With My Spirit, you can overcome *any* challenge and provide much value to many people.

The Fruit of the Spirit can only be created by the work of the Spirit says God. 'Not by might nor by power but by My Spirit'.

That is why I keep drawing you back to the formula* says God. The Spirit in *greater measure* is the accelerator you are seeking. That is your

461

catalyst for exponential growth in every area of your life on earth, as well as your *power and protector* in the spirit realm.

Keep pressing, let your faith override your questions or it will cause you to delay decisions.

Boldness, under the leading of My Spirit brings many blessings and humility and many crowns and rewards.

My Spirit permeates the atmosphere around you at all times, breathe it deep into the depths of your soul. Feel its cleansing power and then through your prayers let it lead you to a glorious victory.

Pray, think, breathe, act and walk with confidence that exudes My Spirit of all conquering love and power".

*See message #1

Colossians 3:2
Zechariah 4:6
Daniel 10:12-13
Isaiah 40:29-31, 55:8-9
Ephesians 4:13, 6:12-13
Proverbs 3:5-6

214

BELIEVE

"Strive always for excellence and choose to be excellent at everything you do. If you have a deadline, be ahead of it. If you make a commitment, honor it. Regardless of whether it was to yourself, each other, or to someone else, you must always do what you say you are going to do when you say you are going to do it says God.

Wear your integrity like a hat that everyone can see. Be direct and accurate in everything you say. Be firm and truthful. Do not be a people pleaser because you will end up being displeased with the outcome.

There is a truth to the management of finances that you must adhere to. Spending money that you do not have is a form of a lie. Paying interest here and there is like a pipe with a hole in it. Your supply is constantly diminished by the leak.

A plan that is not written down in specific minute detail is nothing more than a collection of vague ideas. A specific plan that is not actioned and adhered to is like My Word in the hands of a fool. It may even sound good to the ear but his lack of wisdom and of understanding make it ineffective. Plan your work, then work at your plan diligently to complete it. This will give you direction and focused daily action steps to take. It is time to make progress every day now. Measure your activity constantly and the outcome will delight you. Never look behind, I'm always ahead of you as a light of hope and expectation. The enemy is mainly behind, trying to draw you back to old habits, old failures and things that can keep you from moving forward. Keep your eyes focused on My Light.

My Word and your prayers make it brighter and easier to see the right path. Remember the importance of the things you cannot yet see. Your shield of faith will make the way for you.

Believe, believe, believe, for only the faith filled believer will touch upon the true greatness that I have made available.

The prize for the disciplined application of this level of spiritual focus is beyond your worldly comprehension for now and that is why your faith requires constant fuel.

Build it stronger and never question the outcome, as the smallest seed of doubt is like the iceberg to the unsuspecting vessel. Crush the doubts with bold declarations of faith and expectation. Visualize the outcomes you desire constantly.

Form the victories in your thoughts, verbalize them and act on those words. You are a co-creator, so start creating."

John 8:12
2 Timothy 4:7-8
Matthew 5:7
Hebrews 11:1, 12:2
Philippians 3:13-14
Psalms 119:105

215

STAY CONNECTED

"It is always easy to cry out in a moment of despair says God. True love is when you reach out or call out purely from the love within you and not because something has gone wrong or because you are in need. If I am able to fix things that are broken, how much more can I add beauty to things that are not. Blessed is the man that cries out for My help when he needs it. However, there are extra blessings for those that reach out from their own love, who ask so that they can share with Me their delight in being guided by My spirit.

After all, if they are not being led by My Spirit, they are either leading themselves to destruction or they are in the midst of deception from the enemy.

This is why My Word calls for *prayer without ceasing*.

It is that constant *double check* to clarify *who* is doing the leading, which is only possible to discern from a spiritual perspective.

Be constantly connected to Me.

The longer you detach yourself from Me during the course of a day, the more you become tainted by the dirt of the world. This makes the cleansing more difficult than it needs to be.

Keep constant contact in the Spiritual realm and accomplishing things in the natural will be easier than you ever thought possible. Look at all challenges as 'easy' because they will inevitably become what you think they are. Your power lies in the connection that I have placed in you. Stay connected says God and wonderful things will happen".

Ephesians 5:26
John 15:3

216

LEAVE NO ROOM FOR REGRETS

"You already know the answers says God.

If I am the same, yesterday, today and tomorrow, why would I now come up with a different plan? The formula* is like the engine of a beautiful high-tech car. If you take out one part, it either will not run at all or it will run, but not smoothly. Either way, it has to be rebuilt with all the parts so that it will run again. Revisit My previous instructions and follow them says God.

I will make the way for you. You know what happens to 'faith without works'? Obviously, ideas in your head will remain just that until you speak them out, write them down and act to make them happen.

The world is full of 'we should have or could have, I wish we had done this or that, I always wanted to .....'. This is all idle chatter with no fruit.

You only produce fruit when you take the seed and firmly *plant* it and then water and nurture it, then love it and prune it and cherish it, fertilize it and allow the light to cause it to flourish. I remind you about the power behind spoken words.

Your thoughts form them, you write them down so that you can continue to speak them over and over the same way. Even My commands were given to the people in the same way. Confess them with faith and purpose.

Faith allows you to *call things that are not as though they were* and see them manifest in the natural.

The formula* is just a pathway to keep you centered and focused on the journey. All the pieces to the puzzle are now in your own hands. Put them together to see the beautiful picture", says God.

*See message #1

Romans 4:17
Proverbs 10:31
Matthew 12:36-37
James 3:5-6

217

DO NOT DOUBT

"Not by might, nor by power but by My Spirit says God. Every goal can be achieved and any desire made manifest by a man of faith who steps boldly forward with the confidence of victory.

The enemy is looking for your doubt and hesitation, for that little seed of discouragement that he can sprout into a tree of stress and uncertainty. You cannot allow that to happen. You have to walk daily in the truth and follow the formula* that I gave you.

See the end even before the beginning and keep focused on that picture. There are many wonderful blessings waiting to break through, but blessings only come to the faith *full* not the faith *half full*. The outcome will truly be the one that you expect so be sure to only expect things that develop your purpose.

There are many today that have tremendous opportunities, but they let fear hold them back. Whether it is fear of failure, fear of what others think or the lie from the enemy that I cannot or will not help them. It does not matter which because anyone of these destroys the potential.

Stand strong through this testing time. Walk with *definite purpose* and *certainty of the outcome* that is common with all of My Warriors. Keep the ascendancy in the spiritual realm and it will manifest in the natural realm", says God.

*See message #1

James 1:6-8
Zechariah 4:6

218

CHANGING THE MIND

"Do not be like the man who knows exactly what picture he wants to paint but then picks up the wrong brush. If you bring an old brush and the same old paint to a new canvas, the picture will lack the 'spirit of life' says God. Everything must be new. That is why I speak so emphatically of repentance. Because only through heartfelt repentance can the mind be renewed.

Remember that your situation today reflects your thinking up to this point. When someone sees their life picture as incomplete or lacking, they must address the thinking that has created that image. The same thinking can only continue to produce the same images. The same mind can only produce the same thinking. In order to change the mind, it has to be made new. It can only be made new through repentance says God, there is no other way.

Many add *new* thinking, and this can produce temporary change and very often a temporary improvement in results. However, when the *old* thinking is left in place, that diseased mind will emerge again at some point and lead you right back into the old habits which lead to destruction.

As you have said to others, 'tomorrow will be the same as today unless you do something to make it different'. You have to realize that it applies to you the most! How can you encourage change in others if you cannot change yourself? How can you teach others to succeed without being able to show your own success? You have to *out* pray, *out* work and *out* shine every day. Not to make yourself look better than others, but to be a living witness to the power of a changed mind that is driven by the right ruling of My Spirit. The guidance and instruction I have given you in the past contains every ingredient needed to live a life of richness, a life that will build upon your foundation in the way that leads to righteousness.

If you do not break completely free from the ways of this world, they will keep affecting your direction and cause you to be double minded. This journey requires great faith because the desired outcome will not be clearly in focus at the outset. That is why you must have a clear picture of it and move towards it by following My Spirit".

1 John 1:9
1 Corinthians 14:18
Matthew 3:8
Luke 5:33-39
Romans 12:2
James 4:4
Psalms 51:17

219

THE FALLEN NATURE

"I always hear your prayers, but I do not give you the power to create anything outside of My purpose for your life. However, I cannot prevent a person from doing so if they choose to do things from their own free will pursuing ideas that come from the enemy.

Every idea conceived outside the protection of My Spirit is from the evil one. There is good and there is evil, they are the two choices. The good produces only good and the evil produces only evil. There are never more than two choices, says God.

The human spirit is fallen by nature. A fallen spirit can never produce good, only evil. It may seem overly simple to the world, but it is just that simple. If My Spirit abides with you everything you say and do will be good and directed toward producing good fruit.

My Spirit within you has to constantly contend with the fallen nature with which you were born. It is a constant, never ending battle and you cannot afford to drop your guard for even a moment. It is the greatest challenge for all, which is why most will just stop striving.

For most, it is easier to just go the way of the world. That is the *wide* path and you know the outcome of that choice.

Indeed, this is a long journey of small steps and it is an arduous and continuous journey that requires *consistent focus and effort* to keep you on the right path.

Watch for the side paths that look like they may provide a *shortcut* or an easier route. These are traps that will ultimately lead you back onto the wide easy path. Anytime that happens, you must return immediately to the point from which you departed the narrow way and get back on track. Check each day what steps you have taken to be sure that you are still on the right path.

Do not be surprised that these instructions do not change. My Way has always been clear. The plan of the enemy is to keep presenting new ways to distract you and to keep you off track. You have to be able to see these deceptions and only looking with your eyes guided by My Spirit will empower you to do so."

Matthew 7:13-14
Hebrews 12:2-7

220

SYSTEMS AND ACCOUNTABILITY

"The person that does not hold himself accountable has no standard to uphold, that way he can neither fail or succeed, he is just 'doing'. You are a *being* not a *doing*, but you have to have a plan and a system to implement it in order to know where you are. The farmer has to plan his field, then he has to prepare the soil, then he has to prepare the seed. He must sow in a certain pattern, then water and feed and nurture. Eventually there will be a plentiful harvest.

If he did not *plan* his field or *prepare* the soil or the seed, or sow, or nurture, feed and water at the correct times, there could be no harvest. He is accountable for every step just as you need to be today.

There is no way around this. Everything in the universe known and unknown works on systems that have required elements. Disrupt any of these elements and the system no longer functions to its optimum potential and the result is decay and destruction. That is why excellence in all things is essential. Excellence determines that every step is followed, checked and double checked. Excellence records the results, looks for any shortcomings and adjusts immediately, before the fruit is spoiled.

Excellence promotes righteousness and overcomes even lack of skill and talent. My Spirit combined with a heart of excellence will always accomplish greatness and produce fruit of the highest quality.

We have often talked about accountability says God.

Fruit is a consequence of following a certain process. First, the seed has to be acquired, then the ground into which that seed is to be planted has to be prepared. Once it has been prepared, that seed is carefully put into place and covered for protection. Then it has to be fed and watered.

The food is all contained in that which was prepared which highlights why the correct preparation is so important. It has to be watered, which is symbolic of pouring My Spirit upon it. *Rivers of living water.* Then the seed will take root in that soil and a plant will emerge and break through in search of the light.

This is not the end, it is really the beginning says God and now the real work starts. That little shoot now requires constant love and nourishment to cause it to grow to its potential. It needs more water and nutrients to help it get stronger and thrive. In the natural, these nutrients are made available by nature, in the supernatural they are found in the Truth of My Word.

If you are inattentive to this vulnerable plant, it will quickly wither and die and you have to start right back at the beginning with a new seed. Even when you do manage to help it to grow stronger, it does not mean that you are going to be harvesting fruit right away. It will depend on the type of plant you are nurturing, but you have to keep supplying the nutrients indefinitely if you want to be able to keep harvesting.

There is no point in time where you no longer have to give in order to receive. Nothing in My Creation works that way. Everything is in a constant state of motion, it is either increasing or declining. I can only make the systems and processes available to you. The *action* has to come from your side. If you look at anything that did not work out the way you expected, you will find something that you did not follow properly that caused the result. There are no mysteries here, the enemy will wait for you to allow holes in your hedge and then exploit them.

Your best defense is to make sure that the holes do not appear in the first place and you already have all of the tools necessary for that.

Examine your intentions, be sure that they are clear, and be sure that you both share the vision. Revisit the preparation of your soil, be sure that it is properly ready. Check your seed supply and decide which fields are to be planted. Do not plant two that require the same amount of work at similar times or neither of them will produce fruit. If more than one is planted, they must complement each other in this regard.

Plan out each project and do the required work. Use an accountability system to measure the progress on each project and be sure to complete each project.

When harvesting fruit, always set aside adequate seed for future projects. Bring your plans and your progress reports to Me each day and together we can walk a righteous path.

As you have seen, attempting everything in your own strength is foolish and bears no fruit. Let us get back to the basics and look forward to a time of abundant produce. It is also time for carefully planting seeds that will permanently produce fruit provided that you follow the formula* and give those trees the right attention.

A man's ability to grow wonderful life-giving produce is not determined by how many times he has done it wrong in the past, but by what he does right in the present. Doing the right thing in the present, will always produce the right result in the future. There can be no other outcome. Only wrong actions or lack of action can produce undesirable results.

You know what is right, you know how to do what is right, now you have to walk in Truth and do what is right.

Consistently plant good seeds with good intentions, consistently follow the formula* I gave you for success and use My word as your guide, this will cause My Spirit to work through you and then things will be different, says God.

This can only take place if you are willing to be different. I provide everything you need but the control of the *will* is in your hands. That is how a man can create his own outcome. There are many that cry out 'Thy will be done' but then do everything through their own will and cannot understand that they are entirely responsible for their own undoing. Even if they have achieved great worldly success, it will be of no value in the coming Kingdom. The *will* therefore is in your hands. The only unanswered question then is what are you going to do with it? The choice, as always is yours"

*See message #1

2 Corinthians 9:10
Hosea 14:8-9
Psalms 106:3
Proverbs 19:21
2 Thessalonians 1:5
1 Corinthians 3:1-9
Colossians 1:11-12

221

FREQUENCY AND ACTION

"All the notes, the plans and intentions are useless without implementation says God. Action is the most vital ingredient in every aspect of your life. Spiritual or physical works the same.

There is no point in *thinking* about prayer, you have to *act* to *speak* it out. To create the resonance that produces breakthroughs in the spiritual realm requires the correct frequency and this is only established by speaking and through music and singing.

This frequency has a beautiful fragrance to it. My Messengers are tuned to this same frequency and through it, you can communicate and receive guidance and help.

Look to your calendar of days so that you can follow My *flow* of times and events as there is great restorative power in those. More Word will bring more Wisdom. It is the only true source.

If there were millions of wells but only one that contained life-giving, life-changing water, which one would you want to drink from? In order to teach others how to pursue their quest for the Kingdom, you have to first be pursuing your own.

You cannot say 'here's how you do it' and not be doing it yourself. Every thought, word and action that is not Kingdom focused is wasted. You will never know how many people I can help through you unless you commit to being willing to help them.

You cannot wait to become this person. This is who you are, what I called you to be. You just need to stand up and *be* the person and stop waiting for something to happen. It is *cause and effect,* but you are looking at it inversely. It is not that 'once certain circumstances fall into place', you will be able to act on your calling. It is acting on that calling that will create the necessary circumstances. Start walking and I will order your steps" says God.

Psalms 37:23

Proverbs 3:6, 4:5-7, 16:9

Acts 17:28

222

APPLY THE TRUTH

"You cannot let complacency creep back in.

Constant relationship with My spirit is a proactive experience which requires effort on your part says God.

If you do not make a point of constant focus you will find the connections diminishing as you slip back into the flow of the world. If you are going to instruct people about their diet and health, you have to live it yourself.

The same applies to teaching people about the Truth in My Word. You have to apply these truths in your own lives. You cannot tell people something that is not reflected in your own actions.

People will watch *what* you do as the first clue to your sincerity. Walk in the truth every day and people in the world will want to know what you know. Look to shine the light of truth into every situation, that light is found only in My Word" says God.

Matthew 5:16

223

WISDOM

"Your prayers and My Word are an unstoppable combination says God. Remember the importance of your faith. It is that faith that causes you to issue the prayers with the full expectation of their fulfillment.

Faith activates your words and brings them alive. Human passion can make prayers *fervent* but only faith can make them *effective*. My Word will fuel your desire for spending time in prayer as it is the portal through which we connect. It is not enough to strive to be righteous. As it is written; *'The righteous shall live by faith'*.

It is time to develop a true hunger for My Word. Read it, consume it, sing it, speak it out loud, write it down, share it with others at every given opportunity. Become obsessed with it and revere it above everything. It should be more desirable to you than any earthly entertainment, for that cannot add one jot to your understanding and not one iota of anything of value to your foundation.

You ask for wisdom but fail to immerse yourself in its Source.

All the wisdom you desire is in My Word and you must diligently harvest it. Wisdom is motivated and activated by My Word and the more it is on your lips, the greater presence wisdom will have in and around you.

Wisdom abhors chaos, uncertainty and double mindedness. Wisdom will also promote *faith and love* to work alongside you. This further compels you to increase your depth of knowledge regarding My Word. That's why *Word* is the first ingredient in My Formula*. It leads you to everything else," says God.

*See message #1

Proverbs 8:10-21

James 5:16

Proverbs 8:1-36

2 Thessalonians 1:11-12

Hebrews 10:38

Romans 1:17

Habakkuk 7:4

224

REFLECTING HIM

"You cannot share the power of a relationship with Me if you do not *live* that relationship yourself on a daily basis. You have to become a reflection of My grace, love and kindness says God.

When people look at you, the way you carry yourself, the way you behave, when they listen to what you say, it should be apparent to them that there are things in your life that they would want for their own lives. Why would they be attracted to see more of Me if all they see in you are the same things they already have or that others have?

This is what it means to be 'set apart', to be *in* the world without being *of* the world. You know by now what is required to make this happen.

The more time you give to the worlds meaningless pursuits, the more meaningless life becomes. It has its moments of fun, entertainment and sometimes even what appears to be joy. However, most of the time, you should end up asking, 'what has this added to my foundation? and 'how is this showing others the grace, love and kindness that I can bring into their lives'?

This is a hard road to follow and satisfying the flesh and building the ego is so much simpler. It may bring the instant gratification that human nature craves, but from an eternal perspective it is worse than useless because it adds nothing to your foundation.

My Living Word is the answer. Keep looking for ways to *be* that Word.

To *do* the things that My Word makes clear are the *necessary* things to do in order to follow My will for your life and not your own.

When you are *being* the Word by *doing* the Word, you will surely then *have* all of the wonders promised to you in it says God.

This takes a modern day, esoteric teaching and brings it to life in a way that has massive eternal consequences. Help others onto this path but you can only achieve it through example. Let people *see* My glory at work in your life".

1 Peter 2:11-12
James 4:4
Matthew 5:16
2 Thessalonians 1:11-12
1 Corinthians 3:10-15, 9:24-27
1 Peter 1:7
Colossians 1:13-29
1 John 2:3-6
2 Corinthians 6:4-10

225

LIVING WATER

"The Word, The Word, The Word.

Keep feasting upon the most powerful nutrient that ever was, is, and will be says God. My life sustaining Word. In this, is the total healing for every ailment, physical or spiritual.

It is literally the Living Water of Life. The purifier, the cleanser and the healer.

Search to find the truth in all situations and the Word will guide you to the place you need to be. Keep My Word as your constant guide and companion. Become one with My Word so that I may become one with you. Perfection is the man who lives in My Word in everything he does, demonstrating My ways, expressing My heart and My values.

This will be a perfect man, pleasing in My sight. Remember the importance though to be a *doer* of My Word. Hearing or reading but failing to apply, is like buying the finest clothes and shoes and then never wearing them in public. Adorn yourself with the brilliant light and power of My living Word and you will be shining lights in the world, bathed in truth and bringing hope and encouragement to others.

It all starts with the nourishment of My Word", says God.

Hebrews 1:3
Isaiah 40:8

Psalms 18:30, 33:4, 119:130
Matthew 4:4, 7:24, 24:35
Philippians 2:14-16
James 3:2

Philippians 2:14-16

[7] But whatever were gains to me I now consider loss for the sake of Christ. [8] What is more, I consider everything a loss because of the surpassing worth of knowing Christ Jesus my Lord, for whose sake I have lost all things. I consider them garbage, that I may gain Christ [9] and be found in him, not having a righteousness of my own that comes from the law, but that which is through faith in Christ—the righteousness that comes from God on the basis of faith. [10] I want to know Christ—yes, to know the power of his resurrection and participation in his sufferings, becoming like him in his death, [11] and so, somehow, attaining to the resurrection from the dead.

[12] Not that I have already obtained all this, or have already arrived at my goal, but I press on to take hold of that for which Christ Jesus took hold of me. [13] Brothers and sisters, I do not consider myself yet to have taken hold of it. But one thing I do: Forgetting what is behind and straining toward what is ahead, [14] I press on toward the goal to win the prize for which God has called me heavenward in Christ Jesus.

CONTACT INFORMATION AND RESOURCES

For more help and information about following God's plan and purpose for your life please visit us at
http://faithwithoutreligion.com

Join our Kingdom Quest Facebook group

To get "The Kingdom Quest" Podcast go to:
http://faithwithoutreligion.com

To contact Frank directly: frank@frankatkins.com

Speaking Information: To have Frank speak to your group:

http://frankatkins.com

Made in the USA
Middletown, DE
27 August 2020

16540042R00293